SEXUAL VIOLENCE

My heart is moved by all I cannot save; so much has been destroyed.
I have to cast my lot with those who age after age,
perversely, with no extraordinary power,
reconstitute the world.

Adrienne Rich

SEXUAL VIOLENCE

The Sin Revisited

MARIE M. FORTUNE

THE
PILGRIM
PRESS
Cleveland

For
Sr. Margaret Farley (RSM),
my teacher and mentor,
who gave me the tools
and challenged my mind and heart
to seek justice

In memory of
Marian Lovelace
1947–2000
A courageous survivor of sexual abuse by priests,
she finally did not survive to see
the changes in the Roman Catholic Church.
May her memory and powerful witness
be a blessing and inspiration to us.

The Pilgrim Press
700 Prospect Avenue
Cleveland, Ohio 44115-1100
thepilgrimpress.com

Printed in the United States of America on acid-free paper

10 09 08 07 06 05   5 4 3 2 1

Library of Congress Cataloging-in-Publication Data
Fortune, Marie M.
    Sexual violence : the sin revisited / Marie M. Fortune
      p. cm.
    Includes bibliographical references and index.
    ISBN 0-8298-1668-2 (pbk. : alk. paper)
    1. Sex crimes – Moral and ethical aspects. 2. Sex crimes – Religious aspects – Christianity.
    3. Violence – Religious aspects – Christianity. 4. Sexual abuse victims – Rehabilitation.
    5. Church work with victims of crimes. 6. Church and social problems. I. Title.
    HV6556F67 2005
    261.8'3272 – dc22
                                        2004065048

Contents

Preface

When I wrote *Sexual Violence: The Unmentionable Sin* in 1980, I was unemployed. The funding for what was then called the Prevention of Sexual Violence Project in Seattle had been cut and the Project was on hiatus. So it seemed a good time to write a book. I had been thinking about a book for some months but had had no time to write. The loss of funding made possible the opportunity I had been looking for. Sometimes it works out that way.

My concern had been to examine the Christian tradition as it related to sexual violence, a heretofore virtually unexplored topic. Hence the title: *Sexual Violence: The Unmentionable Sin*. The anti-rape movement had begun in the early 1970s. Though there were a few rape crisis centers and hotlines, and though Andrea Dworkin, Susan Griffin, Susan Brownmiller, and Angela Davis had begun the conversation in print, sin, rape, and sexual abuse were as yet unmentionable, particularly in church.

I was at a retreat in the late 1970s and sat at dinner with a group of seven women. We were getting to know each other, and one asked what I planned to do in my newly ordained ministry. So I explained this project to try to address sexual violence in my work in the church. The conversation stopped; every woman's head was turned towards her plate. Finally one woman spoke and told her story about being raped in high school. Then another talked about her mother's assault when she was a teenager. And the next about being sexually abused as a child by her neighbor. Every woman at that table had a story to tell about themselves or someone very close to them. This was the confirmation I needed to write that book.

What had been unmentionable for so long became mentionable in a place where other women understood because we all have a story to tell. I wanted to help encourage this breaking of silence. I went to Paul Sherry, who was publisher at Pilgrim Press (and later became the president of the United Church of Christ). He agreed that it was time to break the silence in the church, and he gave me a chance. I wrote with pastors in mind. I wanted to provide something that could give them theological and ethical grounding for their pastoral care of victims and perpetrators. What I didn't really realize at the time was that survivors of sexual assault and abuse would find the book useful as well.

Sexual Violence: The Unmentionable Sin has been in print from 1983 to 2004. It has been used in seminaries and clergy training workshops, by support groups and by individuals. I think it has accomplished its purpose: to begin a conversation within the church about sexual violence that could inform our practical and pastoral responses to victims, survivors, and perpetrators.

After more than twenty years, a new purpose emerged. Some twenty-five years after the anti-rape movement began, sexual violence has become mentionable. Laws have been changed. Many children have been educated to protect themselves or ask for help. There are fewer excuses and more research to understand why so many men and some women sexually exploit others. We have discovered the widespread problem of sexual abuse by clergy because of the courage of many survivors to come forward and confront the church. Many have organized to call for justice and vindication just as the widow did in Luke's Gospel (Luke 18:1–8). So it seemed time to revisit this topic; hence the new title, *Sexual Violence: The Sin Revisited*. We have learned much that nuances the discussion.

As I reviewed the original book, *Sexual Violence: The Unmentionable Sin,* I realized that my basic analysis and efforts to deconstruct and reconstruct the Christian tradition as it relates to sexual violence had changed very little. Yet I found myself more interested in the complexities of our collective ethical thinking in this culture, about how we really decide what is acceptable and unacceptable, and how we communicate or even enforce these common values among us. Law, religion, pop culture, music, and sports all both reflect and shape our norms about sexual violence. How in a postmodern culture do we even think about sexual violence, and for those of us who are Christians, is there anything in our tradition and sacred texts to inform and guide us? I believe there is, and I wanted in this new edition to go deeper in considering the interplay of ethics, scripture, and theology as resources for directing our strategies and actions.

In a very real sense, I believe that nothing is different but everything has changed. The dominant culture of our time, which we describe as patriarchy, persists, without a doubt leaving destruction and harm in its wake. But it does not go unchallenged by women and men, children and teens who see through its thin façade and who choose another path. These are the people who dare to say, "I would rather be in genuine relationship with other people; I would rather put my energy into finding ways to live justly and compassionately with family, friend, and foe."

This book is about changing hearts and saving lives — the hearts of individuals and of institutions. So many women and men are now engaged in responding to and preventing sexual violence, I am sure that we will prevail. Isaiah urges us forward:

> Do not remember the former things,
> Or consider the things of old.
> I am about to do a new thing; now it springs forth, do you not
>   perceive it?
> I will make a way in the wilderness and rivers in the desert.
> (Isaiah 43:18–19 NRSV)

In the early twenty-first century, _Sexual Violence: The Sin Revisited_ is a contribution to the ongoing conversation so necessary within the church and without. Let us reach deep into our history and traditions of resistance and justice making to make a way where there was no way, to continue to question the way things are, and to live our lives as they can be, even now in this moment.

Acknowledgments

As most authors do, I want to acknowledge with deep gratitude the many hands and hearts that have supported me in this book. First my life partner of so many years, Anne Ganley, to whom the original book, *Sexual Violence: The Unmentionable Sin* was dedicated. She still sustains my spirit and empowers my ministry. Also Faith-Trust Institute where I work, which gave me a sabbatical to work on this book. And to the staff there, particularly Ko-Eun Kim and Sandra Barone, who support me every day. Finally, Pilgrim Press, who kept *Sexual Violence: The Unmentionable Sin* in print for more than twenty years.

My old friend and colleague, Carol Adams, continues to be my best critical reader. Judith Beals from Boston ensured that I stayed on track and did not overlook significant material. My colleagues Mary Hunt, Traci West, Andy Smith, Nantawan Lewis, and Carol Adams through our work at the American Academy of Religion offered valuable critique and support. Vanessa Barone took care of the needed permissions with skill and ease. The fact that she was just an infant when the first book came out and now is a woman with clarity of vision and purpose encourages me greatly. My appreciation for Sweet Magnolia Woolley de Fortune (known to many as Ms. Maggie) whose wet nose and warm fur often kept me grounded in the here and now. And particular gratitude to my editor, Ulrike Guthrie, whose skill and focus made this a much better book. Finally, thanksgiving to all whose lives have been affected by sexual violence who have graciously taken the risk to share their experiences and insights with me. You are the teachers who make projects like this possible.

Prologue

Unnatural Acts

In the beginning... If one were to start at the beginning, at least at the beginning as Genesis tells us, we would begin with "So God created humankind in his [sic] image, in the image of God he [sic] created them; male and female he [sic] created them" (Genesis 1:27 NRSV). Our scripture does not begin with "In the beginning, God created victim and victimizer and saw that it was good."

How unlike the beginnings we are given, for instance, in early psychological theories that viewed the male sex drive as uncontrollable. In those discussions of sexuality by Sigmund Freud, Havelock Ellis, and others we find what amounts to an elaborate apologia for male sexual aggression.

One of the core themes of this book is that sexual activity has been confused with sexual violence. Out of this confusion arise mistaken ethical stances, egregious pastoral responses, and misinterpretations of biblical passages. This confusion does not arise only from religious culture, though the Christian church can choose either to perpetuate this confusion or to challenge it. We have to look elsewhere to understand how such a viewpoint became accepted.

Madison, Wis. (AP) — Amos Smith was sentenced to 14 years in prison for sexual assault yesterday despite his attorney's argument that violence against women is acceptable in American culture. His attorney, Roger Merry of Belleville, argued that Smith, 30, should not be sent to prison "for being a victim of culture." "Hostility toward women, I think, is something that is culturally instilled in men," Merry said. "It's part of our culture that has been for hundreds of years, that violence against women is not unacceptable."[1]

In discussing pornography, psychoanalyst Robert Stoller comments: "An essential dynamic in pornography is hostility.... One can raise the possibly controversial question whether in humans (especially males) powerful sexual excitement can ever exist without brutality also being present."[2] In response, Irene Diamond suggests that "Stoller has recognized the complexity of the prevailing pattern of male 'sexual' behavior in patriarchal society, but he has not acknowledged the possibility that the 'natural' dynamic may in fact be structured by patriarchy."[3] We can only hope that Diamond is correct. Otherwise, we are left with the fatalistic belief that male sexuality is by nature violent and abusive, and that male sexual desire *is* dependent on the subordination of another.

In fact we know, through cross-cultural analyses, that rape and other forms of sexual violence are not universally found through all cultures. Anthropologist Peggy Reeves Sanday, for example, conducted cross-cultural studies of rape[4] and concluded that rape is hardly universal; in 47 percent of the societies she studied rape was absent or rare. Seventeen percent were what she categorized as "rape-prone" and used rape to punish women. Thirty-six percent were categorized as "rape-present," that is, rape exists but the incidence is unclear. Sanday concludes that rape comes not from a biological drive but is a learned response that comes from the way societies are organized. Certain behavioral patterns and attitudes are common to rape-prone societies, such as the Mundurucu, who live in Brazil.

[These societies] tolerate violence and encourage men and boys to be tough, aggressive, and competitive. Men in such cultures generally have special, politically important gathering spots off limits to women, whether they be in the Mundurucu men's club or the corner tavern. Women take little or no part in public decision-making or religious rituals; men mock or scorn women's work and remain aloof from childbearing and rearing.

These groups usually trace their beginnings to a male supreme being.[5]

In contrast, rape-free societies (such as the Ashanti of West Africa) evidence respect for women as influential members of society, a primary female deity or a male/female deity, full participation of women in religious life with an equal role in ritual activities, cooperation between women and men in work and decision making, and harmonious existence with the environment. Women's qualities of nurture and fertility are highly valued. In this context of socialization for men and women, rape becomes an aberration.

Although rape is not a given in male human nature, it is a given in Western culture to such an extent that it is difficult to imagine what life would be like without sexual violence. The fact that sexual violence is endemic to our society leads people to conclude that it must be "natural." There are those whose self-interest is served by persisting in this belief.[6] For if rape is natural and therefore inevitable, then men who rape never have to take responsibility for their behavior. All society can ever hope to do is to control or limit sexually violent behavior; it can never hope to eliminate it because, well, men are just like that, so this argument goes. In other words, men are a hopeless, lost cause, and sexual violence is a fact of life.

Persistence in believing that sexual violence is primarily sexual in nature leads to the erroneous conclusions that it is then inevitable; that rape is part of human nature; that all men are potential rapists; that "biology is destiny."

Curiously, those who seem to have the most hope for men, those who are in effect willing to say that not all men are rapists, are feminists who believe that rape is not inevitable but rather is unnatural. Basic to this belief is the conviction that men can and must take responsibility for their behavior, especially their sexual and aggressive behavior. Feminists are particularly critical of contemporary social mores and have greater expectations of men as a group than does the rest of society; inherent in this position is a high regard for men. It assumes that men, like women, are moral agents capable of responsible human interaction and it expects responsible behavior from men as well as women.

In contrast to such an optimistic viewpoint one finds the writing about sexuality and sexual violence that formed the basis of the field of psychoanalysis. Some scholars, such as Kathleen Barry, propose that an ideology of cultural sadism[7] exists, and that there is a conspiracy among such as Sigmund Freud and Havelock Ellis to justify male sexual aggression. Their work on sexuality contributed heavily to the "normalization of sexual violence," that is, male sexual aggression was regarded as normal, healthy, and natural.[8] Men could not be held accountable for what they did. What was considered abnormal by Freud, Ellis, and their ilk was not aggression but repression. As a result, they defended the sexual violence of the Marquis de Sade and viewed him as a liberator who fearlessly overcame sexual repression.

De Sade's erotic life was considered the ultimate manifestation of the normal, healthy, and natural male sexual aggression. Even though his pleasure came from acts of violence toward others, de Sade was convinced that no limit should be placed on his efforts to satisfy his sexual drives and to achieve his own sexual pleasure. He had no trouble justifying assault against women:

> It appears beyond contradiction that Nature has given us the right to carry out our wishes upon all women indifferently; it appears equally that we have the right to force her to submit to our wishes, not in exclusivity, for then I would contradict myself.... It is beyond question that we have the right to establish laws which will force women to yield to the ardors of him who desires her; violence itself being one of the results of this right, we can legally employ it. Has not Nature proved to us that we have this right, by allotting us the strength necessary to force them to our desires?[9]

By defining sexual aggression and sadism as "natural" and a male prerogative, the apologists successfully removed men's responsibility for their sexual behavior. Freud concurs: "The sexuality of most men shows an admixture of *aggression,* of a propensity to subdue, the biological significance of which lies in the necessity for overcoming the resistance of the sexual object by actions other than mere courting."[10] And Barry concludes:

> Freud's theories of sexuality and sadism are totally deterministic: people act from an indefinable instinct and an unknowable unconscious which was determined in unremembered sexual drives of infancy. The responsibility for behavior is moved from the individual to the instinct and the unconscious. Both sadistic and masochistic behavior is defined in terms of unconscious instinctual *needs.* The concept of unconscious instinct precludes morality and divorces psychology from the concept of victim or assailant. The social situation or milieus, the conditions that give rise to sexual violence have been reduced to a discussion of internal psychological mechanisms.[11]

If we add to such views the erroneous belief that women are by nature masochistic and unconsciously desire to be raped and beaten, we have a perfect match. The assumption is that men are naturally sexually aggressive and desire to subdue and dominate women and that women love that kind of treatment.

This view, unfortunately, has all too often found a neat fit with Christian teaching. One example that we shall look at more closely is the life and death of St. Maria Goretti, who died forgiving her rapist.

> The legends and myths of virgin martyrs reinforce passivity and the victimization of Catholic girls and women. In these accounts, the passive female exhibits a potential that is activated by the male. Women are potentially dangerous in themselves for what they might incite men to do. When a man murders a virgin in the course of a sexual assault, he facilitates for her the eternal reward of heaven that is promised to virgin martyrs. But women are responsible for men's actions. When women don't incite, but

resist, they help men to be good. Thus the virgin martyr is an ideal woman — for men.[12]

If women were really responsible for men's actions, there would be no such thing as sexual abuse and violence: no offense, no victims, no offenders, and no need for an ethical discussion or legal sanctions.

Fortunately Kinsey challenged this notion with the thesis that sexual interest and erotic response are learned.[13] Yet this insight does not solve the problem created by Freud and others because their *belief* in natural, uncontrollable male sexual aggression is part of what is learned. Barry comments:

> The first definitive experiences of the fully developed, learned sex drive are in adolescence when, according to Kinsey, the time between sexual stimulation and response is shortest. From cultural myths boys readily learn, first, that this drive is one that must be fulfilled because it cannot be contained and, second, that they have the implicit right to take girls and women as objects to fulfill that drive. Sexual power is thereby conditioned in the sex experience of adolescent boys. While boys are experiencing and experimenting with their sexuality, the culture provides them with substantive images of idealized sexual encounter; they often learn that they must live up to pornographic models of sex. As boys, growing into men, experiment with their sexuality free from both restraint and responsibility, that mode of behavior becomes, unchanged, the basis of adult male sexual power.[14]

She suggests that oftentimes men are in fact suffering from arrested sexual development:

> Learned, impulsive, uncontrollable adolescent male sex drive has become for many men the mode of their adult sexual behavior. It is *arrested sexual development,* which stems from a sexuality that has not grown beyond what was acted out at age 12, 13 or 14. Arrested sexual development defines the context for all aspects of their behavior.... It explains the self-centered, exploitative, and bullying behavior that characterizes pimps,

procurers, rapists and wife beaters. These men have learned to take immediate sexual gratification and ultimately any other form of gratification in whatever way they choose.[15]

There is a basis in male sexual socialization for attitudes that perpetuate the normalization of sexual violence. "Boys will be boys." However, these beliefs about male sexuality can no longer be regarded as truths about male sexual nature.[16] They are an insult to men's capacity for choice and moral agency.

The belief that male sexual aggression is natural, biologically driven behavior and "is so overwhelming that the male is the one to be acted upon by it"[17] is a myth that we can no longer afford to perpetuate. It feeds a whole other set of myths about sexual violence: for example, that rape is primarily a sexual act brought on by sexually provocative women and that rapists really are men who cannot help themselves.

Fortunately those who have worked with sex offenders in the 1990s provide us with a more accurate and insightful understanding of the pathology of offenders. In the writings of clinician Nicholas Groth, we find a clearer understanding of rape as a pseudosexual act motivated by aggression and hostility.[18] Likewise, in the accounts of victims and offenders we find valuable evidence of a distinction between sexual activity and sexual violence. Following is the testimony of an offender:

> I was enraged when I started out. I lost control and struck out with violence. After the assault, I felt relieved. I felt I had gotten even. There was no sexual satisfaction; in fact, I felt a little disgusted. I felt relieved of the tension and anger for a while, but then it would start to build up again, little things but I couldn't shake them off.[19]
>
> The crime itself just frustrated me more. I wasn't sexually aroused. I had to force myself. I felt some relief coming off because there was some tension release, but very shortly afterwards the feelings were worse. I blamed the victim and felt it was her fault and that a different girl would give me the satisfaction I craved, so I went out looking for another victim.[20]

For victims, pleasure is not on the agenda. The most common re-action to rape is "I thought I was going to be killed." Fear rather than pleasure predominates regardless of the actual circumstances of the rape itself. Central to this fear is the loss of power in determining one's life and the loss of bodily integrity. Terror and powerlessness shape the victim's experience of rape. Children who suffer sexual abuse express fear and/or confusion and usually a sense of exploitation and loss of control. Contrary to the myth, there is no "masochistic delight" experienced by victims of sexual assault.

For women, the question of whether or not sexual violence is "nat-ural" male behavior is an issue of basic survival. If women accept the belief that sexual violence is natural, that is, part of the created order, then women must also accept that it is God's will that they exist in an alien and hostile environment and are always at risk of attack by men. While many women's experience may be that they do exist in such an environment, accepting this as a natural and God-given real-ity is fatalistic and self-defeating because it discourages women from resisting or changing their environment.[21]

The theological implications are profound: if sexual violence is part of the natural, created order, then women are created to be vic-tims and are by *their nature* always at risk on a cosmic as well as a mundane level. This assumption requires an understanding of God as one who is hostile and cruel to have created two classes of per-sons — the victims and the victimizers. Nothing in the core of Jewish or Christian beliefs can substantiate this conception of God's nature or human nature.

If we understand the biblical metaphor of the Fall as a way of conceptualizing the realization of free choice for humankind, we can begin to understand the nature of sin. Free choice includes the option of *choosing* to victimize another. When a person is so alienated from God and his neighbor that he chooses to strike out, seeking violent conquest rather than loving union with another, he is manifesting the brokenness of humankind and establishing a relationship of victim and victimizer. If we regard this relationship as anything other than a manifestation of brokenness and therefore unnatural and not God's creation, then we allow it to be normative, to shape our relationships, and to justify the behavior of a victimizer as normative. Regarding rape as an unnatural act means that neither women nor men must accept the roles of victim and victimizer as God-given and unchangeable. The cycle need not continue. This is a moral assertion grounded in creation theology.

From _this_ beginning, we can appreciate how theological, pastoral, and ethical approaches that confuse sexual violence and sexual activity are mistaken, and learn from approaches that view sexual violence as a sin that requires ethical and pastoral interventions to challenge it. When I first wrote _Sexual Violence: The Unmentionable Sin_ in 1981, I was attempting to provide a basic resource to pastors to fill the gaps in our theological education and prepare us to effectively minister with victim/survivors and offenders. I offered an analysis then that I retain even now. But my understanding has deepened and widened over the years of my ministry. The complexities of a seemingly intractable social problem like sexual violence abound. Yet I find that I believe more than ever that God does not intend human beings to be victimizers and victims; that we deserve better from one another; that we are capable of making justice and healing in the midst of brokenness. So I offer _Sexual Violence: The Sin Revisited_ as a continuation of the necessary conversation in the Christian community.

SEXUAL VIOLENCE

Chapter 1 ———————————————

Introduction

Sexual Violence Is a Sin

═══════════════════════════════════

Sexual violence is a sin. This direct, yet challenging, sentence is the thesis of this book. This thesis situates sexual violence as a religious issue. Thus, we can and must address it theologically, ethically, and pastorally. Yet the statement, "sexual violence is a sin," is not easily tackled. What is sexual violence? Why is it a sin? Why is the sin of sexual violence at times so difficult to perceive? How do we speak ethically of just relations? Why have Christian ethics and pastoral writings often avoided or misunderstood the justice issues inherent to sexual violence? Is there a relationship between the gender of the majority of the aggressors and the difficulty that Christian ethics has had with identifying the sin of sexual violence? Why are men "supposed" to be sexually aggressive and women sexually passive? Can Christian ethics envision a different possibility? How does the Bible discuss sexual violence and what can we learn from it? And what should our responses be to sexual violence?

In Christian scripture, in both the Good Samaritan story (Luke 10:25–37) and in Jesus's reminder that what we do to the least of our sisters and brothers, we do also to him (Matthew 25:40), we find a generic mandate to give aid to the injured. However, this mandate is not sufficient when we are faced with a lack of clarity as to who is the injured, what is the injury, and who caused the injury. Such is the case with sexual violence. While this generic mandate may call forth a response of compassion, what in the Christian tradition challenges us to a response of justice? How are we to understand and interpret sexual violence as an experience of suffering in light of our faith? How does the relationship between sexuality and sexual violence affect our understanding of Christian sexual ethics? How has our understanding of Christian sexual ethics contributed to our unresponsiveness to sexual violence?

The harsh reality of sexual violence requires a comprehensive re-examination of theological sources including scripture, traditional Christian sexual ethics, and specific Christian teachings about sexuality and sexual violence. This critical examination will lead us to reframe the ethical questions posed by the experience of sexual violence. We can then develop the ethical and theological foundation that is fundamental to an effective and meaningful response to sexual violence grounded in the Christian faith.

In 1983, the original title of the first edition of this book was *Sexual Violence: The Unmentionable Sin*. The truth was that it was a sin that no one talked about. This absence of conversation and context created a vacuum in which victims, survivors, and offenders struggled, often isolated and alone. So one of the most important aspects of the statement, "sexual violence is a sin," is that it is being said at all. This is a step forward in recent years. One of the challenges in addressing sexual violence has been that it is often greeted by silence, and silence means denial, and denial enables injustice.

How did the problem of sexual violence insinuate itself so deeply in the social fabric? The answer is ethical and pastoral. Since 1977, I have studied this issue, educated clergy and church staff, worked with congregations, advocated for survivors, and most important, been a pastor to them. I draw upon these experiences to suggest an answer to the question, "How do we respond to the sin that is sexual violence?" I also incorporate in my answer much of the material from the original book *Sexual Violence,* which appeared in 1983. But much has happened in twenty years in the field of responding to sexual violence, and so I decided that the book must be rewritten in order for it to continue to be a pastoral and ethical resource.

THE VIOLATION OF SEXUAL VIOLENCE

One definition of "victim" is, "a living being sacrificed to some deity."[1] This definition of victim more than any other makes clear the consequence of sexual violence. A living being, a person created in the image of God, is sacrificed to "some deity" every time an adult is raped or a youth or child molested. A person is made to become a victim, a living sacrifice, by an act of another person. One wonders what deity could possibly be well-served by such an act.

As a sin against a person, sexual violence violates the bodily integrity of another, thus denying a person the choice to determine one's own boundaries and activities. Sexual violence violates another's personhood because it objectifies the other, making her or him a nonperson. By rendering a person powerless, that is, by taking away that peson's resources and sense of self, sexual violence creates a victim, someone who experiences the environment as unsafe and is on alert because of never feeling safe within one's own body.

Though it is often times hard to recognize this, sexual violence is also a violation of relationship. Consider this experience of a child, who reported:

> I had been asleep and woke up to find my father being sexual with me. I recall being in a state of terror, not quite knowing what was going on as I lay there for a few minutes and allowed him to touch me.... Mostly a feeling of growing up in an environment that was unsafe...I never felt my body was safe from violation.[2]

A father has violated the unspoken promises that he makes to his child: that he will raise her in an atmosphere of safety. Thus, the offender in sexual violence betrays trust in a relationship, which destroys the possibility of relationship between people. Sexual violence also destroys community, creating an atmosphere of fear and distrust among family, friends, coworkers, and acquaintances.

For many, the realization that sexual violence is a sin has been difficult to accept. For years, the myths have proliferated of rapists who simply cannot control themselves and victims who really want to be raped. In these erroneous stereotypes, the agency of the rapist and the victim status of the victim disappear. It is an old viewpoint, one for instance portrayed in the movie *Gone with the Wind,* in which Rhett Butler forcefully carries a resisting Scarlett O'Hara up the stairs to a bedroom rape from which she awakens happily the next morning, smiling. This now-classic image continues to inform each generation anew.

THE VIOLENCE OF SEXUAL VIOLENCE

Those who have been raped have walked through "the valley of the shadow of death," and most have returned to tell about it. Whether or not physical violence was inflicted, the most common reaction of a victim is "I thought I was going to be killed." Being forced sexually against one's will is the ultimate experience of powerlessness, short of death.[3] The victim is overwhelmed and overpowered physically and/or psychologically by the rapist. The fear expressed by victims of child sexual abuse is similar. Survivors of child sexual abuse are often haunted by the helplessness she or he felt at the hands of the molester who sought control and exploitation.

That is why we must begin here: sexual violence is, first and foremost, an act of violence, hatred, and aggression. Whether it is viewed clinically or legally, objectively or subjectively, violence is the common denominator. Like other acts of violence (assault and battery, murder, terrorism), there is harm of and injury to victims. The injuries may be psychological or physical.[4] In acts of sexual violence, usually the injuries are both.

That a child responds with fear when confronted by physical force from a stranger is not surprising. But with someone known and trusted, the child is overwhelmed, overpowered, and terrorized even without overt physical force. In addition to the terror that comes from the experience of coercion and force, the child may experience the betrayal of a family relationship. These are the consequences of a violent act. It has been largely through victims' telling of their experiences that society has undergone a revolution in consciousness about sexual violence since 1970.

RAPE DEFINED

The word "rape" is from the Latin root *rapere,* "To seize." The focus in English is "to seize and carry away by force" and/or "to force another person to engage in sexual intercourse." The contemporary legal and applied definitions are gender neutral and clearly indicate that either rapist or victim can be of another or the same gender. Thus rape is the *forced* penetration of the mouth, anus, or vagina by a penis or an object regardless of the gender of the perpetrator. However, because of the social inequities imposed because of gender, race, age, and sexual orientation, the most frequent victims of rape are women and children of all races and nondominant men.

Although legal definitions of rape vary from state to state, the most comprehensive definition refers to forced penetration by the penis or any object of the vagina, mouth, or anus against the will of the victim. Lesser forms of forced sexual contact are dealt with as assault and battery. This legal definition represents a significant improvement over earlier rape laws, which specified vaginal intercourse forced by a male on a female. This definition describes what actually happens in rape situations and does not limit rape to penis-vagina intercourse. The current inclusive definition provides for oral or anal sex against the will of the victim. In addition, it does not specify the gender of the victim or offender as the previous laws did. Thus male-male rape can be prosecuted as rape rather than under the old sodomy laws, which made male rape of a male an illegal *sexual activity* rather than an assault.[5] Rape by a female offender would include using an object or fingers to penetrate a victim.[6] The more recent laws place the emphasis on the assaultive aspect rather than on the sexual nature of the act.

Rape can be categorized according to the relationship between the rapist and victim. Acquaintance rape, the most common, describes an assault against someone who is known to the assailant, usually friend, coworker, neighbor, and so on. Date rape specifically describes an assault against one's dating partner.[7] Marital rape describes an assault against one's marriage partner or intimate. Stranger rape, the least common, occurs when a rapist attacks someone who is a stranger. (This would also include acts of rape carried out in wartime as acts of terror against a community.) Rape is an act done *to* a victim, against her or his will. Rape uses sex as a weapon to injure to another person. The fact that the sexual contact is inflicted against the will of the person and causes injury to that person makes rape a violent act.

THE BIBLE TELLS THE STORIES

The Rape of Dinah

Hebrew scripture tells the story of sexual violence in multiple forms. As such, it is a powerful witness to the victim's experience and to the difficulty that family and community had in responding. The first story of rape in Hebrew scripture appears in Genesis 34.[8] We are introduced to Dinah, daughter of Leah and Jacob, on her way "out to visit the women of the region." While she was visiting, Shechem, son of Hamor, saw her; he then "seized her and lay with her by force" (v. 2).[9] Following the assault, Shechem expresses love and tenderness to Dinah. He goes to his father, Hamor, and asks him to get Dinah for his wife. Hamor then goes to Jacob to discuss the matter. But Jacob's sons had also heard about what happened to their sister and were angry because Shechem had "committed an outrage in Israel by lying with Jacob's daughter, for such a thing ought not to be done" (v. 7). It appears that the outrage is that Shechem "lay with" Dinah — that is, he, an uncircumcised male, had sexual contact with her, not that he attacked her.

But Hamor said, "Give your daughters to us, and take our daughters for yourselves" (v. 9), so that they might all live together harmoniously in the land. Hamor and Shechem offered to do anything Jacob asked. In exchange, Jacob's sons, seeking to deceive Shechem, agreed only on the condition that he and all the males with him be circumcised.[10] The arrangement was agreed, to and all the men of Hamor's tribe were circumcised. Three days later Dinah's brothers attacked the city and killed all the males, including Hamor and Shechem. Then they seized their wives and children along with the rest of their property. Jacob confronted the brothers saying, that they had brought trouble on him because the other tribes might now retaliate, but the brothers said, "Should our sister be treated like a whore?" (v. 31)

If we were to derive an ethical understanding of sexual violence based on this passage from Genesis, we would say that sexual violence is wrong because it violates the property rights of men. At no point is the reader provided with any information about Dinah's experience or reaction to the assault. Neither are we provided with any information about Dinah's life afterwards. Since she lost her virginity and her potential husband was killed by her brothers, what man would have her? And without a man to provide for her, what would happen to her?[11]

The sexual attack on Dinah is the dramatic backdrop for the struggle between Jacob's and Hamor's families. The attack is not acknowledged as an offense against Dinah herself, but as a property violation against Jacob and his sons. The response to this violation was collective, vengeful violence. The emphasis in the description is on the sexual nature of the violation: he "lay with her," "defiled her," and treated her as a "whore."

The first lesson we draw from this example is that rape is often misunderstood and misattributed. We often see rape not through the perspective of the victim but through the perspective of those around her, or from the perspective of the attacker. And the response — that Dinah might marry her rapist — places this passage squarely in a contemporary dynamic of the confusion of sexual activity and sexual violence.

The Incest of Tamar

Generally child sexual abuse is categorized as either incestuous abuse in which a child is sexually abused by a member of her or his family or as child molestation in which a child is sexually abused by a friend, an acquaintance, or a stranger. This abuse may involve an adult or older teen touching the child sexually or getting the child to touch the adult or teen sexually. It may also include taking photos of the child in sexualized poses (which often is linked to the child pornography industry) or prostituting the child (that is, forcing a child into prostitution for the commercial benefit of the adult). Child prostitution is a very serious problem in many Asian countries, where the popularity of sex tourism combined with the fear of AIDS create a high demand for child prostitutes.[12]

While rape usually represents a clearly assaultive situation — that is, where the victim is physically forced — child sexual abuse is more often coercive than assaultive. The offender — whether a stranger, someone known to the child, or a family member — takes advantage of the vulnerability of the child and coerces her or him into sexual activity. Therefore, the term "abuse" rather than "assault" is a more common designation. However, as in rape, child sexual abuse is a form of violence, for it results in both psychological and physical injury to its victim.

Legally, child sexual abuse is described using various terms. It may be considered rape if physical force is used and penetration takes place, or statutory rape if force is not used but the victim is underage and thus unable to give legal consent.[13] Sexual abuse without penetration (touching, fondling, masturbation, etc.) usually is described as "indecent liberties."

Clinically, child sexual abuse is the sexual exploitation of a child who is not developmentally capable of understanding or resisting the contact, and/or who is psychologically and socially dependent on the offender.[14] Two criteria provide the parameters for understanding child sexual abuse as a form of violence and aggression. The first (as in rape) is the lack of consent on the part of the victim. However, in the case of child sexual abuse, the lack of consent is a given. Children, by definition, cannot give or withhold consent when approached sexually by an adult because they are immature, uninformed, and usually dependent on the adult. Consequently, they lack the real power to resist.[15] Therefore, any sexual contact between an adult and a child is abusive. The second criterion for understanding child sexual abuse has to do with whose self-interest is being served by the sexual contact and who is injured. Child sexual abuse describes "contacts or inter-actions between a child and an adult when the child is being used for sexual stimulation of that adult or another person."[16] The sexual *use* of a child disregards the child's welfare. The child becomes an object exclusively to meet the needs of the offender. The act is exploitative and, consequently, damaging to the child.

While the particular behaviors that constitute sexual violence or abuse remain the same, the context is an important part of com-prehending the experience. Thus, incestuous abuse (as described above) takes place in the family, which shapes the dynamics of the abuse, often limits its disclosure, and determines any forthcoming intervention.

In 2 Samuel 13, we find the story of incest in the royal family. Although the victim is a young adult and not a child, the family dy-namics are similar. Tamar is a full sister of Absalom and a half-sister of Amnon; all are children of David. In the story, Amnon decided that he "loved" his sister Tamar, but was distraught because Tamar was "a virgin, and it seemed impossible to Amnon to do anything to her" (v. 2). So Amnon tricked Tamar into coming to see him, then he grabbed her and told her to lie with him. She refused, saying, "Do not force me; for such a thing is not done in Israel; do not do anything so vile" (v. 12). Tamar reminded him that she would be shamed and he would be a scoundrel. She told him to speak to King David who "will not withhold me from you" (v. 13). Ignoring her suggestion and "being stronger than she, he forced her, and lay with her" (v. 14).

As with the rape of Dinah (above), we are again told the story of a rape, but this time not only rape, but incestuous assault, that is, sexual violence done by a family member. Yet the violation portrayed in the text is still one of property. At that time, it was possible for a man to marry his half-sister, a practice that was later forbidden under the law (see Leviticus 18:9). Yet Amnon refused to request permission from David to marry Tamar, perhaps fearing that the request would be denied. The folly and shame result from Amnon's rape of Tamar without David's permission. In this story, the reader is provided with Tamar's reaction and reminder that she will bear the shame of this attack.

After the rape, Amnon's feelings shifted dramatically to hatred, and he sent Tamar away. She confronted him, saying that sending her away is an even greater wrong than the assault. Again he ignored her and put her out. Tamar, as a virgin daughter of the king, was wearing a long robe with sleeves. She rent the robe, put ashes on her head, and went away crying. When Absalom saw her he asked if she had been with Amnon. Because it was true, Tamar remained in despair in Absalom's house. When King David heard what happened, he was very angry. Absalom hated Amnon for what he did to Tamar. After two years, Absalom plotted to kill Amnon and commanded his servants to strike Amnon down. Afterwards Absalom fled while David grieved for his son.

Tamar's reaction to her rape is one of public grief and desolation. While this is a common victim reaction to rape, Tamar grieves because she has lost her virginity without gaining a husband to care for her. Because of the property violation, she is left without provision; she becomes damaged goods. In fact, as she points out, Amnon does have a responsibility for her. He refuses, though, to take that responsibility and thus leaves her in shame. This is the essence of the offense described here. In this situation, sexual violence is seen primarily as sexual activity and a property crime; the real offense against Tamar — tricked into a situation she could not control — is overlooked. The primary story is of the conflict between brothers, allowing us to hear Tamar's perspective on the experience only in relationship to this primary story,; and so the sexual assault of a woman is incidental. The reaction of her brother Absalom is the traditional act of revenge ending in murder.

While the story makes clear that the incestuous abuse was destructive to Tamar, her family, and the community and that such a thing should not have been done to her, this judgment is based on the violation of her father's property rights rather than the violation of her bodily integrity. The community never attends to the victimization of

Tamar per se but rather focuses on the economic injury done to her father and brother.

The Vulnerability of Bathsheba

There are numerous situations in which someone is vulnerable because of the inequality of power in a relationship. Under these circumstances, the person with greater power may take advantage of the one with lesser power — for example, a teacher and student, therapist and client, or boss and employee.

Sexual harassment generally refers to conduct that takes place in the workplace between a supervisor and employee or between coworkers. It is "the use of one's authority or power, either explicitly or implicitly, to coerce another into unwanted sexual relations or to punish another for his or her refusal; or the creation of an intimidating, hostile or offensive working environment through verbal or physical conduct of a sexual nature."[17] Specifically, someone who takes advantage of the role of minister, teacher, coach, therapist, and so on, to cross sexual boundaries commits sexual abuse.

Consider the situation of sexual abuse by clergy. It is a violation of professional ethics for any person in a ministerial role of leadership or ministerial counseling (clergy or lay) to engage in sexual contact or sexualized behavior with a congregant, client, employee, student, and so on (adult, teen, or child) within the professional (ministerial or supervisory) relationship.[18] Ministerial violation of boundaries involving sexualization of a relationship can take place in the ministerial relationship or the counseling relationship, as well as the staff supervisory or mentor relationship. When the minister sexualizes the ministerial or counseling relationship, it is similar to the violation of the therapeutic relationship by a therapist. When the minister sexualizes the supervisory or mentor relationship with a staff member or student, it is similar to sexual harassment in the workplace, and the principles of workplace harassment apply. When a child or teenager is the object of the sexual contact, the situation is one of pedophilia or child sexual abuse, which is by definition not only unethical and abusive but also criminal.

The issue at stake here is that those who are entrusted with leadership choose to betray that trust. We find an illustration of this in Hebrew scripture in the prophet Ezekiel's description (chapter 34) of the false shepherds. These are the shepherds that take from the flock they are supposed to be shepherding to meet their own needs and in so doing fail to do their job of protecting and caring for them. Ezekiel bemoans all of this and is speaking to the public figures of his day using the familiar shepherd metaphor — an effective choice because people would understand that it was absolutely contrary to customary practice for a shepherd to take for his personal needs sheep from the flock under his care. The shepherd was entrusted with the care of the flock in order to ensure the well-being of the whole community who relied on the flock as a resource. God condemns the false shepherds for their disregard of the well-being of the flock and for their misuse of their roles.

But we also have a story in Hebrew scripture that epitomizes the betrayal of trust by one who has power. In 2 Samuel 11–12, we find the story of David and Bathsheba. David, the most powerful king of biblical Israel, is attracted to Bathsheba and finally has her husband sent to the front lines of battle where he is killed so that David can have Bathsheba to himself. Nathan, David's advisor, comes to him and tells him a story about a rich man who takes a lamb from a poor man for the rich man's own use. David reacts with outrage and says that the rich man deserves to die and that he should restore the poor man fourfold. Nathan then says, "You are the man!" and proceeds to delineate the ways that David had betrayed the trust that so many, including Nathan, had placed in him. In spite of your great gifts, in spite of your deeds, in spite of your power and prestige, says Nathan, "You are the man." Nathan names the abuse of David's power as king to have what he wants and so to compromise his moral authority. In scripture, David is chastened and sobered and acknowledges Nathan's naming of his sin and betrayal of trust. He accepts the consequences, which include the loss of his firstborn son. For all that, David does not have to deal with the political consequences of his recklessness, for he is after all still king, and goes on to become Israel's greatest king.[19]

To consider sexual violence pastorally and ethically as a sin invariably shapes our understanding and response. We must reframe the ethical questions presented by sexual violence, clarifying the confusion between sexual activity and sexual violence, and asking what is the real violation that takes place when a person is raped or sexually abused. We must name the unmentionable sin and look to resources from scripture and tradition to inform us. We must consider the implications for contemporary Christian sexual ethics. Then we must struggle with the demands that justice makes in response to the sin of sexual violence.

POSTSCRIPT: UNDERSTANDING "SIN" AND "GOD" IN THE DISCUSSION OF SEXUAL VIOLENCE

The use of the word "sin" to describe sexual violence may be initially unfamiliar or misleading for some readers. Too often "sin" is based on an ethical system that emphasizes rules and regulations about specific acts. It often describes the focus of pietistic and moralistic religious beliefs; it may be the bedrock of condemnation. This is not the concept of "sin" used here.

Theologically speaking, "sin" is a state of alienation, brokenness, and estrangement. It is an added dimension of human experience that describes one's estrangement from self, others, and God, which stretches beyond harm as a moral criterion. This estrangement is contrary to the created order and contradicts God's intention for our lives. Persons are created in God's image and created to be in relationship. To know oneself and to be oneself is to be in relationship with others and with God.[20] Affirmation of our relational existence is one of the insights of Jewish and Christian theology.[21] Sin is the rupture of relationship and may be experienced psychologically, physically, spiritually, and socially. All persons know estrangement, brokenness, and alienation at some time in their lives. Salvation (or redemption) overcomes sin and brings healing and restoration of persons and relationship.[22] Moments of healing, wholeness, and new life are moments of grace. As James Nelson observes: "The experience of the new life is a relational reality in which the miraculous and everyday stuff of life are interwoven. The incarnation of God, the divine presence in and through human flesh, is always a miracle."[23] Likewise this experience of grace is accessible to every person who seeks to overcome estrangement and brokenness. God is the source of grace.

Like the concept of "sin," the concept of "God" is troublesome for some and is open to misinterpretation and misuse. God is that dimension of divine presence which is the source of all life (God the Creator), offers persons grace and reconciliation (God the Redeemer), and dwells in and among all persons always (God the Sustainer). This loosely Trinitarian understanding of God emphasizes the "God-within-and-among" and deemphasizes the "God-over-there." It is a God who seeks justice, not revenge. It is a God who stands with the oppressed and over against the oppressor. It is a God who suffers with the suffering of people. It is a God who calls to account those who harm others. This understanding of God, which has developed out of liberation, feminist, and womanist theologies, is the understanding referred to here by the use of the word "God."

Within the theological notion of sin as a dimension of human experience, we must consider the ethical notion of "sins" as the individual or collective acts of those who bring suffering to others. The sinful person strikes out at others in hostility and anger, denying the demands of relationship and violating the personhood of others by treating them as objects or by intentionally inflicting injury. The wages of sin are violence, and the consequences are suffering for all involved.

Redemption is the healing of this brokenness, which may lead to the renewal of the relationship with God, self, and others. In order for this to take place, the one who causes harm must acknowledge and repent; he or she must make changes that are apparent and genuine, and must make restitution for the suffering caused. When these things are done, a context of justice is created and forgiveness can follow. Only then can reconciliation become a possibility.

Chapter 2

The Social Construction of Sexuality and Sexual Violence

A Study in Confusion

RAPE IS VIOLENCE, NOT SEX
  — a button distributed by rape crisis centers in the 1970s

Lately I have begun to wonder about this perfervid insistence that the act [of rape] is not sexual in nature, when every counsel of common sense suggests that it is, at least in part. . . . [One] reason for our reluctance to acknowledge the true character of rape [is] the fact that the atrocity says something disturbing about the very nature of sexuality.
                    — William Muehl, "Rape Is a Sexual Act,"
                              Reflection Magazine, 1976

There are two extreme positions held on the nature of rape: rape is violence or rape is sex. The force with which these two positions are argued makes one pause and consider the meaning of this divergence of opinion. Before 1970, the words used to describe rape would have been mostly sexual words describing a supposedly sexual act, for example, "clumsy seduction," "sex that got out of hand," "perversion," and so on. In the early 1970s, our society began to redefine rape more accurately. The emphasis placed by those in the anti-rape movement (*"Rape Is Violence, Not Sex"*) represented an important corrective to previous beliefs and attitudes. The purpose of this emphasis was to undo the long-held belief that rape is primarily the sexual act of a man who cannot control his sexual feelings. The effort to redefine rape as primarily a violent act succeeded surprisingly well. The most common response to the question "What is rape?" began to emphasize its violent, aggressive source. We began to distinguish between sexual violence and sexual activity in order to create an ethical foundation for a cultural norm that rape is wrong. This was a necessary corrective to the preceding dominant cultural belief that rape was "sexual," meaning that rapists (that is, mostly men) experienced sexual arousal and could not stop themselves from having "sex" with an unwilling partner. This belief served to remove any moral responsibility from the rapist ("he couldn't help it") and often to place moral responsibility on the victim ("she asked for it by her dress, behavior, or demeanor").

But in the early twenty-first century, the eroticization of violence makes the sexual dimension of sexual violence, at least for women victims, very relevant. Sexual violence is both sexual and violent in Western cultural experience. But now when we discuss the "sexual" nature of sexual violence, we need to examine the ways that coercive, violent sexual contact is an extension of the dominant culture's understanding of sexual behavior as some people's right with or without the consent of their sexual partner. Sexual activity and sexual violence are now not only confused, but fused — an even more dangerous circumstance than before.

The relationship between sexuality (specifically sexual activity) and sexual violence is a complex and multidimensional reality that finds expression in numerous areas of our lives. The resulting questions abound: Why is most rape perpetrated by males against females? Why does a man choose to use his penis as a weapon to harm another person? Why are men "supposed" to be sexually aggressive and women sexually passive? Why is so much of the violence inflicted on women and children "sexual" in nature? Why do some people find violence erotic? Why does our society seem to encourage the eroticization of violence? This societal tendency to equate or confuse sexual activity with sexual violence is a predominant reality in our socialization, attitudes, beliefs, and behavior. This confusion must be addressed if we are to succeed in halting sexual violence.

SOURCES OF CONFUSION

The confusion between sexual activity and sexual violence is rooted in a complex set of beliefs integral to the process of male and female socialization. These beliefs promote and sustain the thinking that there is no difference between sexual activity and sexual violence, a view so deeply rooted in our culture that it has come to be regarded as a part of human nature. In fact, these beliefs are indicative of a false consciousness that survives because few people are willing to question the norm. The following beliefs support the confusion of sexual violence with sexual activity.

ERRONEOUS BELIEF NO. 1: _Anything that employs the sexual organs must be primarily sexual in nature._

If I were to approach a good friend and reach out with my hand to touch gently that person's face, the person would interpret that gesture as an act of affection and friendship. If, on the other hand, I approached that person with my hand in a fist and struck him or her on the side of the face, the gesture would be interpreted as an act of hostility and violence. I would be using the same part of my body, my hand, in contact with the same part of the other person's body, the face, and yet I would be acting in antithetical ways toward the other person. Likewise, in sexual activity, a man uses his penis or any other part of his body as a means of giving and receiving sexual pleasure and affection. But in sexual violence he uses the same part of his body as a weapon to violate and assault another person. Just because he is using sexual organs in the process does not make his behavior "sexual" and therefore natural and acceptable.

ERRONEOUS BELIEF NO. 2: _The source of a man's sexual response is external and somehow beyond his control. He is not responsible for what he does with that response._[1]

The colloquial expression of this belief is that "men can't control themselves," and its corollary is that women have to be responsible for men's sexual response (that is, "don't get him turned on or you're in trouble"). If, as the belief goes, even the sight of a woman arouses a man, and if he cannot control his behavior when aroused, then, the belief concludes, if he sexually attacks her it is the woman's fault because she aroused him. Just because a man is sexually aroused and has an erection does not mean that he has to "put" that erection somewhere, that is, into another person against her or his will. He can choose to deal with his sexual feelings and needs in other ways, for example, through masturbation. A woman is not the sole source of heterosexual male arousal. The presence or sight of a woman may be one of many factors leading to arousal, including the individual's socialization and erotic learnings.[2] In no way is she the *cause* and therefore the *object,* willing or unwilling, of his sexual attention. Men do have the capability to be responsible for and with their sexual feelings and behaviors.

ERRONEOUS BELIEF NO. 3: *The widely accepted "romantic love ideal" requires a dominant-subordinate relationship between two people.*

Florence Rush describes the "prototype of romantic love" as containing the "formula of one dominant and one subordinate partner."[3] For example, as prerequisites for romantic interest between a man and a woman, he must be taller, stronger, and make more money; she must be shorter, weaker, and make less money. Supposedly it is this formula of one up and one down that creates and sustains the erotic and emotional interest in romantic love. In heterosexual relationships, the male is dominant and the female subordinate — an arrangement that is accepted widely by both partners without question.[4] Male sexuality seems to be dependent on always being in a dominant position vis-à-vis a subordinate sexual partner, or as Susan Griffin observes, "male eroticism is wedded to power."[5]

The connection of male dominance with male eroticism was clear to me in a conversation I had with a male colleague about sexual assault. I asked him to think of a way in which he could identify with a rape victim. He proceeded to describe an occasion when a female sexual partner had taken the initiative in sexual activity, which had the result of immediately diminishing his erotic interest in her. He did not like what he regarded as her "sexual aggression" toward him. First, my colleague mistakenly identified his experience as parallel to a woman's experience of sexual assault. He equated his partner's sexual initiative with the assaultive aggression of a sex offender. He never imagined himself as actually a victim of sexual _assault_ by a man or group of men. He revealed much more about this culture's prescription for male sexuality than he realized. In this and other cultures, male dominance has become eroticized, as has its corollary, female submission. Male dominance is the key ingredient for male erotic interest and sexual performance. According to the cultural norms, in order for men to be aroused, they feel that they must be in control of the sexual interaction and that their partner should be passive and submissive. The belief is that together dominance and submission and power and powerlessness create the formula that sparks erotic desire in both men and women.

In our society, women and children fulfill the subordinate status necessary to complement male dominance and thus are vulnerable targets for exploitation and abuse. Rush suggests that this dominant-subordinate pattern helps explain why men sexually abuse both women and children: "Since both women and children have been lumped together as helpless, dependent, and powerless, they even share the same 'feminine' gender and consequently both have been sexually abused by men."[6] Any time there is an imbalance of power between individuals or groups of persons, there is the real potential for abuse of the less powerful by the more powerful. If the romantic love ideal in our society is posited on a dominant-subordinate relationship between persons, then it is no surprise that sexual activity and sexual violence have become confused.

ERRONEOUS BELIEF NO. 4: _Men have the prerogative to impose their sexuality on others regardless of others' wishes._

As a corollary to the "romantic love ideal," men's supposed sexual prerogative is the basis of male sexuality as it is experienced in this culture. At the heart of male sexuality, according to James Nelson, is a sexist dualism that posits the norm of male superiority over female inferiority.[7] The established norm in this society is that men have more power than women in all relationships, including sexual ones. The power of the male is what gives him the prerogative to take what he wants sexually. The powerlessness of the female forces her to submit to his wishes and desires, or to use covert means to gain some power in the relationship. Coercion and manipulation become accepted means of interaction. Male sexuality begins to appear predatory in nature — that is, a man takes what he wants when he wants it without regard for the consequences to others.

Male sexuality as defined by the dominant culture includes the following elements:

- a desire that its object be "innocent," that is, powerless, passive, subordinate;
- a need to *objectify* the other in order to avoid intimacy;
- a desire to *use* another person exclusively to meet one's own needs;
- an ability to *rationalize* the experience: "she likes it, wants it, needs it; it's good to teach kids about sex . . . ";
- a lack of regard for the other as an autonomous person;
- a lack of responsibility for one's acts; no one makes any demands or requires any form of accountability;
- an inability to find erotic or emotional pleasure with an equal, male or female, or with someone who takes the initiative sexually;
- a sexual orientation that is predatory and dependent on the subordination of the partner;
- an attempt to avoid rejection by always being in control.

These aspects of culturally defined male sexuality occur in varying degrees and combinations in most men in our society. They are also characteristic of sex offenders and child molesters. To the extent that these characteristics have become the norm for male sexuality, sexual activity and sexual violence have become thoroughly confused.

Theologically, the second and third chapters of Genesis, as they have traditionally been interpreted and generally accepted,[8] provides support for this understanding of male sexuality. According to this interpretation of the story, man was created first and superior. Then God created woman from man's rib *for the sake of* man; she was created to serve his needs and so that he should not be lonely anymore. This understanding of woman's creation underlies the primary assumptions that woman's role is first and foremost to serve man. Woman's job, as the story goes, is to meet man's needs.

The idea that women were created in and of themselves as separate and equal persons who have needs, gifts, and reasons for being outside of relationships with men is absent in this interpretation. The first chapter of Genesis, however, provides a view of the coequal creation and coequal responsibility of woman and man. Woman and man are created simultaneously in this version: God created humankind, male and female. Unfortunately, this creation story is not the one that has most affected our cultural or theological beliefs regarding men, women, and sexuality.[9]

As long as erroneous beliefs about male sexuality go unchallenged, the confusion between sexual activity and sexual violence will remain a predominant reality in our society and will continue to support the conditions that encourage sexual violence. What is most disturbing is the growing tendency to identify male eroticism with violence. The confusion may well become reality; sexual violence may become the norm of sexual activity. As violence becomes more eroticized, "in the spectrum of male behavior, rape, the perfect combination of sex and violence, is the penultimate act."[10] The eroticization of violence means that the acts of violence and abuse themselves bring sexual arousal for some men. The object of the act of violence is almost always a woman or child. This tendency is apparent in commercial sexually explicit materials, in the increasing number of horror films complete with obligatory female victims, in advertising, in contemporary music, etc. The media now both reflects and encourages the eroticization of violence (see the Epilogue).

GROWING UP CONFUSED

Our earliest socialization teaches us to confuse sexual activity with sexual violence. From the beginning we learn attitudes and patterns of behavior that are based on this confusion. Any effort in later life to understand and distinguish between the two goes against the dominant socialized pattern.

Ann Cahill, in her book *Rethinking Rape,* summarizes this disturbing reality:

> The dominant model for all sexual behavior is essentially one of violence, in that the social structure imposed upon sexual interactions demands that girls and women fend off the advances of sexually aggressive boys and men, who are in turn responding to social demands to enact such aggressive roles. The aggressive male attempts to achieve an end that the female (not acting out of self-interest or in response to her own organic needs, but rather engaging in behavior that she has been taught to be socially appropriate and responsible) attempts to foil or at least forestall. Instead, their sexualities are shaped by the mores of a social structure that views sexual desire with at the very least some ambivalence, such that sexual encounters become little more than a struggle for power.[11]

Many men and women grow up with the adages "boys will be boys" and "men are just like that" as significant learnings in their sexual socialization. Translated, these mean that males are naturally aggressive, not trustworthy, will take advantage of women sexually, and there's nothing to be done about it because that's "just the way men are." For example, girls learn that, unlike them, adolescent males have an "uncontrollable sex drive" and that all that men really want from women is sex. Inherent in these messages is a deep suspicion of male behavior, which is not altogether unfounded.

During adolescence, girls learn about "romance" and/or sex from their peers, their experiences, watching movies and television, listening to the radio, and reading magazines and books. Here the message is double-edged. In a heterosexual setting, they learn to desire a romantic, sentimental love relationship *and* to expect a sexually aggressive male who is in control of the social and sexual interaction but not in control of himself. The two become easily confused in the girls' experience: in order to have the romance, they learn to accept the aggression.

Sadly, adolescent males and females begin their sexual explorations already trapped in a dominance/submission paradigm. As Pamela Foa observes:

> Boys and girls have no way to tell each other what gives them pleasure and what not, what frightens them and what not; there are only violence, threats of violence, and appeals to informing on one or the other to some dreaded peer or parental group. This is a very high-risk, high-stake game, which women and girls, at least, often feel may easily become rape.[12]

In the face of a sexually aggressive male, "nice" girls say "no" and a few "nice" boys respect that "no." "Good" girls never say "yes."[13]

Several examples in the Christian tradition exemplify and perpetuate the confusion of sexual violence with sexual activity, such as the story of the Roman Catholic saint Maria Goretti, who was brutally attacked by a rapist at age twelve. Although she successfully prevented herself from being raped, her attacker stabbed her to death. As she died, she forgave her murderer. The church's teaching derived from this event is conveyed in the tone and content of these passages from the homily delivered by Pope Pius XII at the canonization of St. Maria Goretti.

> Saint Maria was born of a poor family in Italy in 1890. Near Nettuno she spent a difficult childhood assisting her mother in domestic duties. She was of a pious nature and often at prayer. In 1902 she was stabbed to death, preferring to die rather than be raped.
>
> It is well known how this young girl had to face a bitter struggle with no way to defend herself. Without warning a vicious stranger burst upon her, bent on raping her and destroying her childlike purity. In that moment of crisis, she could have spoken to her Redeemer in the words of that classic, _The Imitation_

of Christ: "Though tested and plagued by a host of misfortunes, I have no fear so long as your grace is with me. It is my strength, stronger than any adversary; it helps me and gives me guidance." With splendid courage she surrendered herself to God and his grace and *so gave her life to protect her virginity* [emphasis added].

From Maria's story carefree children and young people with their zest for life can learn not to be led astray by attractive pleasures which are not only ephemeral and empty but also sinful. Instead they can fix their sights on achieving Christian moral perfection, however difficult that course may prove. With determination and God's help all of us can attain that goal by persistent effort and prayer.

Not all of us are expected to die a martyr's death, but we are all called to the pursuit of Christian virtue.[14]

The pope seems to regard rape as "being led astray by attractive pleasures." The belief that rape is sexually pleasurable and that its victim is sinful emerges once again. According to this story, it is preferable that a girl die rather than commit the sin of "losing her virginity" because of the rape. The confusion of sexual activity with sexual violence is reflected in this teaching. The attempted rape is seen as a sexual approach rather than as a violent attack, and the agency resides only with the young woman. Unfortunately, this story was used in some Catholic schools to teach young women about sexuality, thus perpetuating the confusion: Sexuality, young women learned, involves a violent, aggressive attack by a stranger. A righteous woman is to protect herself from sexual contact at all costs, potentially including her life.

Unfortunately, this story does not teach women to resist male sexual aggression *for the right reasons,* that is, because it is violent and aggressive, and women have a right to maintain their bodily integrity. The figure of St. Maria Goretti presented by the church is one of the more blatant examples of a confused and distorted view of sexual violence and sexuality, and a source of the view that women have no value except as sexual property.

For girls, the message was that it was better to give up one's life than one's virginity. The secondary messages were equally important. A female's technical virginity takes precedence over her life; her value as a sexual object is more important than her personhood and survival; sexual activity is violent and aggressive and woman's role is to resist and defend her virginity. The confusion between sexual activity and sexual violence is powerfully instilled in this teaching. A more valuable teaching would have been to accurately portray Maria Goretti as a rape victim who attempted to defend herself from attack, and then to distinguish between this and a sexual relationship based on consent and respect. This lesson would help correct the confusion perpetuated in the dominant culture.

Growing up, many girls (and some boys) find themselves the object of sexual advances from adult males. They learn quickly that seldom does an adult believe their reports of molestation, nor do adults protect them from other adults. For example, a girl child's veiled reference to Uncle Harry's fondling of her might bring, not protection, but punishment for "making up bad stories." Women learn very early that sex is something *done to* them by a male, that their proper sexual role is passivity, and that they have no right to determine what happens to them sexually. From an early age many women experience themselves as powerless sexual objects. As they become adults, they learn that they should appreciate this position of passivity as portrayed by Scarlett O'Hara in _Gone With the Wind_. Women learn that forced sexual activity is something to be accepted *and* enjoyed. They learn that sexual activity is an area of their lives over which they have little control.

Both women and men are taught that "women say 'no' when they mean 'yes,'" that is, women say "no" to male sexual advances even when they really want to engage in sexual activity because they are afraid to admit their own sexual desires and needs. In other words, heterosexual men and women learn that relating to each other is a game, which by necessity involves manipulation and coercion.[15] For males, inherent in all the messages they receive is a deep suspicion of female behavior. Men are taught that women will manipulate them to get what they want; they learn that women cannot be trusted because they often do not play the game fairly. Women must be kept at an emotional distance or else they will take over a man's life and he will lose control of the situation. Unfortunately, women do play the game, often in order to survive. They play the passive role to the man's aggressive role. They do not always take responsibility for their own sexual desires and thus on occasion do say "no" when they want to say "yes." But for her to do otherwise would mean being labeled a "whore" or would so threaten her male partner that he would bid her farewell. That risk is often too great for many women. So the game continues.

Many women and men also grow up with the adages "boys will be boys" and "men are like that" as significant learnings in their sexual socialization. Translated these mean that males are naturally aggressive (and have permission to be so), are always in control of a situation, are sexually active with numerous partners, and are not responsible for their own actions. They also learn that virtually any female in any circumstance, public or private, is "fair game." Whether on the street, in school, in the workplace, or in the home, men learn that they have the right of sexual access to almost any woman, that is, any woman not already spoken for by another male. All they have to do is take the initiative in establishing social contact; women are expected to respond eagerly to their attention. Adolescent boys also are exposed to movies, TV, radio, books, and magazines (including sexually explicit magazines and soft/hardcore pornography). They learn through the media that women, as the *objects* of their erotic desires, have to be controlled; and that as men, they are expected to know what they are doing and stay in control of the other person.[16] Women, they are taught, like a strong man to take charge; women like to be sexually ravished and abused; women prefer men who take control of them. Some boys also experience sexual advances by adults — males and/or females. Because, like girls, they learn that rarely will anyone protect them from this exploitation, they resolve early on that they will never allow themselves to be in such a powerless position again. Rather than be exploited some learn to exploit others.

As a result, male sexuality in our culture is presented and experienced as something possessive, aggressive, hostile, harsh, violent, controlling, and with little hint of tenderness, gentleness, mutuality, or respect.[17] This is not to say that all men in our culture have accepted this norm.[18] However, the manifestations of this male image dominate media, advertising, business, politics, and so on. Men are provided with a macho ideal in every generation from John Wayne and Clint Eastwood, Arnold Schwarzenegger and Mick Jagger, Antonio Bandera, and Eminem, to Mike Tyson and others. They are told that to be a "real man" means to be tough and in control, socially and sexually. For those who _have_ accepted this norm, violence is the ultimate means of proving one's manhood, whether on the football field, in the tavern brawl, at the diplomatic conference table, or in confrontation with one's spouse. Subtle and overt violence becomes the means by which men stay in control. A man's masculinity and sexuality become tied to violence.[19]

The confusion of sexual activity with sexual coercion and violence has become the core of male sexual socialization. The implications for society are far-reaching, as Nelson points out:

> A certain code of masculinity is purchased at the price of suppressing tenderness and self-acceptance. Socialized toward a deep fear of homosexuality and toward a self-respect based in considerable measure upon sexual potency and conquest, the young man is torn by both cultural demands and fear about his own sexual strength. The implications for social violence are unmistakable.[20]

More important for this discussion, the implications of sexual violence for all people are unmistakable. Women, as the objects of male efforts to prove their manhood, pay a high price. The resulting homophobia[21] victimizes lesbians, gay men, bisexuals, and transgender people who become the objects of harassment, discrimination, and overt violence in the form of hate crimes like "queer bashing."

T. Walter Herbert describes the function of "others" in the lives of heterosexual men: "Gay men, children, and women become gender scapegoats; they are seen to embody what the man finds 'unmanly' in himself. Punishing them temporarily fends off anxieties by confirming the illusion that the man's troubles come from others, not from within himself."[22] Finally, many men experience the profound alienation from self, from others, and from nature that produces truncated persons motivated by fear, whose only real power lies in their potential to do violence to others and who represent a danger to all of society.

CONSEQUENCES OF CONFUSION

As a result of the confusion of sexual activity and sexual violence, we all inherit beliefs and practices that shape our options and behaviors. Confusion abounds.

Terror or Pleasure

The English language is structured to reify this confusion between sexuality and sexual violence. The definitions of the word "ravish" are very clear: "ravish 1. to seize and carry away forcibly. 2. to rape 3. to carry away with emotion; fill with great joy or delight."[23] No wonder we are confused. In the 1980s, some people believed that rape was a sexual event for the victim as well as the rapist. This attitude was evident in a public comment made by a Spokane, Washington, police captain who was asked what advice he would give to women concerned about an increasing number of rapes in the area. His response was "Lay back and enjoy it."[24] In his mind, there appeared to be no difference between sexual activity and sexual violence.

However, the sexual aspect of this violence is not without relevance. If the victim has an orgasm during the rape (as is sometimes the case), the experience may be very disturbing for the victim. Both male and female victims who have had an orgasm during rape expressed guilt and confusion. They may interpret the orgasm to mean that they *enjoyed* the experience, that they must have wanted it; otherwise, they reason, why would they have had an orgasm? In these situations, orgasm is a physiological response to fear combined with direct sexual stimulation. Sexual arousal to orgasm can be triggered by fear as well as by desire; the physiological response to both is similar.[25] This does not mean that the subjective experience for the victim is pleasurable. In many ways, this is yet another victimization: the victim is powerless to withhold even sexual response and feels betrayed by her or his own body. Still, the overriding experience of the rape victim is fear and violence.

Likewise, the sexual dimension of child sexual abuse contributes to confusion for the child victims.

> I remember the terror I felt and the confused feeling of being turned on [when my father touched me sexually]....Even now [as an adult], what I do recall about my father is that even though I was in a state of terror, it was also in a way very positive, since my father's sexual advances toward me were the only recalled demonstrated love that was expressed to me in my childhood.[26]

The child may experience positive physical feelings, affection, and a sense of self-worth simultaneously with terror and powerlessness. This combination, confusing to the child, encourages self-blame and discourages her or him from seeking help to stop the abuse. Child sexual abuse presents a situation in which sexual activity is confused with sexual violence in the experience of both victim and offender and in the minds of the public.

Blaming the Victim

Many Christians hold the opinion that the sin of sexual violence is the victim's, not the rapist's. This moral acrobatic act goes hand-in-glove with victim-blaming. Arlene Swidler refutes this in arguing that it is no sin *to be* raped. She refers to a news story about a Roman Catholic priest who said that it was "better for girls to die than to submit to rape."[27] Because of this attitude (reflected in the story of

St. Maria Goretti) and others that place responsibility for rape on its victims, many Christians hold the opinion that the sin of sexual violence is the victim's, not the rapist's. In situations of rape, sexual abuse, and sexual harassment the victims been often been blamed for "being sexual": it was what she wore, how she walked, where she was, what she said, and so on, that *caused her to be raped, abused, or harassed.*

Because rape was seen as a "sexual" act and not an act of violence, the belief arose that rape happened when men experienced sexual arousal and could not stop themselves from having "sex" with an unwilling partner. This belief served to remove any moral responsibility from the rapist ("he couldn't help it") and often to place moral responsibility on the victim ("she asked for it by her dress, behavior, or demeanor"). For example, when a fifteen-year-old boy raped a girl in a stairwell at West High School in Madison, Wisconsin, Judge Archie Simonson ruled that the boy was reacting "normally" to prevalent sexual permissiveness and women's provocative clothing. The sixteen-year-old victim was wearing tennis shoes, blue jeans, and a blouse over a turtleneck sweater when she was attacked by three boys.[28] It matters not whether the victim was age ten months, five, twenty-five, or seventy-five years old. The suspicion lingers that because she was attacked or abused, she must have been "being sexual." In fact, it is her *vulnerability* (at any age) that allowed her to be attacked or abused. But actually the *cause* of the attack is with the attackers.

Although there has been some progress in reforming legal statutes regarding sexual assault in the United States, the confusion persists. For example, some states now do not allow information about a victim's past *sexual* history to be admitted as evidence at trial. In the past, under many rape laws, a defense attorney could use the victim's past sexual history as a means of discrediting the victim and undermining the prosecution of the rapist. If the defense suggests that the victim was sexually active prior to the assault, then it can try to convince the jury that the victim really is a "loose" woman who frequently "gives away" her sexual attentions and that this "alleged" rape is really only another incidence of the same. Inherent in these laws was the idea that any woman who is sexually active outside of marriage is unrapable: She cannot be raped because she freely gives away sex. The failure here to distinguish between what is consenting sexual activity and what is sexual violence put the victim at a disadvantage and often resulted in the acquittal of the rapist. At the same time, many of these states, in an effort to be "fair," are also disallowing evidence of the alleged assailant's past arrests or convictions on charges of _sexual assault_. Ethically the woman's history of sexual activity is irrelevant to whether or not she was assaulted, but the alleged rapist's history of rape is very relevant to determine his responsibility for his assaultive conduct toward her. Fortunately, some of the more recent rape laws specify that a victim's past sexual history cannot be used as evidence unless there are extenuating circumstances. These laws try to differentiate between consenting sexual activity and sexual violence.

The dominant culture persists in the belief that "good women do not get raped." Underlying this belief is the idea that if she had been behaving in a proper, righteous manner, she would not have been assaulted.[29] The fact that she was raped or abused in other ways is evidence to the contrary. More specifically, she may believe that if she _were_ "a good Christian woman," God would have protected her from the attack. Her victimization then becomes a sign of _her_ sinfulness. The belief that the rape victim is morally suspect is manifest in the view which combines superstition (the irrational belief that two isolated experiences are causally related) with a belief in a punitive God. The victimization itself is seen as punishment for previous sin. Any prior indiscretion, violation of a religious commandment or law, or act of meanness becomes the cause for the punishment. For example, a woman who was a rape victim reasoned that her rape was God's punishment because she masturbated when she was a teenager.

The commonly held suspicion that the rape victim really did want to be raped persists in the saying, "You cannot thread a moving needle." If a woman had actively resisted, rape would have been impossible, according to this logic. The victim is further blamed by circular reasoning. Feelings of shame or embarrassment in the victim are regarded by others as signs that the victim consented and enjoyed the illicit sexual act for which she now feels ashamed. The fact is that these feelings result from the blame society places on the victim.

Traci West cites a discussion in the early 1970s that illustrates how victim blaming works. In her critique of Calvin Hernton's *Sex and Race in America,* she notes:

> In a curious combination, Hernton condemns the sexual exploitation of black women, but then also assigns black women a pathological unconscious desire to be exploited.... This viewpoint presents the emotional life of women as significant, yet intrinsically distorted. It seems as if the paradigm of sexuality and race which frames these arguments dictates the portrayal of black women as entirely driven by desire, including the desire to be sexually assaulted and exploited.[30]

The myth of the masochistic woman is a deeply held, cross-cultural belief which must be put to rest.

Once advertisers discovered that not only does sex sell, but sex combined with violence sells even better, there was no stopping them. Hence the sharp increase since the 1970s in the use of images that use sex and violence. From music to clothing to cars, the sex-and-violence tandem sells products. Unfortunately, it is selling more than just the product; it is selling the confusion between sexuality and violence.

The use of sodomy laws to prosecute male-on-male rape is yet another example of the confusion between sexual activity and sexual violence. Traditionally, sodomy laws were created to discourage homosexual activity between consenting adult males. According to these laws, sodomy or anal intercourse under any circumstances was illegal. Because most of the old rape laws specified that rape was something that men did to women only, those laws could not be used to prosecute same-gender rape. Instead, sodomy laws, which originally had only dealt with sexual activity rather than sexual assault, have been used to prosecute male-on-male rape. Under these laws, the real offense in male-to-male rape was the same-gender sexual contact rather than the assault that has taken place, a reflection of heterosexism. Sodomy laws have now been declared unconstitutional in the United States.[31] Because rape of a male by a male is in fact sexual violence, the laws pertaining to sexual assault should be used in its prosecution. This is the case under many of the newer sexual assault statutes.

The traditional interpretation of scripture has often been shaped by the confusion of sexual activity with sexual violence. The clearest example of this is the Sodom and Gomorrah story (which is retold in a more complete version as the story of the Levite and his concubine in Judges 19). These are stories about the threatened (and, in Judges, the actual) sexual attack on guests spending the night in a strange town. Yet these stories have virtually always been interpreted in Christian tradition as referring to homosexual contact. This misinterpretation and its influence on Christian teaching has resulted in silence on the sin of sexual violence and inaccurate information and confused ethical teaching on homosexuality.[32]

Similarly in Christian sexual ethics, there traditionally has been an overemphasis on the form of sexual activity, that is, the who, what, when, and where; and almost no emphasis on the context of sexual activity, that is, the power relationship between the two persons and the presence or absence of consent. For example, sexual activity outside of marriage is considered wrong; and sexual activity inside of marriage is considered right no matter what the circumstances. This avoids the reality that marriage per se does not mean that sexual activity within it will be consensual and respectful. In fact it may well be coercive and abusive, but in the eyes of the church such sexual activity is permitted because official marriage legitimizes it. The confusion between sexual activity and sexual violence has encouraged this ethical morass.[33]

It has been held that prostitutes cannot be raped because they are always sexually available. The only possible offense against them might be a customer who got something for nothing, but then that, of course, would not be considered rape but theft. In fact a prostitute can be raped. Even though she may agree to provide sexual services for a fee, this does not mean that she is available for sexual assault against her will. The difference between willingly providing sexual service as a form of consenting sexual activity and being the victim of assault must be clarified. Because of the confusion, prostitutes are highly vulnerable to sexual and physical assault and often have little legal recourse when rape occurs.

Scriptural Sources: "Women Cry Rape Falsely"

Contemporary attitudes in North America that reflect the confusion of sexual activity and sexual violence are deeply rooted in our Western cultural heritage. Many of these attitudes are evidenced in the blame we place on the victim and its corollary, the stereotype of the woman who cries rape falsely. These attitudes have contributed heavily to the inability of society and church to deal realistically with sexual violence. If not their source, they certainly find their reinforcement in scripture.

Unfortunately, of the several references to rape and sexual abuse in the Hebrew Bible and Christian scriptures, the best-known references convey erroneous information and attitudes about sexual violence. For example, the story of Potiphar's wife (Genesis 39) has become the prototype of the woman who cries "rape" falsely. Those stories that are accurate in their portrayal are either seldom referred to or misinterpreted. The story of Susanna, a victim of attempted rape who is falsely accused of fabricating her charge by her would-be rapists, is virtually unknown to most Christians (Daniel and Susanna in the Apocrypha).

Instead, what is fairly well known is the story of Joseph, the hero, who is a servant to the Egyptian Potiphar in Genesis 39:1–23. Joseph was entrusted with the administration of Potiphar's household. Described as handsome, Joseph was invited by Potiphar's wife to come and lie with her. He refused because it would be a sin against God and a betrayal of his master. She insisted and finally one day grabbed his cloak, urging him to have sex with her. Joseph ran away, leaving his cloak behind. When her husband returned she reported to him that Joseph came to her (supposedly to assault her) and that she screamed for help and scared him away. Potiphar was enraged and put Joseph in prison; but even so, "the Lord was with him" (Genesis 39:23).

In this classic story of the woman who cries "rape" falsely, Potiphar's wife has become a prototype of the woman who uses a false charge of rape to get back at an innocent man, not only innocent but the hero whom God especially favors. Potiphar's wife (who is not named) is portrayed as the sexually aggressive female who, because of her class and status, is able to condemn her husband's servant falsely. The teaching is plain: beware of women crying "rape," especially women with status (for example, upper-class Anglo).[34] In reality, false rape charges are a rare occurrence. This story is regarded by many, however, as the "typical rape" with the "typical rape victim" being a vindictive, dishonest woman. This is, in fact, a most atypical situation. Rather than a warning to be aware of false accusations by those with privilege and status, the moral most likely to be remembered is that often women falsely accuse men of rape.[35]

Christian Doctrine

In the Christian tradition, we find only a few direct references to sexual violence. We do, however, find an overall context, patriarchal and often misogynistic, that contributes heavily to the practice of "blaming the victim." The indirect references within this context are often as significant as the specific ones.

The patriarchal bias of the "church fathers" has been carefully examined and documented elsewhere.[36] But it is useful to look at Augustine because he did speak specifically about rape. Mary Pellauer, in her article "Augustine on Rape,"[37] discusses a short section in Augustine's _The City of God_ (written between 413 and 425 C.E.) where he says that consecrated virgins raped by the invaders who sacked Rome should not commit suicide. In this assertion Augustine is arguing against other church fathers such as Jerome. On the one hand, Augustine is trying to exonerate the raped virgins so that they would not feel compelled to commit suicide. On the other, he is concerned about their purity of heart because he also believed that there was always some pleasure for the victim of rape.[38] Challenging the common understanding of the time (that rape victims lost their purity), Augustine "asserted that 'not even when the body is violated is it lost' *provided* that the soul remained 'unsubdued.' It was 'firmness of purpose' which kept 'bodily sanctity' intact."[39] In other words, he was "redefining rape to mean acts in which no trace of sexual pleasure was experienced by victims."[40] So Augustine leaves a mixed legacy in his discussion of rape. He affirms rape victims (that is, consecrated virginal victims), relieving them of an obligation to commit suicide, but he ignores other victims and places responsibility for the "sin" of the rape once again on the victim, that is, her purity of heart and will. In any case, in spite of Augustine's assertions, Pellauer reports that suicide by rape victims continued.[41]

The misogynist attitudes and practices of individual theologians and church leaders are available *ad nauseam* and without apology. These attitudes and practices culminated in the sixteenth century with the publication of *Malleus Maleficarum, The Hammer of Witches*. It became one of the basic texts of the Inquisition. The *Malleus* was first printed in 1586 and reprinted at least twenty-nine times until 1669. Though written by Dominicans and supported by the Roman Catholic Church, it was also later adopted by Protestants as their guide to witchcraft.[42] The text describes women as evil, subject to carnal lust, weak, impressionable, defective, impulsive, and liars by nature.[43] Thus, according to this manual, women were susceptible to witchcraft. Given this view of women, it was not difficult to legitimize the organized persecution of women during and after the Inquisition. By merely labeling them "witches" and thus a seductive danger, church leaders easily justified the torture and murder of thousands of women. The brutal techniques employed in torture included sexual violence and sadism.

In diabolic intercourse, the devil was believed to place a mark on the witch as the sign that he or she was his property. In women this was normally on the breast or genitals. Small protrusions of the body were also believed to be teats by which the witch nursed her familiar. Witches were stripped and shaved. Their bodies were searched and the sensitive parts pricked in search of these supposed bodily proofs of demonic relations.[44] Here the church not only was complicit but actively initiated sexual and physical violence against women as punishment for being born female and being labeled "witch."

In fact, it was frequently the case that women and children who were accused of witchcraft were actually victims of sexual violence. Many who "confessed" to "fornication with the devil" were actually reporting a sexual attack upon them by a man. Rush concludes:

> In a society where sexual abuse went unhampered and people believed in evil spirits, it was not difficult to attribute a sexual offense to a supernatural spirit. [Nicholas] Remy [demonologist and Inquisitor] was satisfied that a child who "could not suffer a man" could accommodate the devil, and in his treatise on demonology he wrote:
>
> > *Although Catherina Latomia of Marche at Haracourt, February 1587, was not yet of an age to suffer a man, he (the devil) twice raped her in prison being moved with hatred for her because he saw that she intended to confess her crime; and she very nearly died of the injuries she received from that coitus.*
>
> Victims of sexual abuse, without recourse, found it simpler to blame or even believe that spectral demons rather than flesh and blood men violated them.[45]

In her detailed study of European witchcraft, *Witchcraze,* Anne Llewellyn Barstow analyzes the sociopolitical context of sixteenth-century Europe within which the witch trials and executions thrived. The victims were usually women identified as vulnerable, often healers or independent thinkers, and the investigations and punishments of them were generally sexually sadistic.

For influential European men, the opportunity to punish in a sexually sadistic way became both a teaching tool and a prime exhibition of control. For this reason we have to consider the men in power as well as the women victims, an investigation that links up with themes of European imperialism and racism. The witch hunts took place at the same time as colonial expansion and the Atlantic slave trade, and they were made possible by some of the same ecclesiastical policies and legal changes.[46] The persecution of women and children as witches provided a backdrop for the church's response to sexual violence during the fourteenth to seventeenth centuries. During this period, the church was not only insensitive to the needs of victims, it proactively persecuted some victims as witches. Blaming the victim was reinforced as standard practice. The confusion of sexual activity and sexual violence went unchallenged.

CONFUSION CLARIFIED: A CHOICE OF CONTINUUMS

There are two ways of looking at the relationship between sexual violence and sexual activity. In the past, rape has been viewed as the extreme expression of sexual activity. On Continuum I it appears as follows:

Continuum I

"normal"
sexual ————————————————————— rape
activity

This paradigm illustrates the definition of rape as "just sex that got out of hand." A line somewhere on this continuum delineates where sex stops and rape begins. While there is no consensus as to where that line falls relative to specific behaviors, it would appear that the delineation has something to do with force. Sexual activity is considered normal as long as it takes place without overt physical force; it becomes rape when one partner physically forces the other in an overt way. The logical implication of this paradigm is that rape is an extreme form of sexual activity in which overt force is used when a man supposedly cannot control his sexual drive or because a woman resists his sexual attention.

A second way of looking at the relationship between sexual violence and sexual activity makes a clear distinction between the two and suggests a normative statement on the nature of sexual activity. In order to illustrate both the nature of and the distinctions between sexual activity and sexual violence, Continuums II and III must be considered together. These continuums make it clear that there is a similar range of human experience and behavior within both and yet a difference between them. Obviously there is more than one style of sexual activity and more than one type of sexual violence. There are degrees of force within sexual violence and degrees of initiative and receptivity within sexual activity. But the two continuums are mutually exclusive. In this paradigm, sexual activity is by definition consensual and takes place in a context of mutuality, respect, equality, caring, and responsibility. Sexual violence involving either adults or children is antithetical to this definition of sexual activity. Sexual violence is by definition nonconsensual and takes place in the context of exploitation, hostility, and abuse.

Continuum II illustrates the escalation of aggression.

Continuum II: Sexual Violence (nonconsensual)

coercive ————————————————————— rape
   "sex"[47]

For purposes of clarification, the extremes of Continuum II are marked "coercive 'sex' " and "rape." The extreme form of sexual violence labeled "rape" is easy to identify: A woman is kidnapped from a parking garage, taken to an abandoned house, beaten, and is subjected to oral and vaginal sexual assault by two men. They then lock her in the trunk of her car, take her to a strange part of town, and leave her with no clothing. Hopefully no one could fail to see that this incident was unequivocally rape: a brutal physical and sexual attack.

The other end of the continuum, which is labeled "coercive 'sex,' " is less easy to identify. For example, a woman goes out on her second date with a man she met through a friend. She likes him and is possibly interested in developing an ongoing relationship. Toward the end of the evening he invites her to his apartment and, upon arrival there, asks her to go to bed with him. She says "no," she prefers not to, but maybe another time. He persists, reminding her that he bought her an expensive dinner and expects something in return; then he gets physically aggressive. She submits to sexual intercourse. Afterwards, he feels some sexual satisfaction but an emotional void. But then sex is like that for him. She feels used and confused. But then men are like that, she thinks. Besides, maybe this means he really does like her and is interested in seeing her again. Many people would argue as to whether or not this was sexual violence. She does not think of herself as a "victim" although she feels many of the same things that victims of rape feel. He does not think of himself as a rapist although he feels many of the same things that a rapist feels. For both of them this encounter is probably interpreted as a minor skirmish in the war between the sexes and, though disappointing, it represents yet another confirmation that "this is what sex is really all about anyway." Yet using the criteria cited earlier for distinguishing sexual activity and sexual violence, it is clear that this incident belongs on the sexual violence continuum and not on the sexual activity one.

Most sexual violence occurs on the "coercive 'sex'" side of the continuum, and much of this is not recognized or reported as such. Victims are more likely to report a rape that is clearly a rape both by legal and cultural definitions. If victims are confused themselves about what occurred, or fear that they will not be believed, or that they will be blamed for the incident, they are unlikely to report it. Unfortunately, for many persons, especially children and teenagers, the only "sexual" experience they have had has been coercive or violent. For them, it is easy to come to the conclusion that sexual activity is by nature coercive and violent, something over which they have no control. This experience provides the basis for their confusion between sexual activity and sexual violence.

Continuum III provides a way of describing sexual activity in contrast to sexual violence.

Continuum III: Sexual Activity (consensual)

receptive _____ proactive[48]
sexual activity   sexual activity

This continuum illustrates the range of differences that a person experiences in sexual activity described as more or less proactive or receptive. When two people share a sexual encounter, one person may be more proactive and the other more receptive. One takes the initiative and suggests or begins sexual activity. The other decides whether or not to consent and, if consenting, receives the sexual attention of the partner and participates freely in the sexual interaction. These proactive and receptive stances often shift back and forth during the sexual sharing so that each person is both proactive and receptive depending on their mood and desire. Frequently in heterosexual activity, sexual sharing is limited to gender roles: the male is expected to be active and take the initiative; the female is expected to be receptive and wait for the male. Fortunately these limited expectations no longer restrict sexual activity. The traditional gender roles are not particularly fulfilling for either the woman or the man. He is under pressure to take the initiative and to perform sexually, satisfying not only his own needs but hopefully those of his partner as well. She is expected to wait for his initiative, dependent on his performance to satisfy her, and unable to express or fulfill her own sexual needs.

Sometimes one person prefers to be primarily receptive and finds sexual satisfaction in the initiative and active stance of his or her partner. At other times, the opposite may be true. A satisfying sexual encounter takes into account the flux of receptive and proactive desires. What is important to realize about this continuum of sexual activity as defined here is that sexual activity is not without powerful and intense physical expression. It is the giving and receiving of sexual pleasure and satisfaction that is often passionate. However, this understanding of sexual activity is to be distinguished from "coercive 'sex.'" The proactive stance in sexual activity is markedly different from the coercive behavior in "coercive 'sex.'" In the proactive stance, one person initiates sexual activity and proceeds only with the consent of the other. In the coercive role, one person initiates sexual activity and proceeds regardless of the lack of consent.

The two continuums of sexual violence and sexual activity are mutually exclusive and do not intersect. As the discussion suggests, they are separate and distinct experiences. The distinction is both qualitative and ethical. One who experiences sexual activity feels different than one who experiences sexual violence. In sexual activity both parties feel affirmed, respected, empowered, and reassured as they share emotional and physical intimacy. In an encounter characterized by sexual violence, the victim feels fear, powerlessness, exploitation, and confusion as sexual contact is imposed with no intimacy. The offender feels powerful, in control, hostile, and dominant. At the same time he or she lacks self-esteem and self-confidence and feels little sexual satisfaction.

Ethically, sexual activity and sexual violence are categorical opposites based on the presence or absence of consent. "Consent" in this instance refers to the informed and freely chosen agreement to engage in sexual activity. "Consent" should be distinguished from "submission," which refers to yielding to the power or authority of another. This distinction is important in understanding the difference between sexual activity and sexual violence. On occasion a rape or an incest victim submits without struggle or resistance to the sexual attack or abuse. However, this is very different than consenting to sexual contact. Consent requires that a person have all the necessary information to make a decision and the power to choose and have that choice respected by others. Thus, a five-year-old who has neither information about sexuality nor power vis-à-vis an adult is forced to submit to sexual contact with that adult. A teenager may have sufficient information about sexuality but not have power vis-à-vis her or his father or employer; thus she/he is forced to submit. An adult who has both sufficient information about sexuality and the power of consent may verbally and physically resist a rapist until the rapist's physical force and/or a weapon overpowers the victim and forces submission.

The area of greatest difficulty for many people in trying to understand their sexual experiences and experiences of sexual violence or abuse focuses on the fine line that often exists between consent and nonconsent. For example, does a woman ever really consent or just submit? This is an especially difficult area for women who have, up until recently, never been allowed to see themselves as sexual persons. Having been well trained to say "no" even when they want to say "yes," how can they know if their "no" is really a "no" or if their "yes" is really a "yes"? Or how do persons who are sexually inexperienced and struggling to explore their own sexuality choose when to consent and when to withhold consent?

The fine line between consent and nonconsent often focuses on the notion of seduction, regarded by some as a polite form of acquaintance rape. Lorenne Clark and Debra Lewis give us a more positive heterosexual definition in stating that "seduction involves persuading a woman to act according to her own desires and contrary to the duties imposed on her."[49] This definition of seduction helps to clarify the difficulty regarding consent. Persuasion or encouragement to act in accordance with one's desires, even though contrary to traditional roles or expectations, still can fall within the criteria suggested above for sexual activity as opposed to sexual violence. In other words, persuasion is not coercion; persuasion finally takes "no" for an answer while coercion does not. Seduction then means approaching someone who has adequate information about sexuality and the power to consent or refuse and seeking to persuade them to engage in sexual activity. The context remains one of respect, mutuality, equal regard for the welfare of the other, and so on.

The other difficult aspect of consent versus nonconsent is: at what point in a sexual encounter does one give consent, and can a person change her or his mind later on? "She said she wanted to have sex with me. So we started to mess around. Then when I got aroused, she changed her mind. What was I supposed to do? I couldn't stop then." The fact is that people do change their minds and often for no apparent reason. Sexual interaction is no different from any other human interaction. For example, a person decides to buy a car and puts money down. At that point, the person consents to the deal made with the seller and promises to purchase the car; however, between the time the down payment is made, the contract is signed, and the purchaser takes delivery, either the buyer or the seller can back out of the deal. If this occurs, the down payment may be lost and one party may be disappointed, but it was assumed at the beginning of the deal that consent could be withdrawn at any time prior to delivery. So why do people behave as if *initial* consent to sexual activity is irreversible?

Sometimes consent is withdrawn because the circumstance of the sexual encounter changes. "I agreed to have sex with him, you know, regular sex. I never knew that he meant anal sex too. When he started that, I told him to back off—I wasn't interested. He didn't listen. He said that I promised him sex and that's what he wanted." Again, drawing a parallel with a business transaction helps clarify this situation. Two people enter into a business agreement under specific terms. When either party modifies those terms, the agreement is void until a new set of terms is negotiated and agreed to. A sexual encounter is similar. If one person agrees to a particular type of sexual activity and the other person modifies the form of activity in a way that is not amenable to the first person, then consent may be withdrawn with good reason.

The ethical issues at stake here are complex. The tendency of our society to confuse sexual activity with sexual violence is deeply rooted in our cultural consciousness and profoundly influences our beliefs, feelings, and behaviors related to sexuality. Continuum I illustrates the confusion between "normal" sexual activity and rape. In fact it is a juxtaposition of Continuums II and III. In this confused view, sexual activity becomes subsumed under sexual violence, and any meaningful distinction between the two is lost: violence becomes erotic and "good" sex is violent. Continuums II and III are used to illustrate the distinction between sexual activity and sexual violence in order to support our claim that there is a difference between the two, and to establish ethical norms based on this distinction.

If we believe that the focus of erotic interests is the result of learning and socialization, then it is no surprise that sexual activity has become confused with violence. When we agree that this development is not in our best interest as a society, we can more effectively name the source and address its cause. When we begin to redefine and differentiate sexual activity from sexual violence, we can achieve the _eroticization of equality:_ both women and men, regardless of sexual orientation, can find erotic pleasure in approaching each other as equals, sharing both proactive and receptive sexual activity. With this alternative, we can begin to repair the damage that has been done to women and men by the confusion of sexual activity with sexual violence.

It All Depends on Your Perspective

Whether sexual violence is seen as an extreme expression of sexual activity (Continuum I) or as a completely different category of human experience (Continuum II) depends on one's view of sexuality.

- If a person begins with the notion that sexual activity is always coercive — that in heterosexual activity the male must take initiative and control the experience; that women really were created to service men, sexually and otherwise; and that the measure of manhood is determined by aggression and dominance in bed — then it is only logical that sexual violence be seen as the extreme form of sexual activity.

- If one begins with the notion that sexual activity is by its nature coercive — that it is something done to one person by another person without regard for the wishes of the first; that it is something over which one has no control; and that women are expected to provide for men's sexual needs whenever and wherever it is requested if they expect to be supported and accepted by men — then it is only logical that sexual violence be seen as the extreme form of sexual activity.

- If, on the other hand, one believes that sexual activity should always be consensual and take place in a context of respect, equal regard for one another, mutuality, choice, equality, and caring — that it is a shared experience which is mutually satisfying, and that any form of force or abuse negates that satisfaction — then it is only logical that sexual violence be seen as antithetical to sexual activity.

- If a man views women as being passive, shallow, emotionally demanding, manipulative, aggressive, oversexed or undersexed, clearly needing a man to protect them, and secretly wanting to be ravished and needing to be controlled "for their own good," and if he has never imagined what it would be like to be overpowered by a man and sexually victimized, then he probably sees rape as "sex that got out hand."

- If a heterosexual woman's first and possibly only subsequent "sexual" experiences have ranged from coercive to violent, and if she has never been in a situation where a man treated her with respect as an equal, she probably assumes that sex is coercive and violent because that is the way men are and sexual violence is just more of the same.

- However, if a person has experienced sexual activity that was consensual, respectful, and caring; if that person has observed men and women relating to each other with real respect and consideration; and if that person knows that she or he can be a victim of coercive, abusive sexual violence, which runs counter to everything she or he believes about how persons should and can relate to each other, then that person probably sees sexual violence as antithetical to fulfilling and mature sexual activity.

Our attitudes and experiences dramatically shape our perceptions of sexual violence. Likewise new information and/or experiences can change our perceptions. In any case, our perception of the nature of sexual violence, the nature of sexuality, and the relationship between the two has a significant impact on our ethical perspective. This effort to reframe the ethical questions surrounding sexual violence begins with the premise that sexual violence and sexual activity are antithetical experiences. This is a moral assertion that values persons, choice, and mutuality over against the prevailing cultural norms of postmodern Western culture.

Chapter 3 ———————————————————

Sexual Violence
An Uneven History of Ethics and Sin

=======================================

THE ETHICAL SILENCE

Sexual violence as a topic for ethical discourse among Christians went largely unaddressed until the end of the twentieth century. There are many complex reasons for this. One reason certainly is the silence on the topic by society as a whole. Ethicists and pastors, like judges, doctors, police officers, and the general public, paid little attention to the problem of sexual violence. Specifically in the Christian community, rape and child sexual abuse were largely overlooked by most ethicists who have shaped traditional and contemporary ethical discussion.

Some might explain the conspicuous absence of ethical reflection on sexual violence by saying that there is no need for it since, like murder, everyone knows and understands that rape is wrong under any circumstance. This explanation is inadequate for two reasons. First, while it could be argued that virtually everyone knows and understands that rape is wrong, there is no consensus as to exactly what rape is or what can be defined as sexual violence. Also, because there is no agreement as to the nature of crimes of sexual assault and child sexual abuse, there is really no unanimous condemnation of sexual violence. *Not* everyone agrees that sexual violence is wrong under any circumstance; hence there is insufficient community pressure to limit its occurrence.[1]

Second, consensus on a social norm condemning antisocial acts does not preclude the need for ethical discourse. The example of murder again makes this clear. Even though we can posit some collective agreement that murder is wrong, there is still an abundance of discussion among ethicists and pastors on this issue, for example, in the controversies surrounding capital punishment, use of weapons of mass destruction, the just war theory, or nonviolent versus violent social change. If, as a society, we shared a collective understanding and condemnation of sexual violence (which we do not), this still would not be an adequate reason to refrain from ethical discussion of the matter. The most significant reason for the historic silence in ethical discourse is that sexual violence was something that was perceived to happen primarily to women and children and, as such, was not a priority for most ethicists. The limitations of a patriarchal bias and male experience (which for most male ethicists probably did not include sexual assault) meant that sexual violence as an experience and as an ethical issue was largely overlooked until women ethicists began to listen to survivors and address the issues.[2]

The question of what is wrong about sexual violence or what is the sin of sexual violence has never been adequately addressed in Christian ethics. Why is it wrong to rape someone or to molest a child? The answer that to some may seem self-evident has, in fact, remained largely elusive. When mentioned at all, the understanding of the sin of sexual violence has been distorted by the confusion of sexual activity with sexual violence, used to condemn victims as sinful, defined as an offense against male property rights, or equated with adultery by interpreting sexual violence as "sexual activity outside of marriage."

SEX, VIOLENCE, AND MORALITY

The historical development of ethics as related to sexual violence and a theological understanding of sin is important if we are to deconstruct that which creates confusion and passivity and to construct a useable ethical framework. For Christians, scripture and the history of Christian ethical discussion in this matter (limited though it is) are primary resources.

For example, the attempt to distinguish between "unnatural" and "natural" sins is found in the "moral manuals" that Christian confessors used during the fifteenth to nineteenth centuries to guide their counsel of parishioners on sexual matters.[3] These manuals heavily influenced people's attitudes about sexuality, and most of their teachings promoted "a highly negative, juridical, and act-centered morality, which all too easily proclaimed moral absolutes with little regard for person-oriented values."[4] A common theme found in the manuals is the distinction between sexual sins "in accordance with nature" and those "contrary to nature." The criterion for natural sexual sins is that the theoretical possibility of procreativity be present, that is, that a child may be produced. Thus fornication, adultery, incest, rape, and abduction are all regarded as "natural" sexual sins. Although they are sins, they are less sinful than "unnatural sins." "Unnatural sins" are masturbation, sodomy, homosexuality, and bestiality. None of these has procreative possibilities; therefore, they are "unnatural" and as such were considered much more serious. This hierarchy of sins uses procreation as a criterion for judging the seriousness of sexual acts. It suggests that sexual acts, for example, homosexuality, are in the same category as sexually violent acts, for example, abduction and rape. In the natural/unnatural paradigm, incest, rape, and abduction are considered sinful not because they are in violation of the rights and bodily integrity of the individual, but because they are seen as "sexual activity outside of marriage." These acts are considered less "sinful" than sexual acts, which _by their nature_ have no victims, for example, masturbation and homosexuality. This paradigm reinforces the confusion of sexual activity with sexual violence by regarding acts of sexual violence as _sexual_ sins and seeing their sinful nature as related to sexual _activity_ outside of marriage.

The use of procreative criteria as the basis for sexual ethics is an inadequate and counterproductive standard. It results in little regard for the quality of relationship between the persons involved. In addition, the procreative norm (if it can produce a child, it is somewhat justifiable) minimizes the injustice and suffering experienced by victims of sexual assault and condemns sexual activity which _by its nature_ is not harmful or destructive, for example, masturbation. The prevalence of this ethical teaching has contributed once again to the confusion and distortion of our understanding of sexual violence and sexual ethics.

Clearly if we are to understand the nature of sexual violence and posit ethical norms in the face of it, we must also look to the secular discussion, that is, philosophical ethics, for input. In fact, within this secular discussion we find a far more extensive and nuanced discussion than we do in a religious context.

Inevitably two issues are at work here: the nature of rape and the wrong of rape. These two issues form a circular framework and we can see the historic development of their interaction. The late-twentieth-century argument within feminist ethics reflects the dilemma: "rape is violence, not sex" (Susan Brownmiller), and "the line between sex and violence is indistinct" (Catharine MacKinnon).

For a while we were relying on the nature of rape to determine the wrong of rape. This suggests how difficult it is to make a moral argument against sexual violence in a patriarchal culture. In other words, if a rapist is motivated by a desire for power and control and uses violence to achieve that end, then we can condemn the behavior and hold him or her accountable for it. This argument rests on the assumption that violence against another person is wrong and unacceptable. If, however, a rapist is motivated by sexual desire, that is, is aroused and forces another person sexually, the moral argument gets more difficult because sexual desire is viewed as "normal," a moral good. It also shifts the focus to the victim, that is, the "source" of the rapist's arousal: what was she (or he) wearing, doing, saying that "caused" the rapist to be aroused? Hence the moral question was turned on its head: it became about the victim's behavior rather than the rapist's behavior. Our ethics turned on our clinical assertions about the nature of sexual violence.[5]

This is why in the 1970–1980s, the anti-rape movement in the United States spent so much energy focusing on "rape is violence, not sex." It was a valiant attempt to carve out a moral stance from which to work for legislative and judicial changes. It was also an effort to reeducate the public and to appeal to a new ethical norm.

In many ways, the effort was successful. Public consciousness did change. Laws did change, for example, many jurisdictions enacted rape shield laws that attempted to prevent a rape victim's sexual history from being admitted as evidence at trial. Rhetoric shaped consciousness but didn't tell the whole story.

This is why MacKinnon's rebuttal of "rape is violence, not sex," is so important. She was willing to name the obvious: rape _is_ the extreme expression of a male-defined sexuality of dominance in a patriarchal culture. Sexual violence is normative, not deviant or aberrant behavior. The evidence abounds: the widespread occurrence of sexual violence in multiple forms, the largely ineffective legal response, the overwhelming acceptance by society that "the way things are is the way they have to be."[6]

When I wrote the first edition of this book in the early 1980s, I did so to help reshape the cultural, political, and ethical norms, to make the case that "rape is violence, not sex." In my presentation of competing continuums, I pursued that argument suggesting that we have two options of how we might view the nature of sexual violence. I now realize that I was part of the effort to carve out an ethical stance from which to work against sexual violence in a culture that fundamentally accepted it as normative. I have no regrets about this position. I continue to argue _as a moral norm_ that sexual experience should take place in a context devoid of coercion and grounded in equality and choice and that sexual violence is the opposite of this.

However, wishful thinking cannot overcome the fact that rape is about sex in patriarchal culture. In order to successfully counter, prevent, and confront sexual violence, we have to recognize that it _is_ about violence _and_ sex in a culture where violence is eroticized. Brownmiller and MacKinnon were both right. But I continue to argue from a theological perspective that, often contrary to experience, the coercive nature of sexuality is not an ontological reality, which is to say that it is not natural or part of God's created order for men or women. I realize that at this moment in history this claim may be more of a statement of faith than anything else. But it is where I have to stand as a woman determined to survive and to change the culture into which I was born.

WHAT *IS* THE MORAL WRONG OF RAPE?

If I were to pose this question of what is the moral wrong of rape to a group of undergraduates, the responses would range from "everything" to "nothing." Much depends on one's social location and experience.[7]

Various ethical arguments have been made to address this question. Together they paint a picture of the struggle to derive ethical norms in a patriarchal culture. For example, Ann Cahill observes:

> The problem of the sexual nature of rape is only one among many difficulties ethicists have faced in their attempts to delineate the precise wrong or wrongs of rape. Due to a host of factors — the historical oppression of women, the particular constructions of feminine sexuality, the imposition of a compulsory heterosexuality, the inherent contradiction between the ostensibly grave manner in which rape is considered ethically and the sheer prevalence with which it occurs — the determination of not only how, but also whether rape is wrong is fraught with uncertainties. The differing ways rape has been approached ethically are reflections of the social and political status of women as well as the underlying assumptions concerning sexual difference and sexual hierarchy.[8]

Establishing ethical norms regarding rape that are more than theoretical presents a challenge. A review of the various attempts is revealing.

Whose Property?

The Hebrew scriptural laws (Deuteronomy 22:23–28) address three specific situations of sexual assault and deal with them differently depending on the circumstances of the situation and the marital status of the victim.

- If a man "lies with" a betrothed virgin *in the city,* both shall be stoned to death: the woman because she did not cry out and the man for violating his neighbor's wife. The assumption here is that if the victim was in the city and cried out, someone would have intervened and prevented the attack. There is no recognition that force or fear may have prevented her screams or that her screams may have gone unheard. So if the attack is carried out without someone intervening, the victim must not have cried for help. This means that she must have eagerly participated in a sexual encounter and thus deserved to die because she "belonged" to another man (vv. 23–24).

- If a man seizes and "lies with" a betrothed virgin *in the country,* only the man shall be killed because although the woman cried out for help, there was no one to save her, "for this case is like that of someone who attacks and murders a neighbor." Only here is the violent nature of the crime emphasized (vv. 25–27).

- If a man encounters a virgin not engaged and "seizes her and lies with, *and they are caught in the act*" (v. 28 NRSV), the man must give *the father* of the woman fifty pieces of silver and *marry her (and may never divorce her) because he has violated her.* The rapist's punishment is to be married to his victim for the rest of his life.

All of these laws address the sexual assault of a woman as a property crime against the man to whom the woman "belonged," in other words, the husband or father. Consequences for the victim depended on the locale of the crime and disregarded the actual circumstance. If the woman is a virgin and still "belongs" to her father when she is assaulted, the assailant must pay the *father* restitution and *the victim is condemned to marriage* to her assailant. Consistently these laws regarded rape as a property crime. The one exception is the reference to the analogy between the rape and murder of a neighbor. Unfortunately, this assessment is overshadowed by the other references.[9]

Some clergy refer to these laws in their pastoral counseling of rape victims to determine whether or not the woman was really raped. "Did you scream? Did you fight back?" become the criteria by which the pastor evaluates the victim's credibility. If she did not scream or fight back, this pastor feels it is his or her task to confront the victim with her "sinful" condition. (See below.) This literal interpretation and this pastoral application betray a lack of understanding of rape and an insensitivity to the needs of the victim.

In Leviticus (18:6–18) we find references specifically to the sexual practices of the Hebrews. The prohibitions included here proscribe sexual contact between persons already related by blood since that would amount to "union with one's own flesh."[10] These laws were also intended to separate the Hebrews from their Canaanite neighbors who practiced these sexual activities.

In this passage, the phrase "to uncover the nakedness" of another is used to describe the prohibition: "None of you shall approach any one near of kin to uncover nakedness" (v. 6 NRSV). "To uncover nakedness" implies some degree of sexual contact that is prohibited because of the close kinship between persons. Types of relationships included in this prohibition are specified: son-mother, father-granddaughter, brother–sister, son-father, brother-half sister, nephew-aunt, son-stepmother, father-in-law–daughter-in-law, nephew–aunt by marriage, brother-in-law–sister-in-law. Finally, a man cannot have sexual contact with the daughter or granddaughter of a woman with whom he has had relations. It would appear that this passage is an example of the incest taboo, which is often assumed to be universal. Yet there is a conspicuous absence of prohibition against father-daughter or father-son sexual contact. The prohibitions here refer to contact between a male and a female who is the property of someone else.[11] Again the property violation dictates the prohibition of sexual contact. We can speculate that the absence of the father-daughter and father-son prohibitions results from the fact that children were regarded as possessions of their father, which meant that he had sexual license with them. The major concern in these laws is the protection of property from misuse, not the protection of individual persons from exploitation.[12]

In all of the scriptural examples that refer to acts of sexual assault and abuse, the authors are concerned with the offense as a violation of male property rights.[13] We can only assume that the authors' attitudes reflect the views of the community.[14] The irony is that even though rape as a property crime completely ignored the well-being of the victim, it did carry with it a response exacting accountability from the rapist and often severe punishment as well, including capital punishment.[15]

Framing rape as a property crime against an owner ignores the real victim and her experience of violence and violation of personal autonomy. It is an ethical wrong based on trespass or theft. Rape as a property crime isn't about women at all but in fact about men's relationships with other men as they jockey for social, political, and economic power (for example, the rape of Tamar, the rape of Dinah, and the rape of the unnamed concubine).

The Problem with Consent

On the one hand, it would seem that the absence of consent would be a strong basis for establishing the wrong of rape. Ann Cahill notes that this was the basis of early feminist ethical arguments; she quotes Carolyn Shafer and Marilyn Frye:

> We shall proceed to presume that rape is sexual intercourse performed without the consent of the woman. Since _we share the public view that rape is morally wrong and gravely so_ [emphasis added], and since we would not want to say that there is anything morally wrong with sexual intercourse per se, we conclude that the wrongness of rape rests with the matter of the woman's consent (1977).[16]

Authentic consent (see chapter 4, "A New Sexual Ethic") assumes genuine choice in a context of a peer relationship. Thus not only force but any type of coercion (including threats to others) render consent impossible. Acquiescence may well pose as "consent," but it is not the same.

The fundamental problem here is that women are placed in a catch-22.[17] Historically, women have not had the rights of legal and social standing (ownership of property, the vote, etc.), and even now those rights are partial.[18] So is the possibility of authentic consent only illusory? Ann Cahill describes the dilemma for women in heterosexual marriages:

> As an institution that legally, socially and historically endows the husband with greater authority than the wife, marriage demands from a woman a consent to limit her possibilities of consent.... To accede to the offer that a man makes, to accept a given situation, to consent to it, is strikingly different than to seek out a certain situation and to choose it for oneself.[19]

Is this circumstance different in same-sex relationships? Yes and no. While gay or lesbian partners do not carry the gender difference framework in the intimacy of a relationship, nor the baggage or benefit of marriage (in the early twenty-first-century United States), the patriarchal context is nonetheless operative. Because of a variety of factors, same-sex partners may not function as equals in relationship. So consent may or may not be an authentic option.

Social location serves to limit ethical options whether related to age, gender, race, or physical ability. Authentic consent (the choice to say "yes" and participate in a particular activity) means that a person also has the option to say "no" and not be punished for it. Consent is only real if the choice to withhold it is respected. If there are punitive consequences for saying "no," then "consent" was an illusion to begin with.

Finally, the practical problem with basing the wrong of rape on the absence of consent is that it rests on the victim's effectiveness in *communicating* nonconsent, whether as a legal or ethical question.[20] Once again this ethical theory shifts focus to the victim's behavior and ignores the agency and responsibility of the assailant. Consent theory alone does not offer a strong foundation for establishing the ethical wrong of rape. However, authentic consent as an extension of choice remains a critical component of sexual ethics.

The question of using consent as the basis for establishing an ethical norm carries with it the issue of moral agency for the victim. In 1992, an Austin, Texas, woman brought a charge of rape against a stranger who broke into her apartment, held her at knifepoint, and raped her. Before he raped her, she asked the rapist to wear a condom (which she provided). He agreed. The grand jury refused to indict the man because he argued that since she asked him to wear a condom, she was consenting. Subsequently the prosecutor refiled the case, and the man was indicted, prosecuted, and convicted.[21]

The initial refusal to indict this man was an indicator that the grand jury regarded the woman's act of requesting that the man wear a condom in order to protect her from disease and pregnancy as a sign of her consent to have sex with him. Her acting as a moral agent to protect herself as much as possible from a man holding a knife at her throat was interpreted as consent. "If she didn't want to have sex with me, why did she ask me to wear a condom?" To save her life. In fact, what was going on here was that _any_ agency at all on her part rendered her no longer an "innocent victim" in the eyes of the grand jury. She then is not only consenting, she is culpable for his actions. No doubt the fact that she possessed a condom in the first place indicated to the grand jury that she was a sexually active adult woman, which rendered her "unrapable" in their eyes.

In fact, moral agency requires that we possess power and resources. We must have knowledge and awareness in order to exercise sound judgment. We cannot exercise choice if we do not have options and the ability to act. Anything that denies or compromises these resources undercuts moral agency. Sometimes those who have the capacity and resources to exercise moral agency attempt to deny their ability in order to avoid responsibility for their actions. The father who explained that his daughter came up to him and unzipped his pants and "What else was I supposed to do?" in order to justify his sexual abuse of this four-year-old child was denying that he had power and responsibility. He refused to acknowledge that his response to her should have been to zip up his pants and leave her unmolested. It is a paradox how often those who have the most resources and opportunity to exercise moral agency (usually offenders) seek to deny it and those who have the least opportunity (usually victims) seek to assume it.

Rape as Assault

If we view the ethical wrong of rape as primarily that of assault (sexual), again we find advantages and disadvantages. Assault has a strong historic and legal rationale that focuses on physical force or threat of force resulting in physical harm as a moral wrong. Even here are significant issues of degree that the law sometimes recognizes in "simple rape" and "aggravated rape."[22]

This emphasis on "assault" helps to minimize the distraction of traditional "sexual" connotations that undermine clarity regarding the moral wrong. It also supports a gender-neutral ethical norm with regard to victim and perpetrator. However, the focus on "assault" carries the temptation to minimize or overlook the sexual impact of rape *on the victim*. If we are to take seriously the double-edged reality of rape as both violent and sexual as it relates to the perpetrator (and his or her motivation, etc.), then we also have to consider the sexual nature of the assault for the victim. With or without "physical force," the trauma is profound and can be highly subjective. How do we measure "harm" on multiple levels: personal, bodily, emotional, spiritual, social? Rape is not merely a variety of assault, although it is assault. But it is *sexual assault*. The adjective here is critical in our consideration of moral wrongs.

MEANS, ENDS, AND CONTRACTS

The use of a person as a means to another's ends raises concerns within a context of traditional Western secular ethics. This approach presupposes a relationship of equals, which explains why this argument did not prevent the development of slavery in the eighteenth and nineteenth centuries. Cahill suggests:

A Kantian approach to rape, such as that taken by Raymond Belliotti (1979), would argue that the crime constitutes a clear violation of the ethical principle that prohibits the use of another human being as a mere means to one's own ends. What is wrong in the case of rape is that the victim is utilized as a mere mechanism for the achievement of the assailant's sexual ends (or, it may be argued, for the achievement of the assailant's political ends, if by that term we mean a general desire for power over another person).... This contractual analysis, unlike the models of consent theory, presents the parties involved as equally self-interested beings, who arrive at a mutually beneficial contract that stipulates a set of rights and responsibilities that adhere to each.[23]

So this argument might be strong in a situation of male-male rape where the value of both parties is acknowledged and the violation is one of a contract not to use the other as means to an end.

But the flip side of using a contractual model within a patriarchal setting and a heterosexual situation is problematic, especially if combined with consent theory. If a woman consents to go on a date with a man — if the man buys dinner, and so on, and assumes a contract of exchange of goods for sex, so he expects the date to include sexual intimacy, and the woman refuses — he can argue that she violated the implicit "contract" under which he was operating. Thus "date rape" could be justified and defended against in judicial proceedings. Once again the social and political differences in power between men and women as classes in patriarchal culture shape the interpretation of ethical wrongs.

THE CONTEMPORARY CHRISTIAN TRADITION ON SEXUAL VIOLENCE

In order to comprehend the impact of the Christian tradition on our understanding of sexual violence, we must look at the ways that the tradition addresses sexual violence historically and contemporarily.

Most contemporary Christian ethicists who do address sexual violence at all do so in a cursory yet revealing manner. Here we often find a contradiction of constructive ethical insight and traditional ethical confusion. For example, in an article on sexual ethics, John T. Noonan Jr. described rape as

> the most universally abhorred sexual act; ... it inflicts fear, bodily harm, and psychological trauma; ... it creates the possibility of conception; ... it invades the victim's privacy; ... it expresses hatred.... It is the touching of the genital zone accompanied by animosity, threat and trauma which makes rape *repulsive* [emphasis added].[24]

He identifies rape as an abhorrent *sexual* act but then describes a *violent* act. "Repulsive" is an unusual adjective to use to assert an ethical norm.

In his discussion of sexual sins, Karl Menninger devotes one sentence in his book *Whatever Became of Sin?* (1973) to the subject of rape: "Rape, for example, is characteristically less a sexual act than a form of assault and mayhem — a form of hurting, debasing, and destroying another person for power-drive satisfaction. That's sin!"[25] He is attempting to clarify the confusion between sex and sexual violence.

Like many traditional legal definitions, *Baker's Dictionary of Christian Ethics* (1973) defines rape as "a man's unlawful carnal knowledge of a woman, without her consent, by resort to force or fraud."[26] This definition emphasizes the important issues of consent and force, but adds that "corroboration by evidence other than the woman's testimony"[27] is required. A doubt remains as to a woman's trustworthiness. It also is interesting to note that this definition limits rape to male-female assault and does not recognize same-gender rape or female-male rape.

The Dictionary of Moral Theology (1962), a Roman Catholic resource, emphasizes the violent nature of rape: "In the terminology of modern theologians, *rape is* a violent sexual relation.... Violence is understood not only as a physical but moral force (serious threats, deception)."[28] Added to this definition is the injustice of the "violation of the right of a woman to use her generative faculty according to her own choice."[29] But then it goes on to say that the rape of a virgin is a greater injustice because "virginity is a good of greatest value, distinct from the right that she has to the use of her own body according to her free choice."[30] Here the concern for sexual chastity overrides the principle of women's right to bodily integrity and autonomy. This concern is further emphasized: "In a case of violence, the woman is obliged to use all the means at her command to avoid _the sexual act_ [emphasis added], short of exposing herself to the danger of death, or to other grave harm."[31] This is one step short of the example St. Maria Goretti gave the world. Finally, the ethical concern expressed here focuses on the maintenance of a woman's sexual chastity, which, at its core, is a concern for male property rights.[32]

> The unjust aggressor is obliged to make reparation of all damages due to his crime. In particular, he must enable the woman to contract marriage in the same manner as if she had never been violated, _even by marrying her himself_ [emphasis added], provided that all other conditions are favorable... _Often the best form of reparation is marriage_ [emphasis added], if it can be properly arranged and offers a reasonable prospect of success.[33]

Published in 1962, _The Dictionary of Moral Theology_ echoes Deuteronomy with its suggestion that a rape victim _marry_ her rapist, and that such a marriage would make reparation _to her_ for the crime![34]

In the _Biblical View of Sex and Marriage_ (1960), Otto Piper goes to the extreme of traditional interpretation and describes rape (along with masturbation) as that which results "when a normal satisfaction of the sexual desire is impossible."[35] He regards insatiable sexual need as the source of sexual violence and "never a conscious volition."[36] If never a conscious volition, then, we can conclude, rape is nothing for which a rapist can be held accountable.

In late-twentieth-century Christian ethical discussion, even less attention was given to incest than to rape. The primary concerns expressed were the potential for hereditary defects in children of an incestuous union[37] (although the scientific basis for this genetic concern is questionable), the impact of incest on the parents' relationship, and the need to maintain the "natural order of procreation."[38] These sources of ethical discussion made no reference to incestuous abuse being destructive to child victims or to it being a violation of the parent/child relationship.

Unlike *Baker's Dictionary* and the *Dictionary of Moral Theology*, Noonan does raise the ethical issues posed by comparing rape and incest. In his discussion, however, there is a mixture of accuracy and inaccuracy that limits its usefulness.

> Except where it merges with actual rape, incest is not necessarily attended by fear or bodily injury. In the paradigm case of father and pubescent daughter, it is typically attended by trauma for the child. It creates the possibility of a conception without responsible parents. *It does not invade the child's privacy without her consent* [emphasis added]. It does not express hatred. It does distort the relation of a father to a daughter. It does involve a betrayal of the child's trust. The infliction of the trauma, the risking of a pregnancy, the distortion of the parental role, and the betrayal of trust are injuries to the individual and to society.[39]

Fear and bodily injury can both be present even without penetration. In fact, the onset of father-daughter incestuous abuse typically occurs between the daughter's age of three to six years old. There is definitely trauma for the child. For the pubescent female child, the possibility of enforced conception is very real and must be addressed by the church. Noonan describes the damage and yet suggests that no invasion of privacy underlies the damage done. While the incestuous abuse may not express hatred, it expresses a total disregard for the well-being of the child. Noonan accurately sums up the nature of the injury and its consequences, but he erroneously believes that the incest taboo is functioning to prevent incest.[40] Again there is minimal understanding of the ethical questions of consent, power, and powerlessness, harm, and the protection of children.

In _Dirt, Greed, and Sex,_ William Countryman makes perhaps the strongest theological and ethical assertion:

> Theft of sustenance or space is the most obvious kind of violation of property; yet, violations of that trust which is the foundation of human community or of the freedom of choice are at least as grave. . . . When committed by a stranger, it violates the victim's freedom of choice; when committed by a family member or presumed friend, it violates the bonds of human community as well. The metaphorical space which surrounds each of us and which we characterize as "mine" is of the essence of our being human. It offers some protection for the freedom to develop and become what God is calling us to be, which is the principal goal of being human. When it is opened voluntarily to another, it is also a means of community. But when it is broken into by violence, the very possibility of being human is at least momentarily being denied to us. As there is nothing more precious to us than our humanness, there is no sexual sin more serious than rape.[41]

He rightly places the discussion in the context of theft, not of property, but of self.

In _Embodiment,_ one of the most useful books on Christian sexual ethics written in the late twentieth century, James B. Nelson cites rape as a social justice issue and as a crime of "violence used to keep women 'in their place.' " This is a valuable insight, but beyond this, his treatment of rape is minimal.[42] In Nelson's later anthology (with Sandra P. Longfellow), _Sexuality and the Sacred,_ they do include three articles on sexual violence and pornography.[43] In the 1990s, we began to see some attention to sexual violence in the discussion of sexuality and ethics.

Despite lip service to the contrary, it appears that twentieth-century Christian teaching, like traditional teaching, viewed sexual violence generally as either a sexual impropriety or a violation of male property rights. The occasional exceptions to this view are too few to significantly challenge the dominant position of both scripture and tradition.

The Christian tradition itself offers even less than the scripture in providing clarity and direction for an ethical perspective on sexual violence. Too often the teachings of the tradition confuse sexual activity with sexual violence. In doing so, they focus on the sexual rather than on the violent aspect of sexual violence; they blame the victim; and they fail to hold the offender accountable. They ascribe agency to the victim and not to the perpetrator. There is virtually no mention of the victim of sexual assault as the one who is offended directly. The context of justice is almost never put forth. Restitution *for the victim* is rarely mentioned. While there is some concern in scripture for the impact of sexual violence on the whole community, the implications of this are never drawn. The tradition treats sexual assault as an embarrassing individual experience rather than as a cause for community outrage. Moreover, the traditional teachings contribute to the negative, ill-informed, and contradictory attitudes about female sexuality and homosexuality.

This critical review of scriptural and traditionally oriented contemporary sources leads to the conclusion that scripture and Christian tradition are inadequate for helping to address sexual violence as an ethical issue. Thus in order to engage constructively in ethical discourse, we must be willing to discard that material which is ill-informed and perpetuates confusion, and draw more deeply on our faith and experience.

Using these resources, we must then reframe the ethical questions presented by sexual violence, clarifying the confusion between sexual activity and sexual violence, and asking what is the real violation that takes place when a person is raped or sexually abused. We must name the unmentionable sin. Then we must struggle with the demands that justice makes in response to the sin of sexual violence. Finally, we must consider the implications for contemporary Christian sexual ethics.

Establishing the Moral Wrong of Sexual Violence

We come full circle in considering the ethical wrong of rape. The question of harm as the strongest criterion remains, which specifies negative consequences for the victim as central to an ethical argument. The early work of Ann Wolbert Burgess and Lynda Lytle Holmstrom, who presented "rape trauma syndrome" to begin to describe and measure the harm of rape on victims, represented an effort to develop a clinical and hence objective measure but was in fact also a moral argument. Judith Herman's work on linking rape to post-traumatic stress disorder emphasized the particularity of sexual violence by calling it "complex post-traumatic stress disorder" and continued to make the case for "harm" as a violation of a moral good.[44] In Ann Cahill's extensive discussion of ethics in _Rethinking Rape,_ she examines the question of harm and summarizes her view of the wrong of rape:

> In the act of rape, the assailant reduces the victim to a non-person. He (for the overwhelming majority of rapists are male, another aspect of the sexually differentiated nature of the act) denies the victim the specificity of her (for the overwhelming majority of rape victims are female) own being and constructs her sexuality as a mere means by which his own purposes, be they primarily sexual or primarily motivated by the need for power, are achieved. . . . The victim's difference from the assailant — her ontological, ethical, and personal distinctness — is stamped out, erased, annihilated.[45]

The focus on the _harm_ done to the victim is the primary measure of moral wrong. Although this in some ways highly subjective norm may be a problem in establishing it as a legal norm — which typically has objective, behavioral measures — it is nonetheless appropriate in shaping a pastoral or therapeutic response. It may also be significant in shaping the response to the perpetrator in an appeal to his or her empathy for the consequences of his or her actions on another person.[46]

A focus on harm done to the victim also is not entirely dependent on the "victim's" perception. The community has an overriding interest at points in positing harm done even in contradiction to the "victim." For example, in statutory rape, the law specifies that sexual contact is illegal between an adult and teenager even if the teenager sees herself or himself as "consenting." This social and legal norm based on the inability to consent because of the imbalance of power asserts that sexual involvement with an adult harms a teen.

Beginning with the question of harm done to the victim is an insight from the secular discussion that strengthens our consideration of the theological and scriptural foundations for positing specific ethical norms related to sexual violence.

THE SIN OF SEXUAL VIOLENCE

As we move from the ethical language of wrong and harm to the theological language of sin, we are able to place the discussion in the context of brokenness and rupture of relationship. The problem of confusion between sex and sexual violence (chapter 2) still overshadows any discussion about the nature of the sin of sexual violence. In order to clear a space to discuss the sin of sexual violence, we need to reiterate what it is not.

Fundamentally, rape or sexual abuse are not sins simply because they are "sexual," that is, because there is some form of genital contact, and specifically outside of marriage. So "adultery" is not the ethical category within which to consider sexual violence.[47] Neither is homosexuality, although confusion on this point is rampant. As indicated in the discussion of Genesis and Judges 19 above (Sodom and Gomorrah; the unnamed concubine), historic and contemporary interpretations of both of these stories focus on the "sexual sin" of homosexuality. This appears to be based on the fact that the gang of men in each case threatens to assault other men, the male guests, which would involve genital contact between males. In fact the stories vividly describe sexual assault, first threatened against men, suggested against the daughters, and carried out against the concubine. All of this mayhem occurred in the context of a profound violation of the hospitality code and of the concubine herself, which are the real ethical issues at stake here.

In neither the scriptural interpretation of the stories nor in more current hermeneutics do we hear any reference except among feminist biblical scholars[48] to the sin inflicted upon the woman, that is, the violation of her bodily integrity and sacrifice of her life. Certainly no one asked the concubine whether she would choose to offer herself to a gang of rapists in order to protect her master from this fate. Once she found herself facing the gang, it was apparent that the gang's purpose was to violate and destroy her, not even because she was a person in her own right, but because she was the property of the guest. Because the master was the real target of the gang of assailants, assaulting the concubine, his property, was the next best thing to being able to assault him directly.

The sin of sexual violence is a violation of the victim that causes physical and emotional harm. Why is it unethical to violate the sexual boundaries of another person?

Sexual violence is a _personal_ sin:

- a violation of bodily integrity that denies a person the choice to determine one's own boundaries and activities.

- a violation of personhood because it objectifies the other, making them a nonperson.

- an act that creates a victim, that is, renders a person powerless by taking away her or his resources and sense of self.

- an act that distorts and misuses sexuality.

Sexual violence is a _relational_ sin:

- a betrayal of trust in a relationship, which destroys the possibility of relationship between people.

Sexual violence is a _social_ sin:

- an act that thrives in an environment of sexism, racism, and heterosexism to sustain subordinate or dominant relationships that encourage or silently condone individual acts of sexual violence, creating a hostile environment, particularly for women and children.

- an act that destroys community because it creates an atmosphere of fear and distrust among family, friends, coworkers, and acquaintances.

In a nonpeer relationship in which there is an inequality of power (for example, a relationship between parent and child, teacher and student, pastor and congregant, etc.), there are additional dimensions to the sin of sexual violence:

- with a child, a violation of the adult role vis-à-vis the child. The adult should be protecting and providing for the child's welfare.

- a misuse of the power and authority of the adult or leadership role.

- taking advantage of vulnerability.

- denial of authentic consent.

In sum, sexual violence is a sin because it causes harm to another person and brings suffering. Toinette Eugene summarizes the sin of sexual violence from a womanist perspective:

A womanist-informed definition of sexual abuse is constructed in terms of the experiences of African-American women within a historical context, and in terms of the ethical, religious, and psychological issues regarding sexual violence. Therefore the elements of sexual abuse are the violation of one's bodily integrity by force and/or threat of physical violence. It is the violation of the ethic of mutuality and care in relationships of domination. It is a violation of one's psycho-spiritual-sexual integrity by using sexual abuse to control and express violence. Sexual abuse is the violation of the Spirit of God incarnate in each of us.[49]

For Christians, this contradicts God's purpose attributed to Jesus in John's Gospel: "The thief comes only to steal and kill and destroy.

I came that they may have life, and have it abundantly" (John 10:10 NRSV).

In addition, the responsibility articulated by the prophet Ezekiel in chapter 34 draws on the Hebrew hospitality code, which mandated the entire community to protect those who are vulnerable: orphans, widows, and sojourners (Psalm 146:9). This important mandate was given to the Hebrews with a reminder: because *you* were once slaves in the land of Egypt (Deuteronomy 10:19). The reminder is that all humans experience vulnerability at different times in our lives and so we are to protect one another in those circumstances.

Sexual violence is a sin against the community. Hebrew scripture refers to an offense that disrupts community life. It describes the upset of male property arrangements that resulted from sexual violence. But reinterpreted from the perspective of the victims, we can better understand the disruption of the community to mean the fear, mistrust, and limitations that sexual violence imposes on all members of the community. In Hebrew scripture, the words describe the havoc, folly,[50] and emptiness that result from sexual assault. A picture emerges of a hostile, alien environment that diminishes the possibility of meaningful relationships within the community, particularly between women and men. From a Christian perspective, the sin of sexual violence is also a sin against the community of faith as a whole. Through baptism all Christians are joined together as one body, so whenever any one of its members is violated or injured, the whole body suffers the effects of the sin.

STOLEN, NOT LOST

Another common lay interpretation of the wrong of rape or sexual abuse articulated by survivors of childhood sexual abuse or abuse by clergy or other trusted helpers is of having lost something as a way of describing the consequences of the betrayal of trust they experience. In this they are reaching for a moral norm by which to establish the wrongness of their experience. Of course the flaw here is that this language of "loss" completely avoids agency or responsibility on the part of the perpetrator. The passive voice of loss ultimately reflects on the survivor and her or his carelessness in "losing" something valuable. This is a reasonable effort again within a patriarchal context in which support for placing responsibility for an offense (betrayal of trust and violation of boundaries) on the person with power (parent, teacher, clergy, etc.) is unlikely. But it seriously distracts from a viable ethical norm, which should focus on theft. This is not to revert to the property discussion above, but rather to acknowledge that in fact something is taken by the perpetrator that does not belong to him or her. It is not the property of one's "sexual goods" but rather the trust that one carries in one's world, in relationships, and also one's future. The sexual abuse of a child means that that child's future is dramatically impacted and will require some expenditure of energy and resources as an adult to address the childhood experience. A child's future is stolen by sexual abuse, which does not mean that the future cannot be recovered. But if it weren't for the actions of an adult who took something that did not belong to him or her, this child's future would have looked quite different.

A sexual attack makes it clear that something has been taken away: another's power, another's bodily integrity. The power to decide, to choose, to determine, and to consent or withhold consent in the most concrete bodily dimension all vanish in the face of a rapist or child molester. The poem "Stolen, Not Lost," written in 1993 by Marian Lovelace, a survivor of childhood abuse by multiple Catholic priests, illustrates the distinction:

STOLEN, NOT LOST

I learned a valuable lesson today about responsibility.
I now know where to leave the shame and blame.
I am beginning to discover the truth —
Many of my precious gifts were stolen, not lost!

You stole my unquestioned belief in my Heavenly Father's love;
You stole the preciousness of solitude in God's presence.
You stole the joy of coming together to share Eucharist.

You stole my reverence for the deep meaning of a church family.
You stole my ability to be quiet and hear God's voice.
You stole my belief in the phrase "God answers prayers."
You stole the joy I felt in calling myself — "Christian."
You stole my ability to find comfort in going to confession.
You stole my innocence and twisted my trust in mankind.
You stole my hope for a better tomorrow and instilled doubt.
You stole my love of life and wanting to live.
You stole my belief in the basic goodness of people.
You stole a significant part of my childhood and adolescence.
You stole my desire to become a loving adult woman.
You stole my voice and my actions that screamed a loud "NO."
You stole my right to claim my justifiable anger at abuse.
You stole my right to easily risk council without suspicion.
You stole the inner peace I experienced entering God's house.

You stole my many treasures and the blame and guilt is yours.
Someday you will answer to God for your many thefts.
Someday justice will be based on the evilness of your actions.
Today I leave the responsibility at your feet, where it belongs.

Today I was given a profound gift and hope for tomorrow.
I was helped to see your behavior in the truest light.
I choose not to be forever damaged by your multiple thefts.
I choose to fight to regain my stolen gifts, as that is my right.

I will grieve those stolen gifts that will always be blemished.
I will strive to be wiser and not cynical because of your thefts.
I will go forward strengthened in faith as I know the truth —
So many of my precious treasures were _stolen, not lost!_

Finally, the sin of sexual violence brings us back to the Ten Commandments. But it is not the Seventh Commandment that should concern us: "You shall not commit adultery." The problem with sexual violence is not that it represents "sex outside of marriage." Rather is it the Eighth Commandment: "You shall not steal" (Deuteronomy

5:19 and Exodus 20:15). It is not theft in the sense of rape or sexual abuse of a woman or child being the theft of property belonging to the male head-of-household. It is rather the theft by the assailant of the security and well-being of the victim, the betrayal of trust, and the theft of her or his future.

WHAT WRONG? WHO DECIDES?

Some criteria are needed to help judge the seriousness and the sinfulness of human behavior. But the criteria should be based on the degree to which a particular behavior causes harm or suffering to a person. Once the ethical question is reframed in this way, principles and criteria can be formulated to guide behavior and society's response to particular behaviors. Establishing the criterion of harm done to the victim does not rely on resolving the issue of intent or the psychological motivation of the assailant (sex or violence?) to determine the wrong of rape. In fact, it allows us to posit the question: why does the motivation of the assailant matter? If he or she is acting out of a desire for power and control or a desire for sexual contact (or both), and denies the autonomy and choice of another person, he or she has violated an ethical norm and should be held accountable. It is the offender's sin. It is a sin against God, the victim, and the community, with serious ramifications for all.

Still we return to MacKinnon's position that rape is the "normal" consequence of the established social and political domination of women by men. As such it is hard to find an ethical norm to challenge it. It is "the way things are," therefore "normal," therefore moral. The ethical norm is also defined by those with power. Carol Adams quotes MacKinnon and Judith Herman:

> "The fact is, anything that anybody with power experiences as sex is considered *ipso facto* not violence, [that is, not wrong] because *someone who matters enjoyed it*" [emphasis added]. (1987)
> ... Judith Herman offers a confirmation of this: if "the normative social definition of sexuality involves the eroticization of male

dominance and female submission, then the use of coercive means to achieve sexual conquest might represent a crude exaggeration of prevailing norms, but not a departure from them."[51]

This is the tacit subtext to the history of Western thought on the subject of the ethical wrong of rape. It has rested on the experience and interpretation of the one with power and virtually ignored the consequences for the one without, hence the difficulty of establishing and implementing social and judicial remedies for this unjust behavior. The question of "who decides" whether it was sex (that is, normal/moral) or violence (that is, aberrant/immoral) is finally a political as well as an ethical and legal question yet to be determined.

Chapter 4 _____

A New Sexual Ethic

===

As I presented an overview of the Abuse Prevention Materials for Teenagers to parents and youth advisors in a local church, the final question from one of the adults was, "All I want to know is, are you going to tell them what is right and wrong?" Our answer to his question was, "Yes, we are going to tell them that responsible, nonabusive sexual activity is right and that sexual abuse and exploitation is wrong."

The persistent confusion between sexual activity and sexual violence necessitates that any discussion of the ethical questions posed by sexual violence must also include a discussion of contemporary sexual ethics. The confusion of sexual activity with sexual violence has prevented many people from realizing how frequently their sexual experiences are really experiences of coercive "sex." So what is a just relationship? What principles and parameters would support authentic consensual sex between persons?

TRADITIONAL SEXUAL ETHICS: A CRITIQUE

In traditional Christian sexual ethics[1] the issues have focused on the form or type of sexual contact between persons. Consider how the following ethical questions are stated:

- Should persons engage in sexual activity before marriage?
- Should persons of the same gender engage in sexual activity?
- Should persons engage in any nonprocreative sexual activity?

- Should a person engage in extramarital activity?
- Should older persons engage in sexual activity?
- Should a person engage in masturbation?

All of these questions focus on the who, what, where, when, and why of sexual activity. None of them considers the qualitative substance of the relationship (which may include sexual activity), such as the presence or absence of consent and the distribution of power.

While some of the questions require ethical discussion concerning the form of relationships (who, what, when, where, and why), that discussion needs to be directed primarily toward the consideration of commitment and relationship.[2] Thus, for example, the question of extramarital (or extracommitment) sexual activity is more accurately a question of extracommitment intimacy, which may or may not be sexual. The question could be stated thus: is it ethically right and good to engage in intimate activity (sexual, emotional, etc.) outside of one's primary committed relationship? The answer to this question depends on the terms of the primary commitment, the experience of the partners, and the willingness to take the advice of others who may say that it is emotionally impractical to engage in extracommitment intimacy.

Using this broader framework, the issue is not whether it is categorically wrong to engage in extracommitment sexual activity. The ethical concern has to do with the impact of such activity on a marriage or commitment. While it is morally wrong to violate such a commitment, sexual activity may or may not cause this violation. Thus, in considering extracommitment activity, it is not the sexual nature of the activity per se that requires ethical reflection but the intimate nature of the activity and its impact on the relationship. Does intimate activity with another person outside of a committed relationship violate that commitment? Does it break trust in the committed relationship?[3] Does it diminish one's ability to fulfill one's responsibilities to one's partner? While the sexual nature of the activity is significant because it represents the potential for greater intimacy, it is not the central issue. The purpose here is not to discuss the issue of extracommitment sexual activity in depth; however, it does provide an example of a way in which those questions traditionally regarded as issues of sexual ethics can be restated and reexamined.

The question of whether persons should engage in sexual activity before marriage is another example of misplaced ethical focus. The traditional *rule* which said categorically that sexual activity before marriage was wrong implied that sexual activity in marriage was right; no other criteria need be applied.[4] The primary consideration was *when* sexual activity took place. It gave little consideration to the substance or quality of the sexual interaction after marriage. Using this view, it would be wrong for a man to engage in coercive sexual activity with a woman before they were married, and acceptable for him to engage in exactly the same coercive sexual activity after they were married. This ethical stance makes it possible to suggest that there is no such thing as marital rape because marriage assures the husband any form of sexual access to his wife at any time. The questions of the substance and quality of the sexual interaction in the relationship, the presence of consent, and so on, are never raised.

Again, ethical reflection on sexual activity before, during, or after marriage or commitment needs to be reframed. The primary considerations relevant to sexual activity have to do with choice, equal regard for the needs of the other, consent, mutuality, and respect. Does the sexual activity in which one engages in a relationship take these concerns into account? Does this activity enhance and sustain one's commitment to a partner? The issue is not whether sexual activity before marriage or commitment is categorically wrong, but rather, what is the quality and substance of that activity (should the couple *choose* it)? How does it affect their relationship before and after commitment? How does it affect their relationship with God? Two persons may very well decide not to engage in sexual activity prior to a commitment between them based on this reexamination of the issues. But their reasons for doing so would be grounded in their shared values and mutual decision-making process rather than based on an arbitrary, categorical rule. This would prepare them for continuing ethical reflection concerning their sexual activities after the commitment is made.

The concern as to whether or not two persons of the same gender should engage in sexual activity is another example of misplaced ethical concern. At different points in the history of the Christian tradition the church has used misinterpretations of scripture and drawn on prevailing cultural attitudes to condemn same-gender sexual activity. Again the implication is that any sexual contact between persons of the same gender is wrong. The concern here is the question of _who_ is involved in sexual activity. Stated in this way, the question of quality of relationship or sexual interaction is never raised. Using this approach, coercive or even violent sexual contact between persons of the opposite gender may be excused while consenting, responsible sexual activity with the same gender is readily condemned.

To suggest that same-gender sexual activity is categorically wrong cuts short the process of ethical reflection and may well limit the possibility for the formation of responsible, committed relationships. In restating the ethical concerns related to same-gender sexual activity, the ethical norms or expectations should focus on the quality of the sexual relationship regardless of gender.

For the most part, sexual ethics have been limited to categorical regulations because of an overriding concern with a procreative norm for sexual ethics. The emphasis on this norm for Christian sexual ethics is rooted in the value the Hebrews placed on reproduction in order to sustain a small, struggling population. To a large degree, sexual activity that produced children was encouraged and that which did not was discouraged. Thus polygamy was common; homosexuality and _coitus interruptus_ were discouraged. Although the biblical record does not discuss masturbation as such, the historic position of both the Jewish and Christian communities has condemned it because it is seen as nonprocreative activity. In addition, the influence of Stoic philosophy on the Christian procreative norm is significant. Stoics believed that sexual desire was irrational and that sexual activity could only be justified if it served a rational purpose like procreation.[5]

The position of the Roman Catholic Church today remains that sexual activity should take place only in the context of marriage and preferably for purposes of procreation. However, the approval of the rhythm method by Pope Pius XI in 1930 has made non-procreative (as distinguished from antiprocreative) sexual activity by Catholics legitimate in the eyes of the church.[6] Most Protestant groups have broadened their understanding of acceptable sexual activity beyond a procreative norm to include the use of artificial birth control methods as a means of responsible stewardship. Still the procreative norm remains a significant influence in determining what is regarded as "natural" and "unnatural" in sexual activity. The "natural/unnatural" criteria frequently determine what is regarded as morally right or wrong. For example, same-gender sexual contact is seen as morally wrong because it is "unnatural"; it is "unnatural" because it is not procreative. Thus, the influence of the procreative norm remains a part of the dominant cultural and religious attitudes into the twenty-first century.

The tendencies of traditional sexual ethics to be "act-centered," that is, focusing on form, and using the procreative norm as a primary criterion have meant that little attention has been given to the issues of consent, power, and the potential for harm in sexual relationships. Hence, traditional sexual ethics have often missed the mark by providing a list of "thou shalt nots" and using guilt as a means to encourage conformity to the rules of the church rather than teaching persons how to make ethical choices. To make responsible ethical choices in the area of sexuality requires information, a willingness to communicate and negotiate, a respect for the other's choices, a sense of self-worth, and a sense of one's own power to consent or withhold consent. The church has not adequately prepared people to engage in ethical decision making. Instead it has sought to control people's sexual behavior through fear, guilt, and regulation.

It is far simpler to leave the discussion of ethical sexual behavior at the level of category and regulation than to focus ethical discourse on substance and quality. To do this means questioning some of the most basic assumptions in our culture about men, women, and sexuality. Perhaps this is one reason that most Christian sexual ethics seem obsessed with the who, what, where, when, and why approach to sexuality. The implications of a deeper ethical reflection are complex and often disquieting. However, our unwillingness to reframe the ethical questions surrounding sexuality is a detriment to our lives and to the community and perpetuates the distortion of human sexuality.

THE CONTEXT OF JUST RELATIONS

Fundamental to just relations is the principle of authentic consent, fully informed and freely given. In sexual activity, this should be the basis for any discussion of sexual ethics. Functionally this principle means that a person has the right to say "no" to any form of sexual contact and they have a right to have that "no" respected. Using the principle of authentic consent can assist people in preventing "coercive 'sex' " because it counters the game playing that encourages the " 'no' really means 'yes' " game.

The corollary to the right to say "no" is the freely chosen right to say "yes" to sexual activity.[7] The principle of authentic consent is not antisexual. It does not obligate one always to say "no" to sexual activity. It is the right to say "no" and the right to say "yes" when fully informed and freely acting. Sexual ethics has to do with helping people make responsible choices based on specific principles and with respecting the other person's choice to say "yes" or "no." The bottom line that should guide one's sexual decision making and behavior is "thou shalt not sexually manipulate, abuse, or take advantage of another at any time." All persons have the right, the responsibility, and the capability to make decisions about sexual activity and the right to have those decisions respected, but they can only do this if they have information, self-confidence, and power in their lives. This does not mean that persons will not make mistakes, use poor judgment, or make choices they regret later; however, it does assume that people can learn from their experiences.

Accepting the principle of authentic consent is of special concern with regard to teenagers. Many adults, concerned about preventing teenage pregnancy, sexually transmitted disease, promiscuity, and so on, do not feel that teenagers should have the right to make decisions about sexual activity. The solution, according to some adults, is teaching girls to say "no" to any sexual contact with boys. Few adults suggest teaching boys anything about their responsibilities in these matters.[8] This suggested solution reinforces a damaging double standard in which females are expected to be responsible for male sexuality. Once again, males are not to be held accountable for their sexuality. Furthermore, this "solution" is unrealistic. Teenagers will have some form of sexual contact with peers or adults. Our concern should be whether they experience that contact as consensual and responsible, or coercive and abusive. The nature of this experience shapes their learning about themselves as sexual beings. Unfortunately, they run a high risk of being confronted with a sexually abusive situation.[9]

Working with teenagers on the topics of sexuality and sexual abuse is difficult because their sexual development is in a formative state. They are at different points in their individual development; they are experiencing increased physical and emotional responses, they are bombarded with messages that attempt to shape their consciousness and self-image, and many do not have a strong sense of self-respect and confidence. Unfortunately, for many (especially girls), their first "sexual" experience is an abusive one: child molestation, obscene phone calls, flasher encounters, acquaintance rape, incestuous abuse. These experiences invariably present themselves as "normative," that is, "this must be what sex is all about, something over which I have no control and no choice." Experiences of sexual abuse can have a lasting impact, which make an adjustment to a responsible and fulfilling sexual life later on difficult. This is why it is necessary to have an alternative, positive image of sexuality. Providing teenagers with information and the sense that sex is a gift from God intended to be shared responsibly in relationship to another is one of the most effective means of *preventing* sexual abuse and sexual violence. Perceiving sex in this way teaches teenagers that they have a right to bodily integrity and a need to respect the bodily integrity of others.[10]

If the principle of authentic consent is accepted as the standard for sexual activity and if it is recognized that in order for consent to be meaningful, it must be considered in relationships of relatively equal power, then we must realize that the vast majority of social and sexual relationships between women and men in our society have the potential to be nonconsensual, that is, coercive and abusive. Moreover, we can see why it has been so easy to confuse sexual activity with sexual violence: freely chosen, fully informed, and mutually agreed-upon sexual activity with another might in fact be a rare experience. Coercive and abusive sexual activity may be the norm and thus the most common experience for both women and men. The model of consensual sex is seldom promoted or encouraged in this society.

JUST RELATIONS AND RELATIONSHIPS OF UNEQUAL POWER

A relationship of unequal power (for example, teacher-student or doctor-patient) is not necessarily an abusive or unjust relationship. The quality of such a relationship is determined by the ability of the person with greater resources not to take advantage of the vulnerability of the other. Ethical discussions dealing with just relations involve us in considering the multiple variables that shape any relationship.

Authentic consent is a fundamental norm for sexual intimacy. For example, a twelve-year-old girl who is approached sexually by her uncle does not have the information she needs to choose to consent. Moreover she does not have the power in that relationship to refuse consent and have her choice respected. Because of her age and naïveté and her subordinate status in relation to her uncle, she is being coerced.[11] Similarly, a client in counseling with a therapist or pastor does not necessarily have the option to withhold consent to sexual advances. Most people in counseling are feeling vulnerable to begin with, and the therapist or pastor represents a role of authority and power that can easily be misused to coerce a sexual encounter. Neither an employee approached sexually by a supervisor nor a student approached by a teacher has the needed prerequisites for giving freely chosen consent to sexual contact. By nature of their position vis-à-vis the person who approaches them, they do not have the option of choosing to consent or withhold consent. The wife whose husband demands sexual access to her at any time under threat of a beating may have sufficient information, but she does not have the freedom to withhold consent. She believes her only option is to submit.

Social location serves to limit ethical options whether based on age, gender, race, or physical ability. The key element in these interactions is power and powerlessness. Anytime a person is in a position subordinate to another, that person is vulnerable to exploitation and abuse, and the person in the dominant role has the potential to misuse the power by coercing the subordinate-child, teenager, or adult. The failure to understand the principle of authentic consent in the context of unequal power in sexual relationships contributes to several forms of sexual abuse that are difficult for some to see as abusive. Because of this, some people are engaged in misguided advocacy for the acceptance of incest, marital rape, and sexual contact between clients and pastors or therapists.

Incest

The movement advocating the benefits of incestuous sexual activity between adults and children is one such area. In the 1980s, the movement came to be known as the "Pro-Incest Lobby."[12] Proponents of this position argued that sex between adults and children causes no harm and is beneficial because touching, affection, and intimacy strengthens family love and discourages teenage promiscuity and rebellion. While some of those seeking to legitimize incest are genuinely concerned about the lack of physical affection in families, their solution misses the point. There is a significant difference between affectionate physical contact and sexual contact. In the latter, the needs of the adult family member are met to the detriment of the child. Children know the difference. They know when an adult is giving them affirmation through affection and when they are being used sexually by the adult. They know the difference between an affectionate kiss on the cheek and a French kiss, or the difference between a hug and a hand creeping up the inside of their thigh.

Discussion of affection in the family often raises the defenses of parents who are concerned that their children develop healthy, open attitudes about sexuality. Such parents may give their children lots of physical affection, openly discuss sexual topics, and often are casual about nudity in the home. More than other parents, these parents are likely to recognize their own sexual feelings toward their children. These feelings are neither unnatural nor uncommon. However, acting on these feelings to the benefit of the parent and the detriment of the child is abusive. The parent has the responsibility not to act sexually toward the child in order to protect the child.

For those with clinical experience dealing with victims and offenders, the issue is not affection or conformity to expectations of church or society. The issue is one of abuse and exploitation. Incest, or any form of adult-child sexual contact, takes advantage of a child who is both uninformed and powerless. The child is uninformed simply by nature of being young and lacking the information held by adults. In addition, because the adult has authority over the child, the child is powerless to give or withhold consent to sexual activity. Without authentic consent, the sexual encounter is abusive for the child. Sexual contact between persons is appropriate only when both persons are fully informed and freely choose such contact. This choice is only possible when both persons have the power to choose and to have the choice respected. Children do not have this power in relation to adults, especially with adults who are parents or parental figures. Even when a child solicits sexual contact with an adult or parent, it is the adult's responsibility to protect the child from an experience that is certain to create lasting psychological problems. Although a child may initially see an incestuous experience as positive because she or he is receiving a great deal of attention from an adult, almost all eventually see it as negative. They feel confused, exploited, and/or fearful. The negative psychological effects are difficult to overcome and may last a lifetime.

Instead of a "pro-incest lobby," we need two things: first, a *sexual ethic that clearly and unequivocally requires authentic consent*. Sexual contact between persons is appropriate only when both persons are fully informed and freely choose such contact. This choice is only possible when both persons have the power to choose and to have the choice respected. Children do not have this power in relation to adults. Second, a *taboo against sexual contact with children* is necessary.[13] Children are fragile and vulnerable in many ways and deserve the protection of adults until they are old enough to have the power to act on their own behalf. Adults have the responsibility not to take advantage of this special status by sexually using a child. A strong and consistent message is needed that children are to be protected from abuse and that being an adult, especially a parent, carries with it the responsibility to protect children. Sexual exploitation of children is taboo.

Marital Rape

Marital rape represents yet another contemporary problem that runs counter to the principle of authentic consent in sexual relationships. The predominant attitude is reflected in some state laws which say that rape cannot occur between husband and wife since a husband always has the right to sexual access to his wife. In fact, rape within marriage occurs in at least 14 percent of marriages.[14] If we define rape as the forced penetration by the penis or any object of the vagina, mouth, or anus against the will of the victim, then it does not matter what the relationship is between the victim and offender. Marriage does not make forced sexual intercourse "sex" rather than rape. Marital rape is a prime example of the confusion between sexual activity and sexual violence.

Cultural attitudes, often supported and encouraged by religious teachings, have sustained the long-standing belief that there is no such thing as marital rape. The church is partially responsible for conveying the notion that husbands have conjugal rights and wives have conjugal duties. This belief can lead to coercive sexual activity on the part of the husband. Yet on this point, Christian scripture is explicitly mutual:

> The husband should give to his wife her conjugal rights, and likewise the wife to her husband. For the wife does not have authority over her own body, but the husband does; likewise the husband does not have authority over his own body, but the wife does. Do not refuse one another except perhaps by agreement for a set time, that you may devote yourselves to prayer; and then come together again, so that Satan may not tempt you because of your lack of self-control. This I say by way of concession, not of command. (1 Corinthians 7:3–6 NRSV)

Both parties, according to scripture, have the right to engage in sexual activity or to refuse to engage in sexual activity. The principle of authentic consent should apply to any sexual relationship and certainly to marriage or a covenanted relationship.

In the 1990s, a convicted wife abuser tried to use the U.S. Constitution's First Amendment protection of one's religious beliefs to support his right to abuse his wife. Ramiro Espinosa believed that the teachings of the Roman Catholic Church gave him the right to have sex with his wife whenever he chose because the marriage vows they exchanged signaled her consent to have sex with him and, that once given, this consent was somehow permanent. Espinosa, fifty-four, seemed to equate with legitimate foreplay breaking into his wife's locked room, slapping her, and ripping her clothes. Thankfully, this time the court was not swayed by his defense.[15]

This is yet another tragic example of an appeal to church doctrine to justify marital rape. When approached by the media, church leaders rejected Espinosa's argument, saying that Catholic doctrine teaches that sex should be part of a loving relationship. But they stopped there. In the subsequent silence there was little recognition of the harm done to the woman (which is a sin) and of the need to call the husband to account for his abusive behavior. Mr. Espinosa's understanding of his rights as a husband is evidence of the inadequacy of traditional Christian teaching on sexual ethics and marriage.

Sexual Abuse by Clergy

In the book of Ezekiel, from Hebrew scripture, we hear God instructing Ezekiel to prophesy to the shepherds of Israel:

> Trouble for the shepherds of Israel who feed themselves! Shepherds ought to feed their flock, yet you have fed on milk, you have dressed yourselves in wool, you have sacrificed the fattest sheep, but failed to feed the flock. You have failed to make the weak sheep strong, or to care for the sick ones, or bandage the wounded ones. You have failed to bring back strays or look for the lost. On the contrary, you have ruled them cruelly and violently. . . .
>
> Well then, shepherds, hear the word of Yahweh. As I live, I swear it — it is the Lord Yahweh who speaks — since my flock has been looted and for lack of bothering about my flock, since my shepherds feed themselves rather than my flock, in view of all this, shepherds, hear the word of Yahweh. The Lord Yahweh says this: I am going to call the shepherds to account. I am going to take my flock back from them and I shall not allow them to feed my flock. In this way the shepherds will stop feeding themselves. I shall rescue my sheep from their mouths; they will not prey on them any more. (Ezekiel 34:2–5, 7–10, Jerusalem Bible)

These words were directed at the leadership and, as such, are now directed at those of us in religious leadership as ministers. The shepherd was an important figure in the community with responsibility for the well-being of the sheep, which supported the well-being of the people. So this pointed metaphor represented an unequivocal judgment on the leaders who were exploiting those in their care. The custom of the day was that shepherds did not take from their own flock for their own needs. This principle underlies Ezekiel's critique and informs ours.

The reality of ministry is that all clergy and ministers have friendships with congregants and clients; all clergy and ministers have experienced sexual attraction to congregants and clients; all clergy and ministers have experienced sexual come-ons from congregants and clients; to some extent, all clergy and ministers have violated the boundaries of our ministerial relationships, if not sexually, then emotionally. At first hearing, these may seem like powerful indictments against the ministry and pastoral counseling. Yet to deny these assertions is to fail to comprehend that these realities are facts of life in the ministry and in ministerial counseling. Our professions, unlike many others, bring us in an ongoing way into some of the most intimate, sacred, and fragile dimensions of others' lives. Paradoxically, because of these intimate connections ministers and pastoral counselors face the risk of engaging in inappropriate or unethical behavior with those persons whom we serve or supervise.

From the perspective of the institutional church, which carries responsibility for the professional conduct of its clergy, the task is twofold: to maintain the integrity of the ministerial relationship and, in so doing, to protect those persons — congregants, clients, staff members, students, and so on — because of a variety of life circumstances.

Sexual contact by ministers and pastoral counselors with congregants or clients undercuts an otherwise effective pastoral relationship and violates the trust necessary in that relationship. It is not the sexual contact per se that is problematic but the fact that the sexual activity takes place within the pastoral relationship. The crossing of this particular boundary is significant because it changes the nature of the relationship, and the potential harm that it causes is enormous.

The behaviors that occur in the sexual violation of boundaries include but are not limited to sexual comments or suggestions (jokes, innuendoes, invitations, and so on), touching, fondling, seduction, kissing, intercourse, molestation, rape, etc. There may be only one incident, a series of incidents, or an ongoing intimate relationship over time.

Sexual contact by ministers or ministerial counselors in ministerial, professional relationships is an instance of professional misconduct that is often minimized or ignored. It is not "just an affair," although it may involve an ongoing sexual relationship with a client or congregant. It is not merely "adultery," although adultery may be a consequence if the counselor or client is in a committed relationship. It is not just "a momentary lapse of judgment" by the minister or counselor. Often it is a recurring pattern of misuse of the ministerial role by a minister or counselor who seems to neither comprehend nor care about the damaging effects it may have on the congregant or client.

Although the vast majority of ministerial offenders in reported cases are heterosexual males and the vast majority of victims are heterosexual females, clearly neither gender nor sexual orientation exclude anyone from the risk of offending (ministers/counselors) or from the possibility of being taken advantage of (congregants/clients) in the ministerial or counseling relationship.

The psychological effect on a congregant or client of sexual contact with their minister or counselor is profound. Initially, the client or congregant may feel flattered by the special attention, which feels positive, and may even see herself or himself as "consenting" to the activity. Frequently, however, the congregant or client has sought ministerial care during a time of crisis and is very vulnerable. (It seems very common that persons who are exploited by a minister or pastoral counselor have some history of childhood sexual abuse which may or may not have been addressed. Being a survivor of child sexual abuse only increases vulnerability to further exploitation.) Eventually the congregant or client begins to realize that she or he is being denied a much-needed ministerial relationship and begins to feel taken advantage of. They feel betrayed, victimized, confused, embarrassed, fearful, and blame themselves; at this point they are not likely to discuss this situation with anyone and so remain isolated. When anger finally surfaces, they may then be ready to break the silence and take some action on their own behalf and on behalf of others.

Spiritually the consequences are also profound; the psychological pain is magnified and takes on cosmic proportions. Not only is the congregant or client betrayed by one representing God but she or he may also feel betrayed by God and the church. For this person, the minister or counselor is very powerful and can easily manipulate a victim not only psychologically but morally. The result is enormous confusion and guilt: "But he said that love can never be wrong; that God had brought us together," or "He said we should sin boldly so that grace might abound." This psychological crisis becomes a crisis of faith as well, and the stakes are very high.

The moral agency and otherwise good judgment of the congregant is compromised by the minister or pastoral counselor's manipulation. If the person you rely on as a moral guide explains away any moral question you may have about this activity and requires that you keep it a secret so that you are not able to check this out with someone else who might help you see more clearly what is happening, being deceived is very easy. The result is that many survivors of clergy abuse end up feeling stupid and blame themselves when in fact their moral agency was stolen from them by someone they trusted.

It is a violation of professional ethics for any person in a ministerial role of leadership or ministerial counseling (clergy or lay) to engage in sexual contact or sexualized behavior with a congregant, client, employee, student, and so on (adult, teen, or child), within the professional (ministerial or supervisory) relationship.

Why is it wrong for a minister to be sexual with someone whom he or she serves or supervises? It is wrong because sexual activity _in this context_ is exploitative and abusive.

- _It is a violation of role._ The ministerial relationship presupposes certain role expectations. The minister or counselor is expected to make available certain resources, talents, knowledge, and expertise that will serve the best interest of the congregant, client, staff member, student intern, and so on. Sexual contact is not part of the ministerial, professional role.

- *It is a misuse of authority and power.* The role of minister or counselor carries with it authority and power and the attendant responsibility to use this power to benefit the people who call upon that individual for service. This power can easily be misused, as is the case when a minister or counselor uses (intentionally or unintentionally) one's authority to initiate or pursue sexual contact with a congregant or client. Even if it is the congregant who sexualizes the relationship, it is still the minister or counselor's responsibility to maintain the boundaries of the ministerial relationship and not pursue a sexual relationship.

- *It is taking advantage of vulnerability.* The congregant, client, employee, or student intern is by definition vulnerable to the minister or counselor in multiple ways. The person in the former role has fewer resources and less power than the minister or counselor. When the minister or counselor takes advantage of this vulnerability to gain sexual access to another, the minister or counselor violates the mandate to protect the vulnerable from harm. The protection of the vulnerable is a practice that derives from the Jewish and Christian traditions of a hospitality code.

- *It is an absence of meaningful consent.* Meaningful consent to sexual activity requires a context of not only choice but mutuality and equality; hence, meaningful consent requires the absence of fear or the most subtle coercion. There is always an imbalance of power and thus inequality between the person in the ministerial role and those whom he or she serves or supervises. Even in the relationship between two persons who see themselves as "consenting adults," the difference in role precludes the possibility of meaningful consent.

The summary of an ethical analysis of clergy sexualizing a ministerial relationship is the measure of harm caused by the betrayal of trust that is inherent in each of these four factors. Important boundaries within the ministerial or counseling relationship are crossed, and as a result, trust is betrayed. The sexual nature of this boundary violation is significant only in that the sexual context is one of great vulnerability and fragility for most people. However, the essential harm is that of betrayal of trust.

The stereotype often put forth when this issue is discussed says that, on occasion, a minister's judgment slips and thus finds oneself unwisely involved in a sexual relationship with a parishioner or client. The stereotype contends that this is a one-time event from which the minister recovers when he or she realizes the mistake. After all, everyone makes mistakes. However, this picture does not fit reality. In fact, it appears that most of the professionals who do engage in such sexual activity are repeat offenders. They are persons who seem to be attracted to the helplessness and vulnerability of their parishioners or clients. They do not hesitate to misuse the power and authority of their professional role to coerce or manipulate that person into a sexual relationship. Furthermore, they minimize and deny responsibility for such misconduct. The result is an abusive relationship in which the parishioner or client feels victimized and betrayed.

In 1983, the FaithTrust Institute (formerly the Center for the Prevention of Sexual and Domestic Violence) began to address the issue of professional ethics and sexual abuse by clergy. Between 1983 and 2000 the Institute was receiving three to five calls per week from victims, survivors, offenders, judicatory and seminary administrators, and lawyers. The Institute initiated training for leadership of judicatories and seminaries in order to provide a new understanding of the issues of power and boundary violations.

In the mid-1980s major civil litigation against Roman Catholic dioceses began to emerge. Situations where the lack of diocesan action forced survivors to go to the courts became common. Some involved criminal prosecution as well. The Roman Catholic Church was the first to feel the shock waves of disclosures of long-standing patterns of abuse by priests. At that point the economic impact was not yet really apparent.

In 1986 the first U.S. conference on abuse in helping relationships was held in Minneapolis. Questions and strategies were shared across professional disciplines. The title of the conference was significant: "It's Never O.K." By the end of the conference, we wanted to add a subtitle: "And It's Always Our Responsibility." This is the bottom line — *and* it's never simple. In 1989, *Is Nothing Sacred? When Sex Invades the Ministerial Relationship* was published.[16] This book was the first critical appraisal of the violation of the ministerial relationship that named it an issue of professional ethics and sexual abuse.

In the 1990s survivor groups organized to provide an invaluable network of support and information for survivors. Groups such as LINK-UP and SNAP[17] have enabled organizers to bring change as well as individual support to survivors and their families.

In 2002 the disclosures of sexual abuse of children by Roman Catholic priests reached critical mass. Many dioceses were facing large numbers of complaints from adults abused as children. Finally the U.S. Conference of Catholic Bishops addressed the problem at its meeting in Dallas. The bishops created the Office on the Protection of Children to implement their commitment to prevent child-molesting priests from further access to children in parishes.[18]

Sexual contact between client and professional is clearly regarded as unethical and unprofessional in the secular professions (such as medicine, psychiatry, psychology, and social work) and is addressed as an ethical concern by the profession of pastoral counselors.[19] For parish pastors, however, there is less clarity and there have been few guidelines. For parishioners in particular there has been little awareness that any sexual approach by a pastor is a violation of professional ethics. Moreover, there is little sense of what recourse a person has when faced with such a situation.

The problem of sexual contact between counselors or pastors and clients or parishioners is becoming increasingly apparent. Yet it represents an area of coercive sex or sexual abuse that remains difficult for many people, including its victims, to recognize and address directly. The powerlessness that a person feels in the face of her therapist or pastor, especially when that person represents an institution like the church, is overwhelming. This problem is a profound violation of professional ethics and the principle of authentic consent.

THE NORM OF A JUST RELATIONSHIP

If persons are created by God to be in relationship, then what is the _norm of a just relationship?_ What is necessary in a relationship in order that it be affirming of persons and pleasing to God? A description of just relationship begins within the context of love and justice. The Christian concept of love is _agape_, a love that moves persons to seek union with others (friends, acquaintances, coworkers, partners, family members, and even strangers) and God. The concept of justice requires a relationship that includes mutuality, equality, shared power, trust, choice, responsibility, and respect for bodily integrity.[20] These aspects of a relationship are prerequisites for a just interaction that seeks equal regard for the welfare of self and others.

In evaluating a relationship with another person to determine if it has the qualities of a just relation, that is, is grounded in love and justice, one might consider the following:

* Do I share the power equally in this relationship (that is, are we peers?)?

* Do I respect the wishes of the other person and my own regarding intimacy and physical or sexual contact?

* Do I trust that the other person will not betray or intentionally injure me?

* Do I freely and with full knowledge choose to interact with this person?

* Does the other person freely and with full knowledge choose to interact with me?

If these questions can be answered affirmatively, then persons can assume that the possibility of a just relationship exists between them.

Some relationships, by nature of the roles of the two persons involved, do not include all of the qualities described here. Specifically, this is the case when the roles in the relationship create an imbalance of power between the two persons who are not peers. The relationship between counselor and client, parent and child, teacher and student, pastor and parishioner, and doctor and patient all represent relationships where one person has greater power than the other. The imbalance of power may be a function of role, difference in age, gender, physical size and strength, and so on. This fact does not necessarily mean that the relationship is unjust or exploitative. Most of our relationships in life are not peer relationships. But it is the responsibility of the person with the greater power and authority to avoid misusing the power to take advantage of the vulnerability of the less powerful person.

The person in the authority role is expected to meet the needs of the other person for support, education, guidance, counsel, and information, and to safeguard the other's welfare. The person in the authority role should not expect to have his or her primary needs met in a parental or professional relationship. Avoiding this expectation requires clearly understanding and adhering to one's role and not confusing this relationship with a peer relationship between equals. In addition, the community has a responsibility through statutes, ethics codes of professional organizations or denominations, and so on, to provide checks and balances for parental or professional accountability.

The norm of a just relationship is based on love and justice and ordinarily requires relatively equal power between persons. When there is a legitimate reason for the absence of equal power, as in a professional relationship or a familial relationship between adults and children, then a just relationship is still possible, but only if the less powerful person is protected from exploitation and abuse by the more powerful person. At such time that an unequal relationship is ended and an equal relationship takes its place, this provision is no longer a priority. This would be the case when a child reaches adulthood and a parent gives up the authority role in order to build a new, more equal relationship. This would also be possible when treatment is terminated between doctor and patient, at which time, if both persons choose, a relationship between equals might be established with the full knowledge that the doctor-patient relationship cannot be renewed at a future point.

A word of caution is needed here. Changing a nonpeer relationship to a peer relationship is not necessarily possible. Many therapists refuse to pursue friendships or intimate relationships with former clients. The problem here is that the therapeutic relationship invariably colors the post-therapeutic relationship and so is not in the best interest of either client or therapist. Careful attention to these boundaries helps protect the integrity of both phases of the relationship and can prevent a therapist from misusing her or his role to the detriment of the client or former client.[21]

REAL ETHICS FOR REAL PEOPLE[22]

If we take seriously the reality of sexual violence and the ethical questions that it presents, what would our sexual ethics look like? We would begin with Paul's formulation: "Love does no wrong to a neighbor," and we would affirm the bodily integrity of self and partner and strive to ensure that each person be free from bodily harm within an intimate relationship. Our sexual ethics would then address both personal and social dimensions.

In seeking to discern the best action to do the least harm in an intimate relationship, four assumptions should support our discernment process:

1. Most people live in relationships of varying degrees of intimacy, and most would prefer to do this with integrity.

2. Both women and men are moral agents and both possess the capacity and responsibility for ethical decision making and action. Our perceptions of our options are likely to be shaped by our gender, race, age, and so on, and are likely to be different because of our experiences. But we share capacity and responsibility regardless of who we are.

3. No particular gender or relational configuration is assumed. All persons regardless of sexual orientation or relational configuration are looking for guidance in relationships. Likewise "family" refers to those persons with whom one chooses to live in a committed relationship (which may involve providing care to those who are vulnerable because of age, disability, or infirmity).

4. Healthy intimate relationships are only possible in the open and in community. Secrecy encourages shame and isolation, which make it very difficult to discern ethical choices. The challenging task in an intimate relationship is to find the delicate balance between privacy and community life.

If doing least harm is our goal in relationship to others, what guidelines might assist us in doing least harm? Guidelines allow us to be particular about the values we bring to our effort to do least harm. They provide a framework within which to make daily choices in relationship. In order to work, they must reasonably follow from the principle of "doing least harm." As such, they also provide a short cut to decision making. Once we have arrived at guidelines that reflect our original principle, we can refer to them quickly in our discernment process and more readily make our choices. The development of guidelines or parameters is an ongoing process and is best carried out in community so that we can test our own ideas against others' experiences and concerns.

But what is the difference between guidelines and rules? Rules are externally imposed requirements that may or may not have a reasonable basis. They sometimes represent the common concerns (or prejudices) of society and are usually expressed in legal statutes or codes of ethics enacted by some representative body such as a state legislature. They may be necessary to sustain the common good and protect those who are vulnerable — for example, marital rape laws — or they may be counterproductive and unjust, such as sodomy laws. But rules and laws are not adequate to guide our actions as moral agents and decision makers within our significant relationships. The guidelines I suggest here are the standards by that one can determine one's choices and actions. They are an internal anchor which informs one's decision making in sexual relationships. I believe they are necessary in order to do the least harm in such a relationship.

1. _Is my choice of intimate partner a peer, that is, someone whose power is relatively equal to mine?_

We must limit our sexual interaction to our peers and recognize that those who are vulnerable to us, that is, who have less power than we do, are off limits for our sexual interests.

With this guideline, we recognize that power is always an issue in an intimate relationship and that when power is relatively equal we have the best opportunity to experience authentic consent and choice in a relationship. If there are differences in power because of physical realities such as size or socially constructed realities such as gender, then it is wise to consciously consider how to minimize the impact on a relationship of those differences. For example, a couple can discuss ways they want to relate so that one person's physical size and strength will not be used in any way to intimidate the partner. This might mean agreeing to remain seated during heated or conflictual discussions so that the larger person does not loom over the smaller person. If both persons in an intimate relationship are committed to relating as peers, methods such as this one acknowledge a predetermined difference in power and attempt to minimize its impact.

We certainly experience sexual feelings toward persons who have significantly more power than we do or significantly less power than we do, but whether we pursue those feelings is always a choice. Pursuing such a relationship means that we run a high risk of either being taken advantage of (where we have less power, for example, as a client vis-à-vis a therapist) or of taking advantage of the other person's vulnerability (where we have more power, for example, as a doctor vis-à-vis a patient). The possibility of harm is great in either case.

2. *Are both my partner and I authentically consenting to our sexual interaction?*

Both of us must have information, awareness, equal power, and the option to say "no" without being punished as well as the option to say "yes." The possibility of authentic consent rests upon equality of power in a relationship. Consent should never be confused with submitting, going along, or acquiescing.

Consent is an alien concept to persons whose life experience has been that sex is something someone does to them, where they feel that they have never had any say in the matter. This is the common experience of many women and some men. In sexual interaction, authentic consent requires communication and agreement that "no" means no, "yes" means yes and "maybe" means maybe. "No" must not be punished by withdrawal or more overt coercive tactics. "Maybe" requires waiting for "yes," not cajoling and pushing.

3. *Do I take responsibility for protecting myself and my partner against sexually transmitted diseases and to ensure reproductive choice?*

This is a question of stewardship (the wise care for and management of the gift of sexuality) and anticipating the literal consequences of our actions. This question takes on even more urgency with the possibility of infection with HIV, which can cause AIDS. The issue of protection against unwanted pregnancy is always present for nonsterile heterosexual couples.

If I am to exercise my moral agency and make careful choices about my sexual activity and protecting myself, I require the following:

- Information about sexually transmitted diseases and reproduction. Accurate, up-to-date information is more readily available than ever, but I must read, listen, and pay attention if I am to use it.

- Access to the material means to exercise my moral options. This means access to condoms and all forms of contraception as well as access to abortion regardless of my financial means.

- Communication with my partner. We need to discuss these issues
  before the fact, not during the act. We need to talk about our likes
  and dislikes, the relative risks of each contraceptive method, our
  sexual histories, and the results of any tests we may have had for
  HIV or other sexually transmitted diseases. In other words, we
  need to know each other well before we can make good decisions
  about safer sex.

Taking this responsibility seriously presupposes a relationship:
knowing someone over time and sharing a history in which trust
can develop. This is the best argument against one-night stands. Basically one-night stands are stupid and a dangerous situation to be
in. Having sex with someone you just met means having sex with
someone who may be violent, who may have a sexually transmitted
disease, and who may be untrustworthy. Why take that chance?

> 4. _Am I committed to sharing pleasure and intimacy in my
>   relationship?_

Concern should be both for one's own needs and those of one's partner. The Song of Solomon in Hebrew scripture describes a nonmarital
sexual relationship without procreative purpose in which the erotic
longing and desire of both partners for each other is expressed and
affirmed. Sexual intimacy is given and received by both.

If we genuinely preach and seek to practice an incarnational theology, which means that we believe that our bodily selves are a good
gift from God, then we must affirm sexual pleasure as also good. The
ethical questions that this affirmation calls forth focus primarily on
our responsibility to meet our own needs and to meet our partner's
needs in a context of consent and respect.

> 5. _Am I faithful to my promises and commitments?_

Whatever the nature of a commitment to one's partner and whatever
the duration of that commitment, fidelity requires honesty and the
keeping of promises. Change in an individual may mean a change in

the commitment, which should be pursued through open and honest communication.

If we believe that relationships are worthwhile enterprises and if we choose to enter into a committed intimate relationship, then the question of faithfulness inevitably arises. How do we keep faith with our commitment to an intimate partner? How do we do least harm? These ethical questions shape our actions as moral agents in relationship. Faithfulness can be fulfilled through truthfulness, promise keeping, attention, and the absence of violence. These aspects of a relationship require daily effort.

Any effort to shift the discussion of sexual ethics in our religious communities toward the values of justice, respect, bodily integrity, consent, reciprocity, and fidelity definitely stimulates resistance in some quarters. Some people still quickly look for the litmus questions: what about abortion, adultery, homosexuality, and masturbation (in alphabetical order)? If we are to use Paul's ethical insight as outlined earlier, then these are no longer the defining questions. If we are to affirm and promote the eroticization of equality in intimate relationships, these are no longer the defining questions. The values which undergird the five guidelines suggested here encourage us not to meet our own sexual needs *at the expense* of someone else. These values are also far more stringent than traditional patriarchal sexual ethics. They recognize that there are no simple answers and no permanent resolutions but rather a constant process of ethical discernment if we are to do least harm to those we love the most.

_____

Chapter 5

Scripture Resources for Reframing Ethical Approaches to Sexual Violence

In contrast to Hebrew scripture, Christian scripture does not appear to have any explicit references to sexual violence. However, there are passages that can be used to develop a new ethical response to sexual violence. In addition, there are two passages in the Hebrew scripture that provide a resource for appropriate understandings of sexual violence. We can look to Jesus's parable of the Good Samaritan for a model of how to respond to the victim if we regard the act of sexual violence as an act of assault and aggression that results in injury. In addition, the Gospels consistently regard women as persons in their own right rather than treating them as property. Jesus's ministry was most unusual and puzzling to his followers in that he treated women as persons. Because of this sensitivity, we can assume that victims of sexual violence were not doubly victimized by Jesus's response to them. However, there is no evidence that the confusion of sexual activity with sexual violence had diminished in its influence on the attitudes and practices of the period.

LUST: MATTHEW 5:28

In Christian scripture, Jesus discusses "lust" in connection with "adultery." In a passage from Matthew, Jesus suggests that the ethical issue goes beyond the act to the thought and desire that precede it. "But I say to you that everyone who looks at a woman *with lust* [emphasis added] has already committed *adultery* [emphasis added] with her in his heart" (Matthew 5:28 NRSV).

He seems to be saying that the thought and desire to commit a particular act are as significant as the act itself and that persons are as accountable for their thoughts and desires as for their acts. This significant ethical insight is often clouded by traditional interpretation of this passage, which has focused on promiscuity. It has been taken to mean that any man who has sexual feelings for a woman is as guilty as if he actually has sexual contact with her.

"With lust" means "desiring greatly." "Adultery" was the category used to describe every sexual offense from rape to promiscuity and always referred to the violation of a husband's property rights.[1] So Jesus's literal meaning might more accurately be expressed: "Anyone who desires greatly in his heart to sexually possess a woman has already taken possession of her or stolen her." In other words, he has broken the commandment that forbids the coveting of another man's wife. Even though this meaning of the verse is still skewed by a patriarchal bias, it brings us closer to the truth than does the traditional interpretation.

Building on this literal meaning, an alternative interpretation of what is meant by "lust" and "adultery" can provide new insight to Jesus's teaching. Rather than understanding "lust" to mean "having sexual feelings," "lust" is used to describe the intense desire *to possess or overcome* another person, particularly sexually. Even Augustine supports this interpretation: "The evil of lust, a name which is given to many vices, but is properly attributable to *violent sexual appetite*" [emphasis added].[2] This definition corresponds to the previously described dominant cultural understanding of male sexuality as predatory and dependent on domination of the other person. "Adultery" might be understood to refer primarily to an offense against the woman (rather than against her owner) because the consequence of a man's desire to possess and dominate a woman is to break faith by violating mutuality and respect in relation to her.

Thus we can reinterpret Jesus's teaching to mean that for a man to desire to possess and dominate a woman is an offense against *her*.

It is a distortion of human sexuality that is physically and spiritually abusive. Using Jesus's ethical insight that it is not only what one does but also what one thinks that is important and applying it to the contemporary experience of sexual violence enables the reader to interpret the passage in Matthew as emphasizing not promiscuous sexual activity, but rather the potential for sexual coercion and violence in thought, word, *and* deed.[3]

PROTECTION AND COMMUNITY SUPPORT: HEBREW AND CHRISTIAN SCRIPTURAL RESOURCES

The most useful teaching from scripture which helps to explain God's response and our responsibility to victims of sexual violence is a concept that is not ordinarily associated with sexual violence per se. Widows, fatherless children, travelers, and the poor were designated in Hebrew scripture as deserving protection and support from the community (for example, Psalm 146:9; Exodus 22:21–24; Deuteronomy 14:29; Jeremiah 22:3). If we consider *why* these categories of persons were singled out, we can more easily apply this teaching to our time.

Each of these persons was powerless and vulnerable in their society. The widow and fatherless child (the single-parent family) lacked a male figure to serve as protector, provider, and authority. The sojourner was vulnerable and at a disadvantage because he was traveling outside of his community. The poor lacked the resources to determine their own lives. In patriarchal Hebrew culture, it was assumed that all females were under the authority and protection of a male (father, husband, brother, brother-in-law, etc.) and that this male was responsible for providing sustenance and protection for the female. Any woman who was not related to a male in this way was without protection or any livelihood other than prostitution. Thus a widow who had no father, brother, or brother-in-law to take care of her was powerless, vulnerable, and at the mercy of her community.

The Hebrew hospitality code[4] instructed the people to care for the powerless and vulnerable and provide them with food (Deuteronomy

24:19). The prophets frequently chastised the people for their neglect and oppression of these people.

> Ah, you who make iniquitous decrees,
>   who write oppressive statutes,
> to turn aside the needy from justice
>   and to rob the poor of my people of their right,
> that widows may be your spoil,
>   and that you may make the orphans your prey!
>   Isaiah 10:1–2 (NRSV)

> Wash yourselves; make yourselves clean;
>   remove the evil of your doings
>   from before my eyes;
> cease to do evil,
>   learn to do good;
> seek justice,
>   rescue the oppressed;
> defend the orphans,
>   plead for the widow.
>   Isaiah 1:16–17 (NRSV)

If we understand that the concern here was for the powerless and vulnerable, to provide for them and to protect their rights, and if we ask who among us today is powerless and vulnerable and in need of support and advocacy, we would certainly specify the victims of sexual violence, especially women and children. In Hebrew culture, the widow represented the powerless woman who depended on her community to care for her. The contemporary figure might well be the rape victim or child sexual assault victim, both of whom are at the mercy of those around them for support and advocacy.

With this in mind, Jesus's parable about the persistent widow takes on new meaning.

> And he told them a parable, about their need to pray always and not lose heart. He said, "In a certain city there was a judge who neither feared God nor had respect for people. In that city there

was a widow who kept coming to him and saying 'Grant me justice against my opponent.' For a while he refused; but later he said to himself, 'Though I have no fear of God nor respect for anyone, yet because this widow keeps bothering me, I will grant her justice, so that she may not wear me out by continually coming.' " And the Lord said, "listen to what the unjust judge says. And will not God grant justice to the chosen ones, who cry to God day and night? Will God delay long in helping them? I tell you, God will quickly grant justice to them. And yet, when the Son of humanity comes, will he find faith on earth?" (Luke 18:1–8 NRSV inclusive)

Here we find Jesus giving assurance that God will grant justice to those who cry out. This is then the promise in Jesus's teaching which corresponds to Susanna's experience in the Apocrypha. For the victim, powerless and vulnerable, there is vindication through God.

Finally, two stories from the Gospels describe Jesus's concern for the well-being of children. In Mark, Jesus affirms children in their vulnerability in spite of the disciples' disapproval:

People were bringing little children to him in order that he might touch them; and the disciples spoke sternly to them. But when Jesus saw this, he was indignant and said to them, "Let the little children come to me; do not stop them; for it is to such as these that the kingdom of God belongs. Truly I tell you, whoever does not receive the kingdom of God as a little child will never enter it." And he took them up in his arms, laid his hands on them, and blessed them. (Mark 10:13–16 NRSV)

His action toward children urges us to protect and not abuse children in any way.

This coupled with the teaching from Luke move us toward understanding accountability, justice, and forgiveness in the face of abuse.

Jesus said to his disciples, "Occasions for stumbling are bound to come, but woe to anyone by whom they come! It would be better for you if a millstone were hung around your neck and you were thrown into the sea than for you to cause one of these little ones to stumble. Be on your guard! If another disciple sins, you must rebuke the offender, and if there is repentance, you must forgive. And if the same person sins against you seven times a day, and turns back to you seven times and says, 'I repent,' you must forgive." (Luke 17:1–4 NRSV)

The mistreatment of the "little ones," that is, those who are vulnerable, which always includes children, is a very serious matter. For Christians, the Gospels portray Jesus's advocacy for the vulnerable, particularly children, as a model for us to follow.

ASSAULT: SUSANNA (in the Apocrypha as "Daniel and Susanna" or in the Canon as "Daniel 13")

In all of the scriptural examples that refer to acts of sexual assault and abuse, the authors are concerned with the offense as a violation of male property rights.[5] We can only assume that the authors' attitudes reflect the views of the community. The one exception to this in Hebrew scripture/Apocrypha is the story of Susanna, in which the attempted rape is discussed as an offense against Susanna herself. The offense is acknowledged and she is vindicated. Yet this chapter was placed in the Apocrypha and not included in the Canon;[6] it certainly is not a well-known story. Its ability to supply a corrective to the perspective of the other Hebrew scripture passages is limited. In addition, even when it does appear, the commentaries discount the emphasis on Susanna's experience of attempted assault.

Superficially, at least, the primary purpose of the story is to show that virtue (here in the form of conjugal chastity) triumphs, with God's help, over vice (here in the form of lust and deceit). Inasmuch as this story belongs to the "Daniel Cycle," it also offers another example of this hero's God-given wisdom. Exegetes, however, have sought deeper meanings in the tale.[7]

This virtually unknown story is about Susanna, described as a beautiful and devout Hebrew woman. Her husband was a community leader, and other community leaders often gathered at their house. Two of these men, respected elders and judges, were "obsessed with lust for her" and came regularly to the house to spy on Susanna as she walked in her garden. One day as they watched, she prepared to bathe in the garden. Seeing her alone, the two men came into the garden and demanded that she "yield" to them. They threatened that if she refused, they would testify that she had been there with a lover and she would be condemned to death. If she submitted, she would be sinning against God. Susanna cried out, refusing to submit. The elders then reported that they found her with a lover and she was put on trial. At the trial, the elders gave their false testimony. Susanna was not permitted to testify at all. The assembly, of course, believed the elders and sentenced her to death. She cried out to God to help her. At this point, God inspired Daniel (the hero) to come to her aid. He questioned the elders' testimony and proved it to be false; then he spoke in judgment of the assailants: "Now we know how you have been treating the women of Israel, frightening them into consorting with you; but here is a woman of Judah who would not submit to your villainy." The elders were sentenced to death. Susanna's innocence was vindicated, and Daniel became "a great man among his people."

This story relates to women's experiences of acquaintance rape (assault by someone known and trusted by the victim and her family) and accurately describes the lack of credibility so common for rape victims. This important teaching story, which portrays the double bind of women in the face of sexual assault and gives God's support for vindication, is seldom referred to in contemporary religious teaching. It has been left out of many translations of the book of Daniel.[8] Daniel's strong statement of judgment against the would-be rapists is a welcome contrast to the many other scriptural references.

Yet the legal limits on women as victims are apparent. Although a victim, Susanna stands accused and is not even permitted to testify at the trial. She is vindicated only because Daniel defends her. Not only is she the victim of attempted rape and blackmail, but also of the legal system.

This situation has definite parallels with the contemporary legal system. In some states, when a woman reports a rape and the state agrees to prosecute the rapist, the testimony of the victim (as a witness) is inadequate to convict. An additional witness must be able to testify to the events of the rape. This is a legal bind because most rapists isolate the victim, ensuring no witnesses. This legal provision reflects a deep and abiding suspicion that women who report rape cannot be trusted.

OBJECTIFICATION: ESTHER 1:10–21

In the book of Esther, we find the story of Vashti, which precedes Esther's heroic rescue of the Jews.[9] Vashti was the queen before Esther. King Ahasuerus was celebrating and showing off his wealth and power to the nobles who surrounded him. He summoned Queen Vashti to come "in order to show the peoples and the officials her beauty" (v. 11). She refused to be objectified in this way, which angered the king. So the king consulted his advisors, who were most concerned about the impact of the queen's resistance: "For this deed of the queen will be made known to all women, causing them to look with contempt on their husbands. . . . This very day the noble ladies of Persia and Media who have heard of the queen's behavior will rebel against the king's officials, and there will be no end of contempt and wrath!" (vv. 17–18 NRSV). So they recommended that the king get rid of Vashti and take another as queen. He did, and sent out a decree "to every people in its own language, declaring that every man should be master in his own house" (v. 22 NRSV).

Vashti refused to obey the command of her husband, the king. The court's concern was that news of her resistance would encourage other women to resist their husband's demands as well. So she gave up her status and position rather than be "eye candy" for the king and his friends.

Then Esther was selected as the new queen, now in a position to advocate for the Jews whom the king's advisor wanted to kill. Even though the consequences were grave, Vashti refused to be humiliated and degraded by her husband. Thus we find in this text a rare glimpse at a strong woman's response to sexual harassment.

Even though the victim's voice is rarely heard, we do have some record of these experiences. As Phyllis Tribble notes, these stories are a memorial to the victims of violence.[10] In addition, there is one story that perhaps inadvertently reveals much about the sexual violence endured by women and their resistance to it.

The Hebrew Hospitality Code, the stories of Vashti, of Daniel and Susanna, of the Good Samaritan, and of the Persistent Widow, plus the pointed reference to the protection of children from harm, together provide abundant resources to shape an ethical and pastoral response to sexual violence from a Christian perspective.

Chapter 6 _____

Just Responses to the Sin of Sexual Violence

In the face of the sin of sexual violence, what is the just response? What is necessary to right the relation which is broken by this sin? These questions emerge on parallel tracks in the aftermath of sexual violence. There is the question of a social response within a community but also that of an individual, pastoral response which is discussed in chapter 7.

The first response of justice to the sins of sexual violence is *righteous anger*. When Jesus saw that the moneylenders were misusing the Temple, he forcefully cleared them out (John 2:13–16). His righteous anger moved him to act in the face of the violation of the Temple, and he cast out the offenders. His action was not vengeful; rather he intervened to stop the abuse. The image of Jesus and the Temple is even more powerful if we understand the body to be a temple of the Holy Spirit (John 2:21 and 1 Corinthians 6:12–20). Surely the violation of persons and relationships deserves no less a response.

The second response of justice is *compassion for the victims*. Binding up the wounds, the injured bodies and spirits of the victims, is the critical need. Like the Good Samaritan, the church is called to get involved, expend resources, and take the risk of helping the victims of sexual violence.

The third response of justice is *advocacy for the victim*. To be a victim is to be made temporarily powerless in the face of not only the offender but also the community. This makes it difficult for a victim to deal immediately with the necessary medical and legal systems.

Victims often need someone to stand by them as they seek help from the community.

The fourth response of justice is _holding the offender legally and spiritually accountable_ for his or her sin against the victim and the community. The painful reality of harm done by one person to another is often in the context of the intimacy of relationship. We know how frequently perpetrators try to avoid being accountable for their abusive behavior. Rare is the person who comes forward having molested one's children, acknowledges his or her behavior, and takes responsibility (confession), willingly accepts the consequences (legal or otherwise: penance), and does everything he or she can to ensure that this behavior is not repeated (repentance).

But Walter Herbert describes the usual response concretely:

> As things now stand, men are right to expect that committing rape and sexual harassment will carry scant penalty, if any. Offenders anticipate that answerable officials — in business, the professions [including the clergy], the military, and institutions of higher education — will extend them _post facto_ permission, as will police, attorneys, judges, and juries.[1]

In the face of this socially constructed ethical morass, how do we assert an ethical norm in a Christian context? Psychiatrist Judith Herman observes:

> In order to escape accountability for his crimes, the perpetrator does everything in his power to promote forgetting. Secrecy and silence are the perpetrator's first line of defense. If secrecy fails, the perpetrator attacks the credibility of his victim. If he cannot silence her absolutely, he tries to make sure that no one listens.... After every atrocity one can expect to hear the same predictable apologies: it never happened; the victim lies; the victim exaggerates; the victim brought it upon herself; and in any case, it is time to forget the past and move on. The more powerful the perpetrator, the greater is his prerogative to name and define reality, and the more completely his arguments

prevail.... To hold traumatic reality in consciousness requires a social context that affirms and protects the victim and that joins victim and witness in a common alliance.[2]

We know that a perpetrator puts one's energy into avoiding accountability in order to avoid the painful consequences of misconduct. Perhaps we too are avoiding engaging with these painful consequences. Why is it so difficult to contemplate accountability? Why do we put so much energy into avoiding holding someone accountable?

- Our language shapes our responses. One of the ways that we join perpetrators of violence and abuse in avoiding accountability is in the very language that we use to discuss their behavior. There is a consistent absence of language that indicates agency. For example, "She was raped when she was eighteen years old," or "Witnesses said that she had been beaten up on several occasions," or "The relationship had gone sour prior to her seeking a divorce."

  Each statement is in the passive voice. *Something happened* to her, such as "she got wet when she went out into the rain." Where is the agency? Who raped or battered her? The absence of agency in our language reflects our discomfort at holding abusers accountable. We can't even name the perpetrator as agent, much less hold him or her accountable.

- The perpetrator convinces us that his or her rights should prevail. A man claims that his right to treat his wife and children as he pleases is more important than their right to physical safety. Fundamentally, we do not believe that women and children have the right to be free of bodily harm nor that men who abuse women should be held accountable.

- The perpetrator convinces us that "this is just who I am" so "I am not accountable." The pastor is just a "friendly sort of guy" and so is not accountable for sexual harassment of his staff. The commentator meant no harm by his racist remarks on the air and therefore should not be held accountable or suffer the consequences. The politician who groped women explains that he was just being "playful" and did not know that anyone was offended by his behavior. These are all variations on the "boys will be boys" explanation, which is an insult to all men.

- We hesitate to "judge" and so are tempted to avoid dealing with blatant misconduct by a member of our community. Moderate and liberal Christians certainly shy away from expressing a word of judgment against any individual. (We are more at ease judging institutions, powers, and principalities.) Conservative Christians don't hesitate to judge; they just use the wrong criteria. Cowardice and passivity combined with a misreading of Paul have brought us to this place (see Romans 2).

- We are afraid of the perpetrator. He not only harasses and abuses, he also indirectly terrorizes us as a community. He is often powerful and willing to use his power to threaten anyone who would confront him. The message is that he is not accountable, and he can do as he pleases; there are few consequences for him.

The courts, media, and public attitudes often look for ways to minimize the violence done to women and children and to thereby avoid holding offenders accountable. The other strategy is to revert to blaming the victim in order to avoid holding the abuser accountable.

As bystanders, many of us also resist holding someone accountable for harm done to another in the face of the irrevocable fact of abusive actions. In the midst of conflicting emotions, the singular strategy is avoidance, whether the offender is a regular guy who works at the post office, a prominent banker who molested his child or put his wife in the hospital, or a well-liked athlete who beats his wife. There are two options for avoidance even in the face of strong evidence: (1) denial — it couldn't or didn't happen, and (2) forgive and forget. It is always interesting when these two responses coexist. "It didn't happen but we should forgive and forget." What is there to forgive if nothing happened? We cannot get to forgiveness unless we acknowledge judgment.

In Romans 2, after a long laundry list of wickedness in chapter 1, Paul then says (NRSV): "Therefore you have no excuse, whoever you are, when you judge others," and echoes Jesus's words in Matthew 7 (NRSV): "Do not judge, so that you may not be judged." The problem is that the exegesis stops here, missing the point of these passages. Paul goes on to say, "for in passing judgment on another you condemn yourself, *because you, the judge, are doing the very same things*" [emphasis added]. In this verse he also echoes Jesus's words, which continue in Matthew 7: "For with the judgment you make you will be judged, and the measure you give will be the measure you get." Neither of these passages is about avoiding judging; they are both about hypocrisy. Paul goes on in Romans: "Do you imagine, whoever you are, that when you judge those who do such things and yet do them yourself, you will escape the judgment of God?" (Romans 2:3 NRSV).[3]

The expectation that one's deeds will be judged is a consistent thread connecting Hebrew and Christian scripture. The prophet Ezekiel lays the foundation, calling the people to task in 33:10–20. He carefully lays out the judgment that there are consequences for our misconduct, our wickedness, our harm to others. But the goal is always our repentance: "Say to them, As I live, says the Lord GOD, I have no pleasure in the death of the wicked, but that the wicked turn from their ways and live; turn back, turn back from your evil ways; for why will you die, O house of Israel?" (Ezekiel 33:11 NRSV). It is this same sentiment that Paul picks up in Romans: "Or do you despise the riches of [God's] kindness and forbearance and patience? Do you not realize that God's kindness is meant to lead you to repentance? But by your hard and impenitent heart you are storing up wrath for yourself on the day of wrath, when God's righteous judgment will be revealed" (Romans 2:4–5 NRSV). Paul goes on to parallel Ezekiel:

> For [God] will repay according to each one's deeds: to those who by patiently doing good seek for glory and honor and immortality, [God] will give eternal life; while for those who are self-seeking and who obey not the truth but wickedness, there

will be wrath and fury. There will be anguish and distress for everyone who does evil, the Jew first and also the Greek, but glory and honor and peace for everyone who does good, the Jew first and also the Greek. For God shows no partiality. (Romans 2:6–11 NRSV)

The purpose of judgment is finally repentance by the offender. He or she must first acknowledge what he or she did and the suffering that the action caused both the victim and the community. Then the sign of repentance is change in the offender, that is, a desire to do whatever it takes to change and to not repeat the abusive behavior.

Accountability is the way to stop the abuse and the way to genuinely help those who abuse. Do we really believe that accountability can help perpetrators stop their violence? How does a community hold its members accountable? I was presenting in southeast Alaska a number of years ago, and in dialogue there with native Alaskan members of the Tlingit tribe, I heard them reflect on their history. They have a memory of a time a hundred years ago when, in their tribe, wife abuse was forbidden. The reason was that every member of the tribe was vital to the tribe's survival. The women were not expendable. The community norm was clear: you don't beat your wife. If you violated the norm, there was a predictable response: your family had to make material restitution to your wife's family in a public gathering called a potlatch. Consequently there was rarely ever an incident of wife abuse. It was shameful and expensive. Now a hundred years later, after the arrival of white settlers and alcohol, those community norms have been badly damaged. Now the incidence of wife abuse and alcoholism equals that of the rest of the United States. But the advantage that the Tlingit people have is that they have a memory of a time when the norm of their community supported safety for women. They are now seeking to recover this norm and these values for their community, to bring these values together with the principles of restorative justice in order to actually hold abusers accountable.

This norm used shame and material restitution to make clear that the community would not tolerate the abuse of women. "Shame" is politically incorrect these days, particularly in mental health circles, and a critique is certainly in order. For too long, shame has been used against those who have less power in our communities: rape victims, gays and lesbians, teenage mothers, children and teens who masturbated. You should not feel ashamed if you were raped, if you are gay or lesbian, if you gave birth to a child outside of marriage, or if you masturbate.

But my mother taught me that I should be ashamed of some things, things that caused harm to others or damaged the social fabric — for example, punching the smaller kids, lying, cheating, and stealing. Today this list needs to include rape, child molestation, and battering. Those who cause harm to women, men, and children should be ashamed of themselves (see chapter 7).

The response of justice to the offender who has genuinely repented through rehabilitation and restitution is *forgiveness*. Forgiveness on the part of the victim is a complex pastoral issue, which is discussed in more detail in chapter 8. However, forgiveness, that is, a willingness on the part of the community to allow the offender to begin anew, is the final stage of justice making, which can lead ultimately to the offender's reconciliation with himself or herself and the community. Such forgiveness can only *follow* the offender's acknowledgment of the offense and its impact and his or her repentance. Otherwise, forgiveness is an empty gesture. This is not a time for cheap grace or premature reconciliation. While Christians believe in God's mercy and forgiveness, we also believe that such forgiveness comes to those who are *truly repentant* of their sin. It does not come to those who seek quick and easy absolution or to those who subtly manipulate the concerns of the victim and the community to serve their own self-interest and to avoid responsibility.

Furthermore, forgiveness should not be used by the community as a panacea for its discomfort in having to deal with sexual violence in the first place. Forgiveness by the community requires a clear confrontation and acknowledgment that one within it has been wronged by another and that the offender has to take steps to rectify that wrong. Justice is not served by a wishy-washy response that simply overlooks the offense with the reminder that we all have clay feet and make mistakes sometimes. Acts of sexual abuse or violence are serious and have a devastating impact on the victim, her or his family, and the fabric of the community. Justice requires that the community deal with these acts with appropriate seriousness.[4]

While the offense of sexual violence is serious, and while the community must respond in order to carry out justice and protect its members, retribution — that is, capital punishment for sexual assault, long-term imprisonment without treatment, or complete ostracism — is *not* a just response to the offender. All of these further the offender's brokenness. The ends of justice and reconciliation are never served by retribution, for then the cycle of violence is never broken.

The fifth response of justice is *prevention*. Society needs to take responsibility for the ways in which it sustains an environment that seldom challenges and often encourages sexual violence. Justice requires that everything possible be done to prevent sexual violence from ever claiming another victim. This means changes in many areas of persons' collective and individual lives in order to address the roots (for example, sexism, racism, homophobia, child abuse, sexual ethics, economics) and not merely the symptoms of sexual violence.

JUSTICE AND ANTIRACISM

Sexual violence occurs in contemporary society in which racism is an endemic and virulent social problem. Any discussion of a just response to sexual violence must include a discussion of racism and sexual violence. Racism affects society's view of sexual violence, and it consequently shapes society's response to victims and offenders. Racism is manifest in a number of attitudes, beliefs, and practices related to sexual violence.

Most sexual assault occurs *within* racial groups;[5] however, it's commonly believed among Anglos that Anglo women are most likely to be raped by men of color. This belief has been taught to Anglo women and has served to sustain suspicion and fear between Anglos and people of color. It has also distracted Anglo women from realizing that their most likely assailant will be an Anglo man. Likewise for women of color, their most likely assailant will be someone from their own racial or ethnic group. When this is the case (as it usually is), race and class anxieties may also minimize the chances that any woman will report the assault.

RACISM AND THE PROPERTY CRIME OF SEXUAL ASSAULT

As we saw in the discussion of Judges 19 (pp. 66ff.), the earliest Western concepts of the wrong of rape viewed it as a property crime, that is, the rape of a woman was viewed as a crime, not against her, but against the one who "owned" her, the male family member to whom she was most closely related. Even though rape as a property crime completely ignored the well-being of the victim, it did, ironically, carry with it a response exacting accountability from the rapist and often severe punishment as well, including capital punishment.

Of course this response to the perceived violation of a man's property rights was itself problematic. For example, in the southern United States, the social construction of race overlaid the gender construction of rape. Anglo women were the property of Anglo men who protected their women's chastity by punishing any hint of sexual intimacy between an Anglo woman and a black man, including eye contact. This punishment often involved extrajudicial actions such as lynching.

The racism of gender politics in the nineteenth and twentieth centuries in the United States, particularly the South, was built on the foundation of slavery that preceded it. Traci West describes the harsh reality faced by slave women:

> Slave women lived with the threat of sexual violence whether they worked in the master's house or in the fields. Slave women were raped by white masters, white overseers, and black drivers. They also faced forms of sexual violence that were the peculiar

invention of the slave system. For example, as forced breeders they were made to submit to sexual relations with black slave men who were chosen by the master for breeding purposes.[6]

After slavery was abolished, Anglo men continued to presume sexual access to African American women whether in the Anglo's homes where women worked as domestics or in the workplace or community. Anglo social mores permitted the rape of African American women by Anglo men with impunity. Rape and lynching were the primary means of social control of African American women and men, and both were predicated on a view of rape of women as a property crime against men. Lori Robinson credits Ida B. Wells-Barnett, an antilynching activist and journalist, with linking the lynching of black men with the rape of black women: "White men, she explained, unjustifiably victimized Black men for false charges of sexual crimes, while raping Black women with impunity."[7]

Racism also contributes to the minimization of sexual violence against women of color. Some cultural attitudes view women of color as being of less worth than Anglo women, specifically African American women or Latinas as "naturally sexually promiscuous" or Asian American/Pacific Islander women as "naturally obedient and subservient to men." These racist attitudes may cause society not to respond to the victimization of women of color.

Reports to police from women of color are too often regarded as false, or, if regarded as true, unimportant and undeserving of attention. If the offender is an Anglo male, the assumption is that he can take what he wants. If the offender is a man of color, it's assumed by the dominant community that "that's the way *those people* behave normally." In either case, the experience of the woman of color who is raped is minimized, and she is less likely to seek assistance through established resources like police, hospitals, or rape crisis lines.[8] They may avoid these institutions because of a history of insensitivity or neglect by these agencies in response to people of color.

Racism also encourages the use of men of color as scapegoats. If the alleged offender is a man of color, authorities are likely to arrest any man of color whether or not he is the offender, to prosecute aggressively, and when convicted, to sentence heavily. This is especially true if the victim is Anglo. Alice Walker describes the underside:

> Who knows what the black woman thinks of rape? Who has asked her? Who cares? Who has even properly acknowledged that *she* and not the white woman in this story is the most likely victim of rape? Whenever interracial rape is mentioned, a black woman's first thought is to protect the lives of her brothers, her father, her sons, her lover. A history of lynching has bred this reflex in her. I feel it as strongly as anyone.[9]

A double standard of justice persists in which a disproportionate number of men of color are arrested, convicted, and sentenced for sexual assaults of Anglo women while Anglo men who rape are less likely to be prosecuted at all. Capital punishment continues to be disproportionately employed as the sentence for a man of color who is convicted of raping an Anglo woman. Whenever an innocent man of color is convicted and sentenced, not only is a gross injustice committed, but no progress is made in curbing sexual violence: a guilty rapist continues to rape while an innocent man pays a price. The history of rape in the United States sits squarely within the history of racism. Beginning with the colonization of North America, sexual assault was a tool of the colonizers. Andrea Smith describes the ways that Native people were demonized and denigrated so that rape and mutilation of Native people were acceptable methods of genocide. In addition, the history of residential schools in the United States and Canada now reveal extensive sexual abuse of children forced to live in these schools away from their families.[10] Currently, the reported rate of rape of American Indian/Alaska Native women is almost double that of Anglo women.[11]

In addition, the extreme vulnerability of immigrant women coming to the United States makes them easy targets of sexual harassment and assault. Whether they come from Asia, Mexico, Latin America, Russia, the Middle East, or Eastern Europe, whether they are legal or "illegal," whether they come as workers or "mail-order brides,"[12] their victimization at the hands of employers or husbands generally goes unreported.

During and after slavery, most rape laws until recently were property laws protecting the husband or father (or owner) of the rape victim; thus it is no surprise that the legal system was most concerned with the protection of white men's property. Whenever the legal system could not be manipulated to this end, lynching was viewed by the dominant community as an available alternative. Lynching a man of color for supposedly assaulting a white woman served to terrorize the community and limit the activity to change unjust laws and practices. It also made clear to white women that they would be "protected" as long as they kept their place, that is, did not question their status as property of husband or father, albeit a prized possession.

Unfortunately, some white women have acted out of class and/or racial privilege to falsely accuse men of color of sexual assault. The most notable historic case of this was the Scottsboro Trial in the 1930s. Nine black men were falsely accused of rape by two white women at the insistence of a posse of white men who believed that rape had been committed. It took until 1951 to win the release of the last "Scottsboro Boy." A lesser-known incident involved the all-black community of Rosewood, Florida. In January 1923, a white woman from the neighboring town alleged that a black man had raped her, when in fact she had been beaten by her white lover. The white vigilantes organized to find the black rapist but when they did not succeed, they massacred most of the residents of Rosewood and burned the town to the ground. In 1999, the Florida State Legislature paid restitution to the surviving relatives of those who were murdered in this hate crime.[13]

Because of this history, which was not limited to the South or to African Americans, it is no surprise that many men and women of color initially responded with suspicion toward white women who began to organize against rape in 1970. At the same time, Latinas on the West Coast and African American women in the Northeast who were organizing to stop sexual assault were also regarded with suspicion. Social ethicist Toinette Eugene describes this dilemma for African Americans:

> The traditional response of the Black community to violence committed against its most vulnerable members — women and children — has been silence. The silence does not stem from acceptance of violence as a Black cultural norm (a view that the media perpetuates and many whites believe), but rather from shame, fear, and an understandable, but nonetheless detrimental sense of racial loyalty.[14]

Racism and the fears of how the dominant Anglo community may misuse disclosure of violence within communities of color interfere with communities' abilities to address these issues.[15]

Efforts to build a grassroots, multiracial, anti-rape movement in the United States have stumbled at points because of struggles to address issues of class and race. But we must continue to seek ways to organize across race and class if we are to use our resources and actually address the painful realities of sexual assault that exist in every community. Anyone who is genuinely concerned about confronting and preventing sexual violence must always evaluate their efforts in light of the ever-present reality of racism. Otherwise there is the risk of once again seeking to solve one problem only to exacerbate another. Thus, reform of the criminal justice system must go hand in hand with more effective arrest, conviction, and sentencing of offenders. Services to victims must provide for the particular needs and perspectives of every racial and ethnic group. Constant attention to institutional and individual racism will greatly increase the likelihood of developing a truly just response to sexual violence.[16]

Traci West challenges church and society:

> To disrupt this pattern [the colonizing/missionary logic of organized anti-violence efforts] requires a decolonizing of our collective spirits. It can happen, in part, by maintaining a religious emphasis on an anti-racist, public sphere movement to end sexual violence that occurs in places like church school classrooms,

in front of city halls, on opinion-editorial pages of newspapers. This emphasis helps to reject the rooting of "the problem" in a black woman's selfhood, relocating it in the perpetrator's choices and our societal inadequacies that support his choices. It means honoring her right to freedom and dignity of mind, body and spirit as we work side by side to challenge the intimate and social assaults.[17]

This is our shared task as we continue to seek ways to make justice in the midst of sexual violence and abuse.

Chapter 7

The Healing Power of Justice

These passages from the Hebrew and Christian scriptures rarely appear in a text on pastoral counseling, yet they form a foundation for Christians to begin to understand our role in response to victim/survivors and offenders of abuse.

> But wanting to justify himself, a lawyer asked Jesus, "And who is my neighbor?" Jesus replied, "A woman was going down from Jerusalem to Jericho, and she fell among a gang of rapists, who stripped her and beat her, sexually assaulted her, and departed, leaving her half dead. Now by chance a priest was going down that road; and when he saw the woman he passed by on the other side. So likewise a government official, when she came to the place and saw the woman, passed by on the other side.
>
> "But a Samaritan, as he journeyed, came to where the victim was; and when he saw her, he had compassion, and went to her and bound up her wounds, pouring on oil and wine; then he set her on his own beast and brought her to an inn, and took care of her. And the next day he took out $100 and gave it to the innkeeper, saying, 'Take care of her; and whatever more you spend, I will repay you when I come back.' Which of these three, do you think, proved neighbor to the woman who fell among the rapists?" The lawyer said, "The one who showed mercy on her." And Jesus said to him, "Go and do likewise."
>
> (Luke 10:29–37, revised)

Jesus teaches Christians to respond to the needs and hurts of their neighbors. When the neighbor is a rape victim or a child victim of sexual abuse, it is not easy to know how to respond. These situations often seem unfamiliar, disturbing, or too complicated for a pastor or concerned layperson. Yet there is a need for each individual in the community of faith to adopt the role of the Good Samaritan and not pass by on the other side. The task is not easy. The needs of victims and their families are often great and may seem overwhelming: crisis intervention, support, advocacy, information, spiritual guidance, justice making, and so on.

> Jesus entered Jericho and was passing through it. A man was there named Zacchaeus; he was a rich corporate executive and frequently sexually harassed the workers subordinate to him. He was trying to see who Jesus was, but on account of the crowd he could not, because he was short in stature. So he ran ahead and climbed a sycamore tree to see him, because he was going to pass that way. When Jesus came to the place, he looked up and said to him, "Zacchaeus, hurry and come down; for I must stay at your house today."
>
> So he hurried down and was happy to welcome Jesus. All who saw it began to grumble and said, "He has gone to be the guest of one who is a sinner." Zacchaeus stood there and said to Jesus, "Look, half of my possessions I will give to the poor; and to those I have harmed by my boorish and exploitative conduct, I will pay four times what the court might require."
>
> Then Jesus said to him, "Today salvation has come to this house, because he too is a son of Abraham and Sarah. For the son of humanity came to seek out and to save the lost."
>
> (Luke 19:1–10, revised)

Then Jesus told them a parable about their need to pray always and not to lose heart. He said, "In a certain city there was a judge who neither feared God nor had respect for the people. A woman who had been sexually abused as a child kept coming to him and saying, 'Grant me justice against my uncle, the abuser.' For a while he refused; but later he said to himself, 'Though I have no fear of God and no respect for anyone, yet because this woman keeps bothering me, I will grant her justice, so that she may not wear me out by continually coming.' "

Jesus said, "Listen to what the unjust judge says. Will God not grant justice to those who cry out day and night? Will God delay long in helping them? I tell you, God will quickly grant justice to them. And yet, when the son of humanity comes, will he find faith on earth?"   (Luke 18:1–8, revised)

Likewise justice is rarely viewed as the starting point for pastoral care. We tend to only think of justice as an ethical principle removed from everyday life and relationships. Yet if we listen to the needs of victims and survivors, they most often express the need for some experience of justice as part of their healing. I learned this principle of the need for justice from my interactions with victims and survivors. When I stopped trying to give answers and started listening to them, I heard them asking for symbolic and real actions from their community. This is what Luke 18 is discussing. In the text, a widow (and thus marginal member of the community) goes to the judge asking for justice. She is seeking a response from her community, which can restore her to them. Only occasionally is this justice the kind meted out by the judicial system. Fortunately there are other means to help make justice and support healing for victim/survivors and for offenders.

> God sets the rape victim free and opens the eyes of the
> powers-that-be.
> God lifts up those who are bowed down and loves those who
> seek justice.
> God watches over children and upholds the victim and survivor,
> but the way of those who cause harm to others, God brings
> to ruin.   (Psalm 146:8–9, revised)

Jesus said, "Occasions for doing harm are bound to come, but woe to anyone by whom they come! It would be better for you if a cement block were hung around your neck and you were thrown into the river than for you to harm one of these children.

> Be on your guard! If someone causes harm to another, you must rebuke the offender, and if the offender truly repents, you must forgive. If the same person harms you seven times a day, and turns back to you seven times and says, 'I repent,' you must forgive." (Luke 17:1–4, revised)

Jesus also called to account those who had harmed others, giving them a chance to repent and turn their lives around. The needed response to offenders and their families is equally complex: to make justice, to support repentance and restitution, and if possible, to enable movement toward healing and reconciliation (see chapter 8 for further discussion of forgiveness).

The key to a capable and effective response is for both pastor and congregation to work together to be well-informed and prepared to help. It is common for victims of sexual violence to feel abandoned or betrayed by the church. In the past the clergy and laity have been unprepared to help and so have too frequently not been able to respond helpfully. Platitudes are an easy recourse that tell victims they will not receive any real understanding or support from the source. Platitudes work well to keep victims' experiences aloof from the speaker so that he or she can slip by and remain uninvolved. Visualize the priest on the road to Jericho passing along platitudinous advice as he makes his way around the injured person: "Keep praying. God will take care of everything. . . . Read your scripture every day. . . . Everything will be fine. . . . Forgive and forget. . . . God hears your prayers."

Platitudes can also flow towards the offender: "He didn't mean anything by it. . . . He's just a very friendly person. . . . You couldn't help yourself. . . . He said he was sorry. . . . He had a bad childhood." Accountability is what the church can do for an offender. Often in conjunction with legal sanctions, the faith community needs to be clear that abusive behavior is unacceptable regardless of one's social location and act accordingly.

The church can and should be the Samaritan, willing to stop and to expend energy and resources to help victims of sexual violence. But it also is called to confront those who cause harm and call them to repent. Both clergy and laypersons have this pastoral responsibility. The church also has a role to play in seeking justice and vindication for the victim/survivor and accountability for the offender.

PASTORAL NEEDS OF VICTIM/SURVIVORS

When in crisis, most people rely on their basic beliefs and values about the world and their place in it. For religious people, these beliefs and values are often principles of faith or doctrine. Questions like "Why is this happening to me?" "Why is God doing this to me?" "Am I being punished for my sinfulness?" are common reactions to the experience of sexual assault or abuse. For some people, these questions take priority over questions about seeking medical care, calling the police, or filing an ethics complaint. Because these religious questions are a priority, they must be addressed or they will become roadblocks that prevent the victim/survivor from dealing with the more practical issues. In addition, the experience of sexual violence or abuse may become a crisis of faith for the victim/survivor. Because a crisis of faith often is of ultimate importance for a religious person, it may well take precedence over the more practical issues at hand. In this case, efforts at crisis intervention by helpers will be thwarted until the crisis of faith is acknowledged and addressed.

The following situation presents a graphic example of the way in which a person's religious beliefs and practices can be a major block to dealing with a crisis like rape:

> *Two rape crisis counselors answered a call from a rape victim and arrived at her home to find her sitting on her sofa reading from the Bible. The counselors ignored the Bible and proceeded to provide crisis intervention; finally, the woman decided to go to the hospital for medical treatment. The counselors and the victim proceeded to the hospital emergency room, the victim reading her Bible all the way. Upon arrival, the three were taken to an examination room and the victim was prepared for her medical exam. She lay on the exam table, feet in stirrups, and*

continued to read her Bible. When the doctor came in, he noticed her unusual behavior and asked the victim, "Is there something you would like to talk about before I do the exam?" She replied, "Yes, I am a Jehovah's Witness, and I am afraid of what my church will do to me when they find out that I have been raped. May I read a few verses from the Bible out loud?" She read from the Bible, closed it, set it aside, and the doctor proceeded with the examination.

Following the examination, it was determined that the victim was at high risk for pregnancy because of the rape. The doctor recommended the morning-after treatment. The woman knew that she could not take the treatment without permission from her church. So the rape crisis counselors telephoned each of the twelve elders of her congregation in the early hours of the morning to ask their permission. Fortunately, when the situation was explained to them, each was very willing for the woman to have the treatment she needed.

Attention to the victim/survivor's religious concerns in the midst of the crisis can help the victim/survivor understand her or his experience in light of her or his faith, and thereby enable the victim/survivor to use faith as a resource. Strengthened and encouraged in their faith, victims are better able to cope with the immediate crisis of an assault. The task for a pastor or counselor is to remove the roadblock that may be created by a victim/survivor's religious concerns and allow the individual's spiritual resources to be tapped. The experience of the Jehovah's Witness woman is a good example. As soon as her concerns were acknowledged and affirmed, she was able to proceed with the more practical matters facing her. Her Bible and her faith were then a source of support for her. Asking for and receiving permission from her church for the treatment she needed also allowed her to deal with the practical part of her crisis. Not only was doctrinal permission given, but the affirmative response from the elders was perceived by her as personal support. Thus she then felt encouraged to go to her congregation for support as she recovered from the assault. Her faith and her church became resources to her. She did not have to step outside of her faith community to deal with her rape.

In the midst of the crisis of sexual assault, victims primarily need compassion, support, and sympathy. Like the biblical Job, victims need the understanding of friends and family, church and community. Too often, like Job's comforters, those around them misperceive their need. As Kushner points out in *When Bad Things Happen to Good People*:

> What Job needed from his friends — what he was really asking for when he said, "Why is God doing this to me?" — was not theology, but sympathy. He did not really want them to explain God to him, and he certainly did not want them to show him where his theology was faulty. He wanted them to tell him that he was in fact a good person, and that the things that were happening to him were terribly tragic and unfair. But the friends got so bogged down talking about God that they almost forgot about Job, except to tell him that he must have done something pretty awful to deserve this fate at the hands of a righteous God.[1]

This caution is helpful when we encounter someone in the midst of the pain of abuse or an assault. The questions and concerns about faith and theology will come soon enough.

In *Trauma and Recovery* Judith Herman begins by pointing out two kinds of trauma. First is the common trauma brought about by natural forces or accident[2] — floods, hurricanes, tornadoes, earthquake, fire, auto accident, blizzard, volcano, and so on. The thing about this trauma, according to Herman, is that humans know how to respond to it. Amazing though it may seem even in our postmodern world, empathy and sympathy abound in the face of these disasters. Neighbors help one another; outsiders show up with food and supplies. The community pulls together to help us cope with these circumstances. We turn our collective resources to support those most affected by natural or accidental trauma.

This trauma response is an example of what is described in Hebrew scripture as the hospitality code. These community norms were very strong and the expectation was very clear. If you, a Jew, encountered a widow, an orphan, or a sojourner/stranger in your midst, you were expected to care for that person and provide for their safety and their economic well-being. The text is very clear that the reason for this was not altruistic; the reason was that Jews were to remember that they were once strangers in the land of Egypt (Deuteronomy 10:17–19). In other words, this expectation is not about righteousness; it is about remembering that we have been in a vulnerable position and will be there again. So when we are able we help out our neighbor, and our neighbor will be there for us when we need them.

But it gets more complicated. The second form of trauma is clearly caused by the actions of another human being, an agent of trauma. Judith Herman observes:

> To study psychological trauma is to come face to face both with human vulnerability in the natural world and with the capacity for evil in human nature. To study psychological trauma means bearing witness to horrible events. When the events are natural disasters or "acts of God," those who bear witness sympathize readily with the victim.
>
> But when the traumatic events are of human design, those who bear witness are caught in the conflict between victim and perpetrator. It is morally impossible to remain neutral in this conflict. The bystander is forced to take sides.
>
> It is very tempting to take the side of the perpetrator. All the perpetrator asks is that the bystander do nothing.... The victim, on the contrary, asks the bystander to share the burden of pain. The victim demands action, engagement and remembering.[3]

But unfortunately the likely human response to this trauma is to do nothing, except to blame the victim: What was she wearing; what was she doing there; why did she marry him; why did he go there? There is little empathy or sympathy, a deflection of attention away from the perpetrator of the trauma and a tendency to silence or ostracize the victim altogether. The moral substance of this trauma is murky. And since the perpetrator most likely is someone known to both the victim and her or his community, bystanders prefer not to get involved.

Unlike the community's empathic response to natural disaster and accident, with rape and sexual abuse, we have a perpetrator who is usually a friend, neighbor, coworker, or family member. As Herman says, we bystanders are forced to take sides. It's hard to take sides against Uncle George or the coach or pastor who has molested a kid. As a result, a great deal of trauma from abuse remains privatized and thus tacitly accepted as "just the way things are."

In my experience working with victims and survivors of sexual and domestic violence, I have seen that people suffer not only from the abuse they experience but also from the threat of meaninglessness that comes with it. *The only thing worse than suffering is meaningless suffering.* So people who experience the trauma of violence at the hand of another person, usually not a stranger or enemy, struggle to make meaning — and usually in a context of isolation, ostracism, and moral ambiguity, if not moral condemnation and victim blaming.

The first question victims and survivors ask is some version of "Why did this happen to me?" For many the question is theological: "Why did God *let* this happen to me?" This question of why suffering happens at all and, specifically, why does it happen to me is the classic theological conundrum that all the world's religions face. And there is no unambiguous answer. The fact is that suffering does happen to every human being, and it is not God's doing: it is most likely the result of human incompetence, inadequacy, or cruelty. Some of us still refer to this as "sin." But whatever we call it, and wherever it originates, the consequence for many people is traumatic.

I was on vacation several years ago at the beach. On my early morning walk, I noticed all along the edge of the tide on the sand that there were pieces of broken glass. There were small pieces of all colors whose sharp edges had been softened by the action of the water and sand. I reached down and picked up these pieces as I walked along so that when I returned from my walk, I had two handfuls of glass. I tossed them into the trash. The next morning, once again there was broken glass all along the beach. Once again I picked up the pieces not wanting to cut myself or to leave them for the next beach walker. On the third day, there was again glass all over the beach. At this point, I began to consider: where was this glass coming from, and who broke it to begin with?

It is not enough to pick up the pieces, though this is critically important. We must make an effort to put the pieces back together, to provide the glue that restores the bottle or vase or glass to its original shape. But we must also be willing to ask, "Who broke this glass?" and "How can they be held accountable so as not to do it again?" This is where our response to traumatic violence must include a response to the perpetrator. We must be willing to engage the whole community in being the glue that puts the pieces back together and prevents the breaking in the future.

As I have walked with survivors and victims of violence, they have taught me much about what they need in their healing process. Generally I find that they *know* what they need but rarely does anyone who is trying to help take the time to *ask* them what they need. They are often clear and concrete, and their expectations are usually pretty reasonable. If we categorize the things that people often need in their healing process, we might come up with a list that fits under the rubric of justice making.

I do not limit the possibilities of justice making to the actions of a judicial system. All too often the judicial process is not about justice for victims or accountability for perpetrators but about fairness of procedures.[4] I am using the term "justice" in a broader, ethical context. In other words, what does the human spirit need in order to heal and move on? Here we will consider "justice as pastoral care." How can we be informed by scripture, motivated by empathy, and sustained by the community to move from being passive bystanders to becoming active advocates for healing and change?

WHAT SHALL WE *DO*? THE DEMANDS OF JUSTICE MAKING

Justice is not a category of experience usually associated with personal healing or pastoral care. It most often refers to sociopolitical problems in need of a corporate, institutional response (see chapter 6). But in fact, justice is a necessary component of healing from the trauma of sexual violence. It has the potential to free a victim/ survivor from the burden of trauma to seek health and healing. Justice is a broad category of possibilities. On occasion, the judicial system can provide an expression of justice, for example, when a rapist is apprehended and convicted. In other situations, victim/survivors experience no sense of justice from the judicial system, for example, when a rapist is convicted of the assault but then his conviction is overturned on appeal because of a legal technicality and he is released into the community. Experiences of justice often come from sources other than the legal system. For example, a teenager finally reveals to a teacher whom she trusts that her father has been sexually abusing her for six years. The teacher believes her and acts to try to protect her from further abuse. One person standing up for her or him may be sufficient for the victim/survivor to experience justice. Whatever form it takes, justice is usually a prerequisite for a victim/ survivor to move towards healing and forgiveness.

As helpers, we learn about the demands of justice in the midst of trauma if we listen to the victim/survivor. Rather than offering pat answers and platitudes, we should be asking, "What do you think you need to find some healing from this experience of abuse?" Most victim/survivors have a sense of what they need and are able to articulate it. Generally what they articulate is reasonable and possible. What they request falls into several categories:

- Truth telling
- Acknowledgment
- Compassion
- Protection of others

- Accountability for offender
- Restitution by offender
- Vindication of victim/survivor

As we consider these categories through this chapter, we also discuss other aspects of pastoral care and response that relate to each of these.

Truth telling: Victim/survivors often desire to tell the story, to speak the truth about what they have experienced. Herman describes this work as the reconstruction of "the traumatic event as a recitation of fact."[5] But telling the story is not only about "facts"; it is also about feelings and meaning. The victim/survivor needs a safe, private place to "tell the story." The "facts" may shift and change as memories return. What matters at this point is the truth of someone having been victimized by another.

There may be a public forum at a later point where a survivor would "tell the story." In legal proceedings, with the media, or at informal gatherings, she or he may choose to talk about the experience. These settings are always more risky, because the survivor inevitably loses control over the information. But for some, the public disclosure of their victimization helps to lift the burden that silence has placed on them. Traci West identifies this breaking of the silence as an act of resistance, critical to the survivor's renewal of self.[6] Herman describes the survivor's truth telling as "testimony."[7]

MAKING SENSE OUT OF EXPERIENCE

In the aftermath of sexual assault (by a stranger, acquaintance, or intimate), one of the most common reactions from many victims is to try somehow to understand why the violence happened to them. Many people focus on details as a way to regain a sense of control over the situation. If they can figure out *why* it happened, or what circumstances led to the assault, then they think that they can prevent being victimized again by avoiding those circumstances in the future. On the whole, this effort to understand the why of one's victimization is a healthy sign. It is in fact an effort to regain some semblance of control of one's life and environment, that is, to regain that which was lost in the assault or abuse.[8]

In struggling with the question of why the assault occurred, victim/survivors may seek religious explanations that all too often are inadequate and simplistic. It can be tempting for a rape victim or an incest survivor to arrive at an explanation of the experience based on a simple formula that combines self-blame and God-blame. For example:

A fifty-five-year-old woman was raped by a stranger who broke into her home during the night. Her explanation for why this had happened to her was that God was punishing her for having divorced her husband ten years earlier.

A nineteen-year-old woman had been sexually abused by her older brother since she was ten years old. Her explanation was that the incestuous abuse was God's punishment for her being a bad person. In addition, at age fifteen she had an abortion because she had been impregnated by her brother. The incestuous abuse continued, and then she was convinced that God was punishing her for having had the abortion.

A gay man who had just begun to be more open about his sexual orientation was kidnapped and brutally raped by three men. He falsely concluded that God was punishing him for his positive feelings about his homosexuality.

All of these victims see the sexual violence they encountered as God's punishment of them. They justified this punishment by viewing themselves as sinful people who deserved punishment. Self-blame and God-blame together make a simple, yet limited explanation of their suffering that is based more on superstition than on sound theology. Such an explanation once again avoids placing responsibility on the offender.

In these situations, the victim/survivors' efforts to comprehend their experiences in light of their religious faith should be affirmed, supported, and nurtured. However, simplistic or superstitious explanations should be discouraged and challenged by anyone doing pastoral care or counseling.

Some churches promise that if a person lives a good, Christian life (that is, goes to church regularly, prays, reads the Bible, tithes, etc.), she or he will never again experience suffering but will prosper and thrive. Then when people do experience suffering or crisis (as they invariably will), they are faced with two choices: (1) even though they tried to live a Christian life, they must have failed somehow and God is punishing them; *or* (2) although they were living by the rules, they still suffered, so they conclude that the basis of their faith must be bankrupt. In this case, they turn away in anger from their faith. Neither choice adequately explains the experience of suffering. But the church's promise implicitly or explicitly of "no more suffering" sets up people to face this double bind. Simple answers are inadequate to address the complexity of the suffering of sexual violence and cut people off from the resources of their faith.

Other churches emphasize a theology of suffering that acknowledges suffering as part of life and preaches God's presence as the constant in the midst of suffering. In other words, on one level, our experience of suffering will be significantly shaped by who we are. If we experience privilege by virtue of our social location, then the suffering of sexual abuse or violence may be interpreted as aberrant. If we experience marginalization by virtue of our social location, then the suffering of sexual abuse or violence may be interpreted as more of the same. Toinette Eugene emphasizes the role of experience in doing womanist ethics and theology: "Doing ethics and theology with the experiences of African-American women at the heart of the liberative effort means that racism, sexism, classism and heterosexism converge in our analysis, and inform our understanding of oppressive experience as socially constructed." She hastens to add: "Experience also includes the liberating praxis Black women employ to reduce and eradicate oppression in their lives and the community."[9]

From a pastoral perspective, the voices of privilege and of marginalization have to be in dialogue in addressing the personal pain of sexual violence. One's social location is most likely shaped by gender, race, class, sexual orientation, age, and ability. So the pastor or helper can help discern the dynamics of a victim/survivor's experience which shape their struggle with meaning and help reframe a theology that is liberative and not oppressive. This is the context for the question of suffering.

WHY IS THERE SUFFERING?

It is important to understand the experience of the suffering of sexual violence in terms of one's religious perspective. To ask the questions from a perspective of faith, "Why do I suffer in this way?" and "Where is God in my suffering?" is to come to terms with oneself in relation to God and the universe. These are profound theological questions that cannot be simply answered with platitudes and then dismissed. The question of why there is suffering at all is a question of classic theological debate to which there is no completely satisfactory answer. Human suffering in the midst of a world created by a compassionate and loving God is a dimension of human experience that is most disturbing. For the purposes of this discussion, there are two aspects of the experience of suffering with which persons struggle when they ask, "Why is there suffering?"

First is the question of cause, that is, the source of the suffering. For some it suffices to say that suffering is caused by human sinfulness, that is, sinful acts bring suffering to others.[10] God *allows* such sinfulness because God has given humans free will and does not intervene when we choose unrighteous acts. People simply live with the consequences of these acts. This explanation may be adequate for situations clearly caused by human negligence or meanness, intended or not — for example, a fatal car accident caused by a drunk driver, chronic brown lung disease in textile workers who are denied protection from occupational hazards, birth defects in families living near chemical dumps, or incestuous abuse inflicted by a father who was himself a victim of child abuse.[11]

For victim/survivors of sexual violence, although the inclination is to hold God or oneself responsible, there is clearly a perpetrator whose actions resulted in suffering. The offender's sinful acts may be understood as a consequence of his or her own brokenness and alienation, but nonetheless the impact of these sinful acts victimizes another person. So the explanation of sexual violence is in some ways straightforward: someone chose to do harm to the victim. The follow-up question may be, "If God loves me, why didn't God protect me and prevent this harm?" Again one's social location shapes these questions.

The second question relating to understanding suffering involves the question of meaning. What meaning does this experience of suffering hold for the victim/survivor? An interpretation of the meaning of one's suffering begins with the differentiation between voluntary and involuntary suffering. *Voluntary suffering* is a painful experience that a person chooses in order to accomplish a greater good. For example, the acts of civil disobedience by civil rights workers in the United States in the 1960s led to police brutality and imprisonment. These consequences were unjustifiable and should never have been inflicted. Yet people knowingly chose to endure this suffering in order to change the circumstances of oppression, which caused even greater suffering for many people. Like voluntary suffering, *involuntary suffering* is also unjustifiable under any circumstances; it should never happen. However, unlike voluntary suffering, involuntary suffering is not chosen and serves no greater good. Rape and child sexual abuse are forms of involuntary suffering. Neither serves any useful purpose; neither is chosen by the victim/survivor; neither should ever happen to anyone.

Yet both do happen, and the frequent question in response is: why did God send *me* this affliction? Frequently responses include: (1) this is God's way of testing my faith, (2) this is God's punishment for my sins, or (3) this is God's way of strengthening my character. To each is added the superficial reassurance that God does not give us a heavier yoke than we can bear. All of these responses imply that God is responsible. Such responses attempt to engender meaning in the suffering itself, for example, to build character. People have difficulty accepting that such painful experiences as rape and child sexual abuse happen *for no good reason.* So they try to create a "good reason" or seek a "greater good."

In Jesus's encounter with the man born blind (John 9:1–12), he is confronted with the question about the cause and meaning of suffering. He is asked by the people if the man was born blind because of his parents' sin or because of his own.[12] Jesus avoids suggesting "a good reason" and interprets the meaning of suffering through other questions. Jesus restated the question: where is God in this suffering and what can God do in this situation?

For Christians, the theology of the cross and resurrection provides insight to the meaning of suffering. God did not send Jesus to the cross as a test of his faith, as punishment for his sin, or to build his character. The Romans crucified Jesus and made him a victim of overt and deadly violence. It was a devastating experience for Jesus's followers who watched him murdered. They were overwhelmed by despair and meaninglessness. They left the scene of the crucifixion feeling abandoned and betrayed by God. The resurrection and subsequent events were the surprising realization that in the midst of profound suffering, God is present and new life is possible. This retrospective realization in no way justified the suffering; it redeemed it. It presented the possibility of new life coming forth from the pain of suffering.

Sometimes Jesus's crucifixion is misinterpreted as being the model for suffering. Since Jesus went to the cross, according to this interpretation, persons should bear their own crosses of irrational violence (for example, rape) without complaint. Rather than the *sanctification of suffering,* Jesus's crucifixion remains a witness to the horror of violence. It is not a model of how *suffering should be borne,* but a witness to God's desire that no one should have to suffer such violence again.

ATONEMENT

Neither is the crucifixion explained or justified as atonement for the sins of humanity. "Substitutionary atonement" is the theological term for the teaching that God sacrificed his only son, Jesus, to "atone" for our sins. Jesus is punished because of us, and he accepts this role of suffering obediently because of his great love for humanity. Somehow through all this, humanity achieves salvation. I have never understood this theology, nor has it framed my experience as a Christian, but it is the dominant theological motif in much of Christianity. Unfortunately it has subsequently been used to justify and accept human suffering at the hands of others.

Rebecca Parker and Rita Nakashima Brock in their pioneering book _Proverbs of Ashes_ confront the Christian theology of the atonement head-on. Parker quotes Hosea Ballou in his _Treatise on the Atonement_ (1805):

> The belief that the great Jehovah was offended with his creatures to that degree, that nothing but the death of Christ, or the endless misery of mankind, could appease his anger, is an idea that has done more injury to the Christian religion than the writings of all its opposers, for many centuries. The error has been fatal to the life and spirit of the religion of Christ in our world; all those principles which are to be dreaded by men have been believed to exist in God.... [13]

Jesus, a Jew, was executed by the Roman state in a definitive act of anti-Semitism. I believe that God was deeply grieved by the death of this son. Jesus, in his prime as teacher and leader, knew and accepted the inevitable consequences of his teaching and his politics, both of which confronted the religious establishment and the state. Jesus lived again and lives today in the hearts and minds of his followers. God did not kill Jesus, nor was his crucifixion a cosmic salvific event; it was an unmitigated tragedy.

It also never really made sense to me to conclude that because Jesus suffered death on the cross that we, as his followers, were condemned to similar fates. Rather Jesus shared in the extremity of human suffering even unto premature death. Suffering happens. He knew the sufferings that we know, and so for Christians as a statement of faith, we believe that he is present with us in those times of suffering.

The fact of sin is the fact of alienation from God and the subsequent moral choices to do harm to another human. Because of the limits of our imaginations and our capacities, brokenness unhealed begets brokenness. This is what I understand and believe about Jesus, the crucifixion, and the reality of sin in the world. This is what I have seen repeatedly in my ministry with victims, survivors, and perpetrators of sexual and domestic violence.

Christian traditions about the atonement have nonetheless been central to the dominant worldview of which we are a part. They represent the struggles of Jesus's followers to make meaning of his death. Unfortunately some of the meaning they have made has translated into a theology that ends up justifying the abuse of vulnerable people and avoiding accountability for those who abuse others. This is especially salient for women and other marginalized people who are looking for a way to make sense out of senseless suffering — and to change the circumstances that allow for that suffering. I have seen much suffering that has resulted from this peculiar theology.

As Brock and Parker suggest:

> Western Christianity claims we are saved by the execution [of Jesus], that violence and terror reveal the grace of God. This claim isolates Jesus, as violence isolates its victims. When the victims of violence are made singular, solitary, unprecedented in their pain, the power of violence remains.
>
> Jesus' death was not unique. The torture inflicted on Jesus had been visited on many. It continues in the world, masked by the words "virtuous suffering" and "self-sacrificing love."[14]

This is the theological distortion that has idealized the suffering of those who are most vulnerable and all too often blinded our ethics to the demands of justice and accountability for the one who causes this suffering.

The resurrection, the realization that the Christ was present to the disciples and is present to us, redeemed the suffering and death experience. "To know that the presence of God endures through violence is to know life holds more than its destruction. The power of life is strong. Salvation is sometimes possible."[15] The people were set free from the pain of that experience to realize the possibility of newness of life among them. In this sense, experiences of suffering, like rape and child sexual abuse, may present a victim/survivor with an *occasion for new life,* that is, the occasion to become a survivor. It is an occasion for learning and maturing psychologically and spiritually. Whether or not the experience of suffering indeed becomes this depends largely on the kind of response that the victim/survivor receives from family, friends, the church, and other institutions that she or he may encounter. A just, compassionate, supportive response will maximize the possibility for healing and new life; an isolating, condemning, disbelieving response will to a large degree preclude such a possibility.

The possibility of new life is also supported by the acts of resistance on the part of the victim/survivor. This reality must not be overlooked or minimized. Traci West rightly cautions: "Overgeneralization about how societal oppression functions can sometimes create formidable barriers to recognizing and understanding resistance."[16] Specifically regarding African American women, West argues, "Too unrelenting a focus on the destructive impact of race and gender subjugation upon black women victim-survivors builds such a barrier."[17] She is pointing to the temptation, often on the part of helpers, to equate "victim" with "helpless." In fact, most victim/survivors are constantly engaged in acts of resistance that have resulted in their survival in the midst of violence or abuse.

A word of caution is necessary. The awareness that a painful experience like rape or child sexual abuse can be redeemed for the victim/survivor is generally a *retrospective insight.* Initially, victim/survivors do not view their experience in this way. As victim/survivors cope with and reflect on their experience, and integrate their responses, then they may start to experience redemption of the suffering. This process can be a long one. Pastors and counselors should not attempt to reassure victims *at this point* that they will certainly grow from their experience of rape or abuse! Such a response at the time of the crisis will be heard as uncaring and superficial and as justifying the abuse. In the recovery process, and with constructive support, most victims do come to the conclusion that they have grown emotionally and spiritually from the experience. However, the realization should not be put forth prematurely. Furthermore, it should not be suggested as a retrospective explanation of God's activity, for example, "God sent this affliction upon you in order that you might know God's redeeming love and that you might find spiritual growth as a result." God does not send suffering in order to produce this result. God does not will that people should suffer. It is a fact of life that people suffer. The question is not "Why?" but rather "What do people do with that suffering?"

The following illustrates how one victim's awareness of growth reshaped her theology:

> *A young woman was raped at age eighteen. As a religious person, she reflected on her rape experience in light of her faith. And as she recovered, she observed that her prayer life had shifted dramatically since the assault. Prior to the rape, she recalled that her prayers most often took the form of "Dear God, please take care of me." As she recovered from the rape, she realized that now her prayers began, "Dear God, please help me to remember what I have learned."*

She had moved from a passive, immature relationship with God, in which she expected God to take care of her, to a more mature, assertive relationship in which she recognized her own strength and responsibility to care for herself with God's help. In addition, her compassion and empathy for others increased, and she was empowered to act to change the things that cause sexual violence. She was able to redeem her experience and mature in her faith as she recovered from the assault with the support and care of her pastor and friends.

Acknowledgment: To be heard and understood by someone who matters, and to have the moral quality of the experience acknowledged. This response of presence, hearing, and acknowledging is the reciprocal responsibility of the bystander to the victim/survivor. Herman calls this the "open-minded, compassionate witness."[18] Anyone can stand on a street corner and "tell" their story: people walk by, cars and buses pass by, and no one hears the story being told. There is probably some value for the victim/survivor in hearing the story come out of one's own mouth: silence is literally broken. But much more helpful is the active response by someone else of hearing *and* acknowledging. This suggests not only passive listening ("I hear you"), but active response ("I believe you") and moral solidarity ("This was not your fault; it should never have happened to you").

This active presence, whether by a minister, friend, police officer, family member, etc., is the beginning of two important aspects of healing: regaining some control over one's world and renewing connection in community. This exchange between victim/survivor and a supportive witness denies the power of the offender (a) to define the experience (which usually involves victim blaming) and (b) to maintain the rupture of relationships for the victim/survivor, creating isolation from valuable resources for support.

GUILT AND SHAME

Guilt and shame are common reactions for victims of sexual violence. Society has effectively stigmatized victims; they are still regarded as dirty, seen as guilty of sexual indiscretion, and blamed for the assault or ongoing abuse. Although these attitudes toward victims are often more subtle than before, they still run deep in the individual and collective consciousness of society. These attitudes are also held by victim/survivors; they have feelings of guilt and shame and do not want anyone to know.[19]

For victim/survivors who are Christians, there may be additional feelings of guilt and shame stemming from religious teachings. Much of the guilt and shame about sexual violence that comes from religious teachings relates to the confusion of sexuality with sexual violence. If a woman accepts the Christian teaching that sexual activity outside of marriage is sinful and that women are seductive temptresses, then she will probably view her victimization as a sexual sin and see herself as being responsible. If a male rape victim views his rape as sexual activity rather than violence and if he has learned from homophobic Christian teachings that any sexual contact with another male is sinful, then he will probably view his victimization by another man as his own sexual sin. Both victims may feel guilty and shamed by the experience because they see the events as primarily sexual.

This feeling of shame is particularly poignant for victims who are sexually inexperienced. Seeing their rape experience as sexual, they feel that they have "lost their virginity." This is most difficult for women in a culture where there still remains a vestige of patriarchal attitudes that regard women as property and regard unmarried women who are not virgins as "damaged goods." Victims in this circumstance are dealing not only with the crisis of sexual assault, but also with their fear that their entire future may be jeopardized. Frequently there are cultural attitudes in family and community that shape the victim/survivor's reactions.

In situations where the Christian victim/survivor of sexual violence feels guilt and shame, pastors or counselors, by acknowledging the guilt and shame that may be present, can help the victim/survivor look for the source of these feelings, that is, erroneous societal and/or religious teachings. Since the chances are good that a victim/survivor will be confusing the experience of sexual violence with sexual activity, this distinction needs to be clarified and discussed. This is most important for sexually inexperienced victim/survivors so that they do not assume that all sexual activity is coercive or violent.

Clarification and discussion distinguishing "sexual" from "violent" is also needed when the victim's primary concern is loss of virginity. While *technically* rape may destroy the symbol of virginity (that is, for a woman, it may rupture the hymen), this experience is no more related to a person's first *sexual* experience than is a woman's first gynecological examination (which also may rupture the hymen). In addition to this clarification, however, some women will need to come to terms with the high priority they may have placed on their virginity, which, unfortunately, is often reinforced by religious teachings (for example, the teaching derived from St. Maria Goretti discussed earlier). For some women this priority means that their identity is based on their value as a sexual commodity.[20]

In fact, when community norms prescribe a woman's value as primarily a function of whether or not she can present herself to a husband as a technical virgin (that is, hymen intact), she may develop a limited and distorted sense of self-worth. A woman is worthy because she is a person created in God's image. Her worth derives from her personhood, not her value as a sexual commodity.[21]

A compassionate presence: The word "compassion" literally means "to suffer with." Compassion here does not refer simply to a warm and supportive presence on the part of the bystander. Rather it highlights the willingness to listen and to be present to the suffering without "trying to fix it" or turn it away. In theory, this may seem simple but it is in fact very difficult for most of us. The temptation in response to someone else's suffering and pain is either to try to "fix" it by problem solving (referring, or giving "answers" to the hard questions, passing along a book or video, etc.), or to walk away as quickly as possible. Either of these strategies helps us not to have to take in the pain that the other person is presenting to us, which may be scary, overwhelming, and upsetting. Ministers tend to go with the "fix it" approach; congregations tend to go with the "pass by" approach.

Somewhere along the way, someone has to stop and be a compassionate presence with a victim/survivor. It may be brief and fleeting: a sensitive police officer in the way in which he took the report; a thoughtful nurse or advocate who stayed by the victim's side during a medical exam; a supportive sibling willing to hear the survivor's experience in the family, which had been unlike his experience. But whatever form it takes, it is significant; the more, the better.

Victims and survivors often realistically fear being ostracized by the people who matter to them and for this reason hesitate to disclose their experiences or report to authorities. Our job as bystanders (whether helpers or neighbors and friends) is to take the time just to be present and walk this part of the road with the victim/survivor. We can help to carry the load part of the way.[22]

ABANDONMENT

Some victim/survivors interpret feeling alone in the midst of suffering as being abandoned by God. There are two possible sources for their feelings of abandonment. One is the lack of support and involvement by family and friends. When people avoid the victim, she or he may literally experience being abandoned by those closest to her or him. The victim may then assume that God has also turned away. A second source of the feeling of abandonment comes from the victim's experience and understanding of suffering. As discussed previously, if a person believes God to be omnipotent, loving, and rewarding of the righteousness of good Christians, then suffering is either a sign of God's disfavor or punishment or a realization that God does not play by the rules. Either interpretation can lead to the feeling of being abandoned by God. This feeling of abandonment occurs for the victim who expected God to protect her or him from all pain and suffering. When encountering suffering, the victim feels betrayed. The sense of abandonment by God is profound and often creates a crisis of faith.

However, as Traci West suggests, social location and life experience certainly shape a victim/survivor's understanding of God's presence or lack thereof.

> Most black women who rely on Christian faith as a primary sustaining resource do not expect that faith in God will shield them from all the encounters with pain and suffering. For many of them God is a refuge in the midst of suffering, a bulwark of strength that enables them to survive in spite of overwhelming obstacles.[23]

If a victim/survivor's life experience at the margins has included a substantial helping of pain and suffering, sexual violence or abuse may be yet another burden to carry. If the experience of God has been a sustaining presence in the midst of suffering, the victim/survivor she may not feel abandoned by God now. But nonetheless she or he may feel isolated and alone, wondering where God could possibly be in all of this.

If, on the other hand, a victim/survivor has somehow avoided much pain and suffering in life, and has interpreted this as being protected by God's mantle, then the shock of sexual violence or abuse may create the sense of abandonment by God. A victim/survivors' sense of abandonment is expressed in various ways. It may be articulated as having difficulty with prayer: "I pray, but God doesn't seem to hear me" or "I can't ever pray anymore." For a female, the experience may center on a realization that a male God and a male redeemer cannot comprehend a woman's experience of victimization. God's "maleness," reasons the victim/survivor, makes God unavailable to her in her suffering. She feels abandoned by a God who cannot understand. She may simply feel numb and out of touch with God. Subsequently, a victim/survivor may feel guilt: "I seem to have lost all of my faith. It must not have been very strong to begin with." She may feel anger mixed with despair: "Where is God now when I am hurting and need help?"

A pastor or counselor can reassure a victim/survivor that these feelings are normal and a common experience for victim/survivors. The Psalmist was very familiar with the sense of God's absence:

My God, my God, why have you forsaken me?
  Why are you so far from helping me, from the words of my
    groaning?
O my God, I cry by day, but you do not answer;
  and by night, but find no rest....

Yet it was you who took me from the womb;
  you kept me safe on my mother's breast.
On you I was cast from my birth,
  and since my mother bore me you have been my God.
Do not be far from me,
  for trouble is near
  and there is no one to help....

I am poured out like water,
  and all my bones are out of joint;
my heart is like wax;
  it is melted within my breast;
my mouth is dried up like a potsherd,
  and my tongue sticks to my jaws;
  you lay me in the dust of death.

For [God] did not despise or abhor
  the affliction of the afflicted;
[God] did not hide [God's] face from me,
  but heard when I cried [out].

(Psalm 22:1–2, 9–11, 14–15, 24 NRSV, inclusive)[24]

These words of scripture are echoed in Jesus's despair as he cried from the cross: "My God, my God, why have you forsaken me?" (Mark 15:34 NRSV). Here even Jesus's faith faltered; in the midst of the physical and emotional pain of crucifixion and impending death, he too felt abandoned by God: "Why have you left me here alone? Why have you given me up to this terrifying experience?" The fear that we will be left totally alone to face suffering and even death reaches to the depths of our being and confronts our faith.

If a person believes that the sign of God's presence is avoidance of suffering, the experience of suffering logically indicates God's absence. This expectation is based on an understanding of God as one who omnipotently intervenes in human affairs, protecting some but not others. While this view of God is often the basis of biblical prayers and requests, it is not the predominant image of God that people experienced. God does *not* promise to protect us from all suffering as long as we behave properly and follow the rules. God knows that we will all suffer. What God does promise is to be present with us even in that suffering—to strengthen and carry us through. God did not reach out and snatch Jesus off the cross in order to protect him from the suffering of death. But God was faithful and present to Jesus through that experience.

As I sat with a group of mothers of incest victims (women whose husbands or ex-husbands had sexually abused their children), the theme of feeling abandoned by God came up several times. Finally, one woman told of her experience: She said that before she was aware of the incest and had to face this crisis in her family, she had pictured her relationship with God like the popular image of two sets of footprints on the beach. God always walked beside her in her life and she knew that God was always there with her. When the incest was disclosed, her picture of her relationship with God shifted. Now she only saw one set of footprints on the beach. In her despair, she assumed that God no longer walked with her. Only later, as the crisis began to be resolved, did she look again at the image and make a different interpretation. In retrospect, she saw that the single set of footprints on the beach were God's footprints. Hers were missing because God was carrying her through the crisis.

A victim/survivor who feels that God has abandoned her or him cannot be convinced of God's faithfulness and presence by even the most persuasive and articulate pastor or counselor. The victim/survivor will only know it through her or his own experience. We can accept and not condemn this feeling of abandonment, mindful of the fact that even Jesus experienced the same feeling. We can identify with the victim/survivor's fear and bear witness to our own experience of God's presence in our lives in times of suffering. Furthermore, our compassionate presence can mediate God's presence during a victim's recovery from abuse.

ANGER

One of the greatest challenges for a pastor, helper, or friend trying to be a compassionate presence to a victim/survivor is the anger which that person expresses. Although usually totally justified, the expression of anger may be difficult for the helper to receive.

Virtually every victim/survivor of sexual violence experiences anger at some point, either during and/or after the assault or abuse. This anger is a healthy response to victimization. Yet for Christians, it is often an uncomfortable feeling that may be repressed. Christians in general and Christian women in particular have learned from various sources that anger is "sinful" and "unbecoming" to a woman. Thus, victim/survivors not only may repress their anger, but may also feel guilty about experiencing it at all. Some victim/survivors are so well socialized not to express anger that it may not surface until years after the abuse. This is particularly common for adult survivors of child sexual abuse who discover their anger as adults when they begin to deal with their childhood abuse.

Providers of pastoral care for victim/survivors can assist them in recognizing their anger and directing it appropriately. For those who are already expressing anger, we can affirm and assist them in focusing it. Affirmation and support for feelings of anger can begin with a clarification of righteous anger. Righteous anger is anger for a right reason and an appropriate response to a situation of injustice. Jesus's response to the money lenders in the Temple was righteous anger (John 2:14–22). Anger is an appropriate and valid response to the abuse of a person. We can give permission to victim/survivors to be angry and not feel guilty.

Revenge, however, is not the same as righteous anger and should be challenged by a pastor or counselor. Not only does revenge cut short any process of justice, it also can easily become self-destructive for the victim. For example, if a victim goes after her rapist a week after the rape and kills him, she will be charged with murder. The victim's act of revenge could result in her imprisonment. Justice is not served by such an act. Willard Gaylin cautions:

> The anger and outrage generated by a sense of ubiquitous injustice could lead to an abandonment of all humanitarian and altruistic concerns for the criminal and, beyond that, for the disadvantaged and disenfranchised in general. We must not attempt to purchase an elegant and individual justice for each person at

the expense of the concept called social justice. It would turn out to be a very costly exchange.[25]

Anger in response to sexual violence may initially be undirected or misdirected. The rage may be so powerful that it immobilizes the victim/survivor. The victim/survivor may need help in focusing and directing her or his anger.

> _A young woman who had been raped expressed strong feelings of anger at God for having "let" the rape happen to her. The power of her anger and the fact that she directed it toward God frightened her. I suggested that she write a letter to God express-ing her anger. I reminded her that God could handle her angry feelings and she did not need to hold back to protect God. She wrote the letter and decided to share it with me the next time we talked. It went on for three pages, lambasting God for al-lowing there to be such a thing as rape and for not protecting her from it._

After this letter-writing exercise, which expurgated much of her rage, we were able to discuss her understanding of God and of suf-fering sufficiently to enable her to move beyond "blaming God." Her anger was affirmed: the world did not end because she lashed out at God. It was then redirected toward the real source of her suffering, her abuser.

Sometimes the anger is directed toward the victim/survivor's part-ner or at a family member. Sometimes pastors or counselors find the rage pouring forth at them. It is important for the persons on the receiving end of the anger to understand that we may be getting it simply because we are there at that moment. It probably has nothing to do with us personally. It can make us feel very uncomfortable or even afraid, which may call forth our defenses. We may be tempted to respond, "Why are you yelling at me? I didn't rape you!" A more helpful approach is to set a limit on being the depository for this ini-tial anger. Once the limit is reached, the pastor or counselor should encourage the victim/survivor to focus the anger on the source of the suffering and to express it appropriately. The anger is affirmed but not allowed to harm others.

When the victim/survivor's anger is directed inward, the result can be self-destructive. For example, an adult who had been a childhood adult survivor of incestuous abuse and who had not been able to deal with this experience found herself in a pattern of heavy drug abuse. Another victim who, as a teenager, suffered chronic sexual abuse by a neighbor and received no support from her family, engaged in periodic self-mutilation. Both of these victims turned their anger toward themselves.

Directing the anger at the source of the suffering is vital if a victim/survivor is to move through the process of recovery and healing. There may be multiple sources: initially, the offender, and, secondarily, the system that may have been nonsupportive or even further victimized the victim; the insensitive police officer or medical doctor who reacted with disbelief to the victim's story; the unscrupulous defense attorney who tried to smear the victim's reputation as a defense for his or her client; the minister who encouraged the victim to pray and "forgive and forget"; the rape crisis counselor who ignored a victim's need to deal with her or his religious concerns. All of these represent the system's responses which could compound the victimization. Victim/survivors may need assistance in identifying the sources and in focusing their anger.

A victim/survivor's anger as a healthy and appropriate response to victimization motivates the victim/survivor to act on one's own behalf. When directed outward toward the appropriate source, anger can energize the victim/survivor.

A victim was hesitant to report her assault to the police because she was anxious about the long, involved legal process that would result. As she got in touch with her anger not only at what the rapist had done to her, but also at what he would continue to do to other women, she decided to report the rape. She went through with the prosecution of her assailant and he was convicted.

Her anger energized her to act and to do what she could to ensure that the rapist would not rape again. As a moral agent, she was able to seek justice in the public arena; this was an act of resistance. She was able to do this because of the support of her community, family, friends, and church.

While righteous anger is a healthy response to victimization, it represents a stage in the healing process, not a way of life. Sometimes the victim/survivor's anger becomes the center of her or his life. This all-consuming rage can drain all of a person's energy and make it difficult to engage in self-care. The elements of justice making discussed in this chapter offer a framework for healing that can utilize healthy anger and lead to real healing rather than self-destructive rage.

A word of caution here: particularly in response to a victim/survivor's anger, a pastor or helper may be tempted to counsel forgiveness to "help" her or him get beyond the anger. This is not helpful on any level at this point. See the further discussion below of forgiveness and its place in the healing process.

Protecting the vulnerable: to protect anyone who might be vulnerable to harm by this perpetrator. Protection is the community's responsibility. Whether formal (e.g., legal sanctions) or informal (e.g., limits on church activities), steps must be taken to do whatever is possible to ensure that the offender does not harm someone again. For a professional who has abused in the professional role (e.g., doctor, teacher, or clergy), the community can suspend licenses or professional standing in order to limit the offender from future access to vulnerable people. In custody proceedings, family court judges can limit a parent's custody or visitation privileges with the children whom the parent abused. When an offender wants to return to participation in a congregation (after incarceration or treatment), a congregation can set limits on the offender's activities and access to vulnerable people.

A desire to protect others from harm is a common motivating factor for victim/survivors to come forward and report an abuser. Our responsibility is to work collaboratively with secular and religious resources to do whatever we can to protect others.

Accountability: to hold the perpetrator accountable. Here we focus specifically on the pastoral response to the offender. Although both religious and secular communities are challenged to hold perpetrators accountable, it is a critical part of the possibility of justice in promoting healing (see chapter 3).

Accountability serves the interests of the victim/survivor, the offender, and the community. Yet it is often the most difficult aspect of the process because it requires action in place of passivity. In terms of the offender, he or she deserves to be held accountable. In his discussion of a murderer, Willard Gaylin argues: "As a tribute and testament to [a perpetrator's] freedom, we must dignify him by making him pay for the evil actions he commits. We show our respect by making him accountable."[26] As Christians, we show our genuine concern for the offender by calling him or her to repentance. The irony is that within the Christian tradition (and building on what we learn from Judaism), we have a framework for this very action: judgment, call to repent, confession, penance, repentance, and the possibility of forgiveness and reconciliation (see below). The biblical, doctrinal, and in some traditions even the sacramental resources are there. We are just hesitant to use them.

To call an offender to account accomplishes two important steps in healing: (1) it is a stand in solidarity with the victim/survivor, and (2) it is a confrontation with the offender, naming the sin and the consequences of brokenness within the community that resulted from his or her actions. As such calling the offender to account offers the offender the chance to change and to make right the brokenness that he or she caused. This is the essence of true repentance and is the preferred response to the victim/survivor.

Every victim/survivor longs to hear these words from an offender: "Yes, I did molest you when you were a child," "It was my fault, not yours," "I am responsible for what I did to you then," "Please don't blame yourself; it was my doing," "Is there any way I can make right what I broke?" or "I am so sorry that I hurt you so badly." These responses to confrontation can be enormously helpful in healing because they represent an acknowledgment and affirmation both of what happened (truth telling) and who was responsible (naming). Tragically few victim/survivors ever hear these responses from their offenders. In lieu of this best-case scenario, the community and/or church can provide these responses in acknowledging the victim/survivor's truth.

CONFESSION AND REPENTANCE

One of the major religious issues in working with offenders as opposed to victim/survivors is the issue of confession and repentance. The willingness on the part of rapists or child molesters to admit what they have done and to acknowledge the harm that their actions have caused another person are significant steps for sex offenders. In religious terms, these constitute confession. A sex offender may seek out a pastor for the purpose of confessing. Too often, however, an offender confesses to a pastor, asks for forgiveness, and, having received cheap grace, walks away believing everything is fine. His confession may be honest, his remorse real, and his desire for forgiveness authentic, but he also wants it to be easy. A word from the pastor, a quick prayer, and all is well; he then believes he will stop sexually abusing children. Seldom, if ever, is this sufficient to stop a sex offender, because his confession has fallen short of repentance. Confession is necessary, but not sufficient. It is only a first step toward repentance. Dietrich Bonhoeffer comments, "A man who confesses his sins in the presence of a brother knows he is no longer alone with himself; he experiences the presence of God in the reality of the other person."[27] Thus, confession can reconnect an offender with God's presence, which can then empower him to repent.

Repentance goes beyond confession, apology, and good intentions. Repentance means to turn around, to change one's behavior, and to not repeat the offense.[28] If one does not do whatever is necessary to change one's abusive behavior, then confession is at best a sham and at worst a ploy.[29] What is necessary for the sex offender in most cases is a long and difficult process of treatment (which may or may not involve incarceration). In a treatment situation, the offender's faith can provide the source of strength and determination he needs to stay in treatment. In addition, the supportive but firm position of the pastor ("I want you to be in that treatment group every week; this is God's will for you now") can encourage the offender's commitment to the treatment process.

Caution is advised for the pastor or counselor especially in the situation where an offender "gets religion" soon after his offense is disclosed: "Now that I've found Jesus Christ, I am a new person. I'll never rape again. I don't need to see a counselor now that I have Jesus in my heart." His sudden conversion may be a ploy to avoid treatment or incarceration, or his religious experience may be genuine, in which case he sincerely believes he will not offend again. In either case, a pastor or counselor must avoid being taken in by either the offender's manipulations or his good intentions. Realizing that the offender *will* offend again unless he or she gets help, the pastor or counselor must insist that the offender seek the treatment needed. All things are possible through God, even the rehabilitation of a sex offender. Repentance becomes real as the effort to change is made. Jeremiah's vision of the potter is a reminder: "So I went down to the potter's house, and there he was working at his wheel. The vessel he was making of clay was spoiled in the potter's hand, and he *reworked it into another vessel* [emphasis added], as it seemed good to him" (Jeremiah 18:3–4 NRSV). Change is possible. But repentance is necessary: "Turn now, all of you from your evil way, and amend your ways and your doings" (Jeremiah 18:1 NRSV).

But for the offender, healing of his or her brokenness is dependent on taking responsibility (confession), doing penance (restitution), and repentance (making real change so as not to repeat the behavior). Whether or not there is literal reconciliation is another matter not under the control of the offender (see chapter 8 on forgiveness). Accountability is the way to stop the abuse and the way to genuinely help those who abuse.

Restitution: material compensation for the losses incurred by the victim; ideally provided by the perpetrator as an act of repentance;

if not, then by the community. Restitution, to be paid to the one harmed, is both literal and symbolic. A victim/survivor often has incurred expenses resulting from the abuse: medical bills, therapy, lost wages, etc. Compensation for these expenses can be very helpful for the victim/survivor's healing. Material things, specifically money, communicate a very powerful message in our society. But then it also did in Jesus's time: when Zaccheus, the dishonest tax collector, repented, he wanted to pay back four times what he had taken unjustly (Luke 19:1–10). This restitution offers a reasonable model for contemporary efforts at accountability.

For the offender, restitution is an act of repentance. Restitution clearly acknowledges the offender's responsibility for the sin as well as the need to make right the injuries done to the victim. Although material or financial means are seldom adequate to restore the victim's complete well-being, payments can assist with real costs. Restitution payments to a rape crisis center or victims' compensation program contribute to services made necessary by the offender's actions. In this way, the offender makes restitution to the community as well.

Even if an offender (whose conduct was criminal) does not repent or make restitution, the community can still hold him or her accountable by due process of law and protect itself by incarcerating the offender.[30] If the misconduct was professional, the community or church can remove credentials to deny the offender sanctioned access to vulnerable people. In other words, the offender does not retain control over the outcome and the possibilities for justice for the victim/survivor.

Vindication: not revenge; rather, to be vindicated is "to be set free"; scars remain but healing is sufficient so as not to continue to be held in bondage to the trauma. When the community (church, family, courts, workplace, etc.) stands with the victim/survivor, she or he begins to experience vindication. This literally means, "to set free." This is what the persistent widow in Luke 18 was asking for from the unjust judge: that he hear her and acknowledge what happened to her in public. Hopefully the response of the community to her vindication was that she was welcomed back without stigma or blame.

In some ways, vindication is the culmination of these responses of justice making. It describes whatever it takes for the victim/survivor to feel sufficient resolution to be able to get on with life. It is unlikely that anyone ever gets all the justice they deserve in the aftermath of sexual violence or abuse. The real question for any victim/survivor is: what is sufficient for my healing? The answer is different for everyone.

An adult survivor of incestuous abuse came to talk with me about her recent memories of sexual abuse by her uncle. She was getting in touch with her anger, which she was also hesitant to share. She quickly moved to the point of wanting to confront her uncle only to be stymied because her uncle was deceased. So she decided instead to write to her father, her uncle's brother, and tell him what had happened. She wrote the letter; we discussed whether she wanted to send it. We explored the possible responses her father might make. She decided that she didn't care how he responded; she just needed to break the silence.

Her father received her twelve-page letter and immediately got on a plane and came to her. He said how sorry he was that all this had happened. He said he didn't know that his brother was abusing her, but he knew she was having a hard time and he didn't check that out with her. He said that he should have protected her because that was his job as her father. He asked how much her therapy had cost her and said that he would send a check for the expense as soon as he got home. When I saw her a week later, she was a different woman. She still had work to do; she stayed in her survivor support group. But her burden had been lifted; she had forgiven, that is, let go of the immediacy of her pain because she experienced justice in her father's response.

In this illustration we are looking at the actions of the community, our responsibilities as bystanders. How do *we* help make justice in order to contribute to an individual's healing process and to a perpetrator's accountability and change? Of course the irony in all this is that as bystanders, we too are served by our engagement. It allows us to *do* something in the face of the potential of powerlessness, to stand in solidarity, to not give in to the violence that surrounds us. These are acts of resistance for us as well.

Our shared efforts to make justice as a means of healing and accountability help to create a possible future. Survivors and offenders both may have the opportunity for a renewal of relationship to the wider community (but not necessarily to each other). Judith Herman describes the final stage of healing for a survivor:

> The survivor must be ready to relinquish the "specialness" of her identity. Only at this point can she contemplate her story as one among many and envision her particular tragedy within the embrace of the human condition.... Commonality with other people carries with it all the meaning of the word _common_. It means belonging to a society, having a public role, being part of that which is universal. It means having a feeling of familiarity, of being known, of communion. It means taking part in the customary, the commonplace, the ordinary, and the everyday. It also carries with it a feeling of smallness, of insignificance, a sense that one's own troubles are "as a drop of rain in the sea." The survivor who has achieved commonality with others can rest from her labors. Her recovery is accomplished; all that remains before her is her life.[31]

Surely this is a possibility for the church as a faith community. This is what it means to be a part of the Body of Christ.

Chapter 8 _____

What about Forgiveness?

In our worship life together, we sometimes rather casually read a corporate prayer of confession usually followed by the pastor's equally casual "words of assurance," which often announce "your sins are forgiven." As a pastor, this has always unnerved me a bit. Who am I to pretend to "forgive" you for something you may have done to your child, your partner, your employee? I cannot. What I can do is to remind you of the Good News, that when we *repent* of the harm that we caused, God is merciful and rejoices with us in the possibility of reconciliation.

A pastor or counselor may question a survivor: "Isn't it time you forgave him? If God can forgive him, surely you can, too." For a victim/survivor who does not *feel* forgiving at this point, these words of advice only leave her or him feeling guilty for not forgiving and estranged from those attempting to assist. Forgiveness by a victim/survivor cannot be hurried, nor can it be orchestrated by those on the outside. To expect people to move quickly from their pain to forgive those who are responsible for it is insensitive and unrealistic. Forgiveness is not merely an act of will, although it may be an intentional, willful act. One cannot just decide "I will forgive" because someone else suggests one *should* forgive.

Forgiveness is a word that has become more and more meaningless in our society. Some people mean that they want to simply forget what happened by just putting it out of their minds. By forgiving, others mean that the offense or injury which occurred is somehow "okay," that is, that somehow it becomes a nonoffense. Neither of these meanings is adequate to the experience of rape or sexual abuse.

A person can never forget these offenses. The memory of the event always remains in the victim/survivor's consciousness. It becomes a part of one's history, as do one's positive experiences. Nothing can ever make the offense a nonoffense. It will never be "okay" that a person was raped or molested. It is forever a wrong done to another human being.

In situations of violence or abuse, forgiveness is the last step, at best. But it can hold a key to healing. In Christian circles, forgiveness is the single most common expectation that is placed on victims of clergy abuse, rape, incest, battering, etc. Many people say to victims and survivors: "The Bible says you must forgive and forget." Never mind that it is impossible to forget the things the abuser did; never mind that "forgive and forget" appears in Shakespeare's *King Lear* (IV: vii), not the Bible. Never mind that it is the worst advice we can give any survivor. She takes it seriously and tries very hard "to forgive," absent any acknowledgment on the abuser's part of the harm he has done, not to mention any effort on his part to change.

Linda Hollies, a United Methodist pastor and incest survivor, summarizes:

> When people say we can forgive and forget, that's a lie. Even when you forgive, to forgive means to take it off your agenda for retribution and put it on God's agenda. That's all it means. I'm going to take you off my hit list. I will not expect you to come back and apologize. I will not expect you to come back and make amends. I will not expect you to feel sorry. I will not expect you to ask for my forgiveness. I turn it loose. You did it. That was yesterday. You will not ruin my today. God knows you will not hold me captive in tomorrow. And so when I think about it, when it comes back, when it's fresh, I have to say, "God, I gave this to you. You keep it." It's never to say I won't think about it.[1]

Most important, forgiveness happens in its own time and cannot be rushed from the outside. It may take one year or thirty. Pastors and counselors can be available to victim/survivors as they struggle with a need and desire to forgive. Pastors and counselors can do whatever they can to mediate justice in the victim/survivors experience. They can bear witness to God's presence and power, but they cannot force a victim/survivor to forgive.

CONDITIONS AND CHOICES

Forgiveness is not unconditional. In human experience forgiveness occurs within a context and takes place when a set of conditions is met. In order to be authentic, forgiveness happens based on the following:

- empowerment of the victim/survivor through God's grace;

- vindication of the victim/survivor experienced through justice.

- a choice on the part of the victim/survivor to let go of that experience of pain and anger.

The choice on the part of the survivor to let go only happens *when she or he is ready to let go*. When the healing is sufficient and the survivor feels safe and strong enough, she or he will be ready to let go and can make that choice. Even then, letting go is not easy. God's grace, which is known through prayer and the presence of the Holy Spirit, can empower a survivor to forgive. Finally, in order to forgive, most survivors need some experience of justice. At some point in the aftermath of a rape or the disclosure of sexual abuse, a survivor needs some concrete expression of the fact that she or he has been wronged, that what occurred should never have happened, and that the offender is responsible. Ideally, the offender's repentance will provide that justice and will free the survivor to forgive.

For most people, some experience of justice is the prerequisite for forgiveness and eventually for healing. It may be a ten-minute conversation with a significant person or a two-year civil or criminal trial. It may be an apology from a bishop. It may be compensation for medical expenses. Such experiences of justice can free the survivor to let go, but this letting go should never be confused with accepting justification for the trauma inflicted on her or him. It is never to "forgive and forget," but to let go and put aside the immediacy of the memories in order to get on with one's life, as Linda Hollies writes. Forgiveness, healing, and recovery only become real possibilities when the community surrounding the survivor creates the conditions for an experience of justice (see chapter 7).

However, if the expectation of who *should* act in response to harm done by one to another is passed *to* the one harmed and *away* from the one causing harm, then three adverse things happen:

- Victim/survivors, whose priority is their own healing, may decide that they have the power alone to bring about this healing by their agency in the "act" of forgiving. This is a cruel hoax for most victims. As a result, a victim/survivor is shamed or cajoled into saying the magic words "I forgive him or her," convinced by the bystanders that now she or he (the victim/survivor) will feel better; now God will love them; and now they can be a "good Christians."

- No one (especially the bystanders) ever has to hold the offender accountable. This is particularly advantageous for the non-repentant offender.

- The bystanders (often the pastor or counselor and many members of our churches) can stand by and do nothing, self-righteously reassured that we have no lines in this play.

The overall result is that the burden "to forgive" is cast upon the shoulders of the victim/survivor, who already carries the pain and suffering of having been victimized. Instead the responsibility of agency should here lie first with the community: we can help make justice by our responses. Second, the responsibility of agency lies with the offender who, when called to account, can repent. Finally, these actions then make it possible for the victim/survivor to be free to forgive, which is about that person's healing process.

WHEN FORGIVENESS HAPPENS:
A GIFT FOR SURVIVORS

For Christians, forgiving is one means of letting go and disarming the power that the offense has over a survivor's life. At some point, a survivor may be freed to forgive and may decide: "I will no longer allow this experience to dominate my life. I will not let it continue to make me feel bad about myself. I will not let it limit my ability to love and trust others in my life. I will not let my memory of the experience continue to victimize and control me." Forgiving means letting go and putting the rape experience in perspective: "I can never forget what happened. But I choose to put it here and leave it behind. If I ever need to recall it, I know where it is. But I refuse to carry the pain any longer."

> *A friend of mine who was raped in her twenties by a police officer reflects some forty years later on her healing. She says that the memory is there, but she keeps it in a locked box. She has the key to it and can open it whenever she needs to. But otherwise it stays locked away in her consciousness so that it can't continue to diminish her life today.*

For some survivors, forgiving may mean acknowledging the humanness of the offender: "I refuse to let his acts toward me prevent me from recognizing his humanity, that, like me, he is created in God's image." But forgiving never means condoning or excusing what he did: "What he did is a distortion of who he was created to be and should never have happened."

Forgiving does not mean allowing oneself to be abused repeatedly: "Be on your guard! If another disciple sins, you must *rebuke the offender* [emphasis added], and *if there is repentance* [emphasis added], you must forgive. And if the same person sins against you seven times a day, and turns back to you seven times, and says, 'I repent,' you must forgive" (Luke 17:3–4 NRSV). Jesus teaches that a person must be willing to confront the offense and be willing to forgive as many times as it takes. But it is also clear in this scripture that a person's forgiveness is dependent on the offender's repentance. If the offender's repentance is genuine, he or she will not repeat the offense. The cycle is broken.

Some argue that we should follow Jesus's model of forgiveness from the Cross in which he unconditionally forgave those who crucified him. Fred Keene offers a more literal and helpful interpretation:

> [The Crucifixion] is a situation where Jesus has no power; he is speaking from a cross about those who have crucified him. What is noticeable is that he does not forgive them. Instead, he asks his Father, he asks God, to forgive them. Having no power within the situation, he can not forgive. . . . This is the one place where, if Jesus wanted the weak to forgive the strong, he could have indicated it. He did not.[2]

Keene's analysis of Christian scriptures on forgiveness provides a valuable framework for understanding Jesus's teaching. He argues convincingly that Jesus's expectation that we forgive applies when we are in a position of power and someone with less power owes us a debt. Jesus does not expect those who have less power, for example, victim/survivors, to forgive the harm done to them until they feel empowered, which is what happens when they experience some form of justice.

For the perpetrator, change or repentance — "get yourselves a new heart and a new spirit" (Ezekiel 18:31 NRSV) — carries the possibility for him or her to be restored to community in some experience of reconciliation.

I was meeting with a group of incest offenders who were in a court-mandated treatment program. I had been asked to discuss religious issues with them because out of the twenty-seven men, twenty-five were Christians and they had a lot of questions. At the end of the evening, they made this request of me: whenever you talk with church people, they said, tell them not to forgive us so quickly. Each of them had gone directly to their pastor after

*their arrest for molesting their children. Each had been prayed
over and sent home "forgiven." They said it was the worst thing
anyone could have done to them because it allowed them to
continue to avoid responsibility for the harm they had done. I
take their plea very seriously. "Don't forgive us so quickly."*

Their witness is a powerful challenge to us all. They are trying to
tell us that justice and accountability are necessary for healing and
before we can even discuss forgiveness.

Unfortunately it is usually the community (family, friends, religious
group) that presses the issue of forgiveness with survivors. Usually
with good intentions, forgiveness is offered as a cure-all, but it is
not a helpful place to begin for either survivor or perpetrator. Quick
forgiveness or cheap grace is not helpful to perpetrators — and it can
be devastating to survivors whose process is artificially cut short.

RECONCILIATION: WHEN REPENTANCE MEETS FORGIVENESS[3]

Reconciliation means to bring together that which should be together
in a just relationship, to renew a broken relationship on new terms,
and to heal the injury of broken trust that has resulted from an
offense inflicted by one person on another. Reconciliation happens
when the offender genuinely repents and the injured forgives, creating
the possibility of a new relationship. Unfortunately, this ideal of reconciliation seldom is manifest, especially in cases of sexual violence.
The victim's hurt may be too deep for her or him to be able to forgive, or the offender's denial and unwillingness to take responsibility
may be too strong for him or her to be able to repent. The offender
may be dead and gone, as is sometimes the case when incestuous
abuse is finally acknowledged, or the survivor may have no interest
in reconciling a relationship with a stranger who assaulted her.

One act that can enhance the possibility of reconciliation between
survivor and offender is restitution on the part of the offender. When
restitution follows from repentance, it is a concrete act that may

indicate the offender's honest intentions and desire to heal the relationship. Restitution may take the form of payment to the survivor for medical expenses or payment to a rape crisis center to support its services. Sometimes restitution is ordered by the court; sometimes it is voluntary. Restitution can be one step that leads toward reconciliation. For example:

A woman who had not seen her father since she had left home seven years earlier decided to write to him and confront him with the sexual abuse he had inflicted on her in her childhood and teenage years. He wrote her back and asked to visit her.

She agreed, somewhat reluctantly. When they met, he acknowledged the abuse and told her that he now realized that what he had done was wrong. She let him know how angry she was and that she was still dealing with the psychological aftereffects in therapy and with physical discomfort from urinary infections that resulted from the abuse. His remorse and sense of responsibility were real. He offered to pay for her medical and counseling expenses. He said he had talked with his pastor, who had encouraged him to meet with her. He asked her to forgive him. She felt herself tighten, afraid once again of betrayal. And then she felt herself begin to let go of the anger. It had served its purpose; it had motivated her to confront her father. She questioned him about other children; had he abused them, too? She found that she had been the only one, an only child, and that he had not gone out of the family. But he realized his problem was still there and his pastor had urged him to see a counselor. He had already had two sessions. Her anger dissipated further. For the first time, she saw him beginning to take responsibility for himself. She said she forgave him mostly so that she could get on with her life. She said she hoped that he would stay in therapy and work on his problems because she couldn't help him. They agreed to visit each other again when both felt up to it. She agreed to let him see her children, his grandchildren, whom he had never met, but only under supervision. She explained that *she had taught them to tell her if any adult tried to touch them sexually. He assured her he would not hurt them. He visited her family for holidays and was able to have a satisfying relationship with his daughter's family thereafter, never forgetting but never discussing again the sexual abuse from years earlier.*

Although the ideal of restitution and reconciliation is difficult and seldom attained, it is worth looking toward as a possibility. In so doing, we must realize that forgiveness or repentance alone cannot accomplish reconciliation. But when both meet, the possibility is real that the survivor and the offender will no longer be defined by the offense, but once again be two persons whose brokenness is healed and who can encounter each other anew.

Chapter 9 _____

Children and Youth

To Such Belongs the Kingdom of God

At first he would just stand by the bed and touch me. Later he began to lay in the bed beside me. Although he began by being gentle, as time went on, his touch became rougher and rougher. He would leave me feeling sore and bruised for days. It was as if he completely lost touch with the fact that I was a child. He was a bully who physically dominated everyone in our family. I saw and heard him beat up my mother so many times that I was in constant fear that he would kill her. I knew that I was no match for him, and I guess I believed that his sexual abuse was somehow better than the physical abuse my mother received. Total detachment became my way of dealing with what went on at night. I would roll into the wall when he came in, pretending to be asleep, trying to be part of the wall. I would cry hysterically in order to get so far into my own pain that I wouldn't notice what he was doing. With the pillow over my face, I taught myself to detach my mind from my body. I could actually see myself from the far upper corner of the room; I saw the little girl crying in bed and felt sorry for her.[1]

People were bringing little children to him in order that he might touch them; and the disciples spoke sternly to them. But when Jesus saw this, he was indignant and said to them, "Let the little children come to me; do not stop them; for it is to such as these that the kingdom of God belongs. Truly I tell you, whoever does not receive the kingdom of God as a little child will never enter it." And he took them up in his arms, laid his hands on them, and blessed them. (Mark 10:13–16 NRSV)

Jesus said to the disciples, 'Occasions for stumbling are bound to come, but woe to anyone by whom they come! It would be better for you if a millstone were hung around your neck and you were thrown into the sea than for you to cause one of these little ones to stumble. (Luke 17:1–2 NRSV)

The sexual abuse of children and youth is perhaps the most disturbing manifestation of sexual violence. Many people have a difficult time imagining that an adult could willfully exploit a child sexually, especially an adult related to the child. As a result, this common childhood experience is frequently overlooked. Freud was so dismayed by the frequency with which his clients reported sexual abuse as children that, rather than face the reality that they expressed, he decided that it was largely fantasy. From this erroneous and unscientific conclusion, Freud developed his theories of female sexual fantasy. His conclusion that the reports from his female clients of sexual abuse by fathers were untrue provided a pseudoscientific basis for the collective denial that children are sexually abused in their families.[2] It is particularly difficult to admit the reality of child sexual abuse, so eyes and ears are closed to its victims who seek help. If no one "sees" it, then it "does not exist."

Statistics show otherwise: 27 percent of females and 16 percent of males are sexually molested by age eighteen.[3] Based on police reports, in 90 percent of the rapes of children younger than twelve, the child knew the offender. For victims eighteen to twenty-nine years old, two-thirds knew the offender.[4] Among high school students, 81 percent reported some form of sexual harassment in school.[5] A child or teen may be assaulted or molested by a stranger, by someone known to her or him, or by a family member. Each of these situations presents different difficulties for the child.

MOLESTATION BY A STRANGER

When a child is molested by someone not known to her or him, it is usually treated as a crisis. A child who has been taught about sexual abuse will more than likely go to a trusted adult for help. The adult's response at this point is critical. If the parent, teacher, family friend, or other adult reacts with horror and disbelief, immediately moving into crisis herself or himself, the child will become anxious for having "caused" this disruption for the adult. The adult's crisis then becomes the focus of responses by friends and others trying to help. An alternative response by an adult to a child's disclosure of sexual abuse is to listen carefully and calmly. Reassure the child that she or he did the right thing in coming to tell you. Repeat that it was not the child's fault. Be clear that you will take care of the situation; you will protect the child. Then call the police and report the incident; call the local rape crisis center and ask for their help as well.

If the offender who abused the child did not use physical force, quick and calm intervention by an adult can help ensure minimal trauma for the child. The child will ordinarily recover quickly from this unpleasant experience. If the offender used force, the recovery is more difficult for the child because the experience itself was more frightening and traumatic. In either case, a calm, sensitive response is most helpful.

SEXUAL ABUSE BY SOMEONE KNOWN
TO THE CHILD OR TEEN

Ninety percent of the time, the child victim of sexual abuse knows the offender, and chances are high that the offender is a family member. Sexual abuse by someone known to the child is less likely to be reported by the child and, if unreported, can become a chronic pattern of abuse that may last for years before being revealed. The abuse usually begins between ages three and, six and if there is no intervention, often continues into the child's adolescence. Child sexual abuse includes fondling; masturbating the child; oral, genital, or anal penetration; or forcing the child to sexually stimulate the adult or older teenager. A child who is being sexually abused by someone they know is not likely to report the abuse for several reasons: the adult (parent) or older teenager (babysitter) is in a position of authority over the child; the child fears being blamed for doing something wrong; the abuser may offer bribes or threaten physical harm; the child may enjoy receiving this special attention, even though it is uncomfortable, confusing, and likely frightening; the child is aware that he or she is dependent on the adult for basic material needs. Too frequently a child has tried to disclose the situation to an adult who either ignored or refused to believe the child. The child then concludes that adults cannot be trusted or expected to help, so the child tries to cope on her or his own.

Child sexual abuse in the family may well extend into adolescence. In addition, the teenager or college student may be raped by someone he or she is dating. Barrie Levy reports that "date rape accounts for sixty-seven percent of the sexual assaults reported by adolescent and college-age women (Ageton, 1983). Young women between the ages of fourteen and seventeen represent an estimated thirty-eight percent of those victimized by date rape (Warshaw, 1988)."[6] Young adulthood is a particularly vulnerable period in a person's life. The exploration of intimacy and relationships can lead to exploitation for females or males.[7]

COPING MECHANISMS OF CHILD VICTIMS OF INCESTUOUS ABUSE

The child or teenager who has been sexually abused and exploited by a family member or other significant adult develops specific coping skills and attitudes in order to survive. These may include isolation and detachment, a mistrust of adults, the confusion of sex and affection, low self-esteem, and self-destructive behavior.

Victims often withdraw from their peers. Because the victim rarely shares the experience with peers, she or he believes that no one else has ever experienced this before; the victim feels isolated from peers as a result. The victim also feels older than one's peers and more experienced because she or he is "sexually active" at an early age. Survivors often talk about never knowing childhood. In addition, they may detach themselves from the abuse experience, pretending that it is all a dream, that the sexual contact is really with someone else and not with them, etc. Thus they may come across as being emotionally flat and removed from what they describe and know.

Child victims learn early not to trust adults. A relationship that should be trustworthy and in which an adult is supposed to care for and protect a child is betrayed by child sexual abuse. Some form of coercion is employed overtly or subtly by the adult to force compliance with sexual demands. Physical size and authority are used to the offender's advantage. If a victim has asked for help from another adult and not been believed, she or he readily concludes that adults in general cannot be trusted.

Children need emotional and physical affection. Child victims learn that the only affection they are likely to get from the offender is sexual. They also learn that this sexual attention is not for their benefit, but is solely for the benefit of the offender. Hence, they feel exploited. They begin to believe that the only way to get affection is through sex and that sex is basically exploitative and something over which they have no control. As a result, child victims commonly lose their sense of self-worth. They feel responsible for the sexual abuse and develop overwhelmingly negative feelings about themselves. Their only sense of personal worth comes from being the object of an adult's sexual attention. They quickly begin to think that sex is all they are good for.

SELF-DESTRUCTIVE BEHAVIOR

A loss of self-worth may move the child or teenage victim to self-destructive behavior. Drug or alcohol abuse, self-mutilation, anorexia, bulimia, and suicide attempts may result. These should all be regarded as severe symptoms of a problem and an attempt should be made to discover what lies behind them. It may be sexual abuse.

I believe that children engage in violent and/or self-destructive behavior for a reason. I believe that when children have pain which is hard to express, they will sometimes do destructive things to themselves and to others in order to be heard. I believe every victim of incest and childhood sexual abuse tried to tell someone, either verbally or by behavior, that something was wrong. We are all so uncomfortable with destructive behavior that we often cannot see beyond it. We deal with the outward, visible signs of feelings because they are more concrete and easier for us to manage than the secret pain or fear that may lie beneath them. As a result, it is often a child's behavior that we confront, rather than what a child is really trying to say. We must learn to do more than just see the behavior or treat the symptoms of incest. We must learn to hear the pain and offer new survival skills.[8]

This is a critical issue for youth ministries. It is not uncommon to find one or more youth group members who are labeled "provocative," "seductive," or "too mature." This label usually comes from the teenager's sexual acting out with peers or adults. The most common response to this behavior (and other juvenile antisocial behaviors) is judgmental and punitive without stopping to assess the source of the behavior. In many cases we have punished juveniles who are themselves victims of the adult behavior we did not want or bother to know about, rather than attending to their needs as victims.

Any child or young teen who attempts to sexualize their interaction with an adult is probably disclosing their victimization. Sexualization of a relationship to an adult may indicate the confusion between affection and sex that happens for child victims of sexual abuse. In other words, a child or teen may learn to relate to adults sexually because they have experienced adults being sexual with them. Rather than punishment or shame, our response should be to try to find out what is going on for that child or youth, and one of the ways to encourage this is education and open conversation about the topic of sexual abuse.[9] The bottom line is that if a young person approaches an adult sexually, we must not respond sexually.

"HONOR YOUR FATHER AND MOTHER"

The Sunday school teaching of the commandment to honor father and mother (Exodus 20:12) presents special difficulty for the child who is being sexually abused by her or his parent(s) and for the parents. If the parent misuses this teaching to demand unquestioning obedience from a child, then the incest survivor is compelled to submit to sexual activity with the parent and to feel guilty if she or he questions such activity. The victim/survivor feels that there is no recourse because not only is parental authority invoked, but also religious authority. The child is misled to believe this is the teaching of the Bible and the church.

Misuse of scriptural teaching is a blatant distortion. In Ephesians, Paul makes very clear the meaning of the commandment:

> Children, obey your parents *in the Lord* [emphasis added], for this is right. "Honor your father and mother" — this is the first commandment with a promise — "so that it may be well with you and that you may live long on the earth." And, fathers, do not provoke your children to anger, but bring them up *in the discipline and instruction of the Lord.* (Ephesians 6:1–4 NRSV [emphasis added])

Children's obedience to parents is conditional; it is to be "in the Lord," that is, consistent with the gospel. Here, in addition to the reminder to children to keep this commandment, there are instructions to parents: guide and instruct your children in Christian values such as love, mercy, compassion, and justice. The caution to the father not to provoke the child to anger is most telling and appropriate. Nothing provokes a child's anger more quickly than abuse by a parent, especially sexual abuse.

A child victim of incestuous abuse (or an adult who was a child victim) may need help in resolving questions about this religious teaching on relationships with parents before she or he can address any other religious concerns. Incestuous abuse clearly violates the parent's responsibility and should not be condoned on the basis of this commandment.

DISCLOSURE

Disclosure of sexual abuse is often frightening and difficult for the child victim. The child fears not being believed or being punished for lying. Most of all, the child fears that no one will do anything to stop the abuse and that she or he will face retribution at the hands of the offender. Furthermore, small children often do not have the vocabulary to explain to an adult what is going on and so will use words or images that adults do not understand and may easily disregard.

A fourteen-year-old girl brought a girlfriend home from school one afternoon. As they walked into the kitchen, the new friend was introduced to the girl's mother, and immediately the girl's six-year-old brother ran up to the friend, grabbed her by the legs and said, "George sucks dicks." He then ran and hid in the hall closet. The mother and daughter were appalled and embarrassed by the six-year-old's behavior. The mother went to find him and reprimand him. He was sitting in the corner of the closet crying and looking up at his mother and said, "Mommie, it's true, it's true."

This six-year-old boy had been sexually abused by a fifteen-year-old neighbor for the past year. He had been afraid to tell anyone in his family because he feared their disbelief and rejection, so he chose to tell a perfect stranger in hopes she would help him. If she rejected him, it would not be as painful for him as rejection by a family member. Children's unconventional ways of communicating distress need to be taken seriously, especially if they have not been provided with vocabulary and concepts which they can use to tell adults about abuse.

Children may not tell directly, but significant changes in the child's behavior may be signals that should not be ignored. For example:

- a shift from outgoing behavior to shy, withdrawn behavior (or vice versa);

- regressive behaviors such as resuming thumb-sucking or bedwetting;

- discomfort or fear of being left alone with a particular adult or teenager;

- precocious, provocative sexual behavior, such as imitation of adult sex play (a child will not act out sexually unless she or he has been taught to do so by sexual contact with an adult);

- running away or drug and alcohol abuse;

- nightmares or sleep disturbances.

Any of these indicators should encourage an adult to explore with the child in a nonaccusatory, sensitive way what has been happening to her or him.

As adults, we are tempted to ignore or punish children's distress stories or indications because we really do not want to know about child sexual abuse. "Recognition of sexual molestation in a child is entirely dependent on the individual's inherent willingness to entertain the possibility that the condition may exist."[10] If we refuse to believe that it can happen, then we will not see it when it does happen and we will conclude that children lie about these things. *Children rarely lie about sexual abuse.* They do not have the details to make up stories unless they have had the experience. The most important thing that we can do when we suspect any abuse is to believe the child and act quickly to intervene.

A report to the police or the state children's protection office should bring an immediate response. This is important especially in cases of incestuous abuse because once the family is aware that the child has told the family secret, the family will close ranks to defend itself from outside intervention. The abuser will deny the sexual abuse, and the child will be pressured to change her or his story. The child may be removed temporarily from the home by authorities for the child's own protection until a decision can be made about what to do. This will be difficult for a child because it will seem that she or he is being punished by being sent away. The child may begin to regret having told.

During this period, agencies can provide crisis intervention and support for the child victim and nonoffending parent(s). The parent and child need each other for support as well in order to follow through on prosecution of the offender so that he or she will get help. Even though the child will be relieved that someone is helping and that the abuse will stop, the child will often be ambivalent because of feelings of love and family loyalty for the abuser. The child may feel guilty and responsible for "breaking up the family." In addition, the nonoffending parent may feel resentment and direct that resentment at the child. Those who intervene need to be sensitive to ambivalence that may be expressed, and see it as ambivalence rather than as an indicator that the child's story is false.

NONOFFENDING PARENT(S) IN INCEST SITUATIONS

Many people believe that nonoffending parent(s), especially mothers, must have known about the child sexual abuse in their family and thus must have colluded with the offender. For example, they wonder how a mother could not know that her child was being sexually abused by the father or father figure in the home. While some mothers may have known, most mothers of incest victims do not know about the abuse. After disclosure of the abuse, they may look back and realize that the child was giving them clues, for example, asking not to be left home alone with her father. At the time, however, the mother may never even have considered the possibility of incest. When faced with the child's disclosure, the mother is then confronted with the difficult choice of whom to believe, her child or her husband. Sometimes a mother chooses to believe the husband, largely because she cannot handle the ramifications of believing the child. But often, with support, she is able to face the reality that her husband is sexually abusing her child and to take the steps necessary to protect the children.[11]

The mother is in a difficult situation. She may be horrified at the thought that her husband could do such a thing to the children, and yet feel emotionally and economically dependent on him and fearful that she cannot survive if she forces him to leave the home. She may be a battered wife and afraid of his violence toward her if she tries to stop his abuse of the children. The mother may have a strained relationship with her child (especially a teenager) who has been acting out for several years or with whom she feels in competition for her husband's attention. This will make it difficult for her to believe and support her child. In her confusion and crisis, she may blame the child for causing this upheaval and jeopardizing the family's future.

Because the nonoffending parent is the primary resource for the child victim after disclosure of the abuse, anything that a pastor, counselor, friend, or family member can do to support them and encourage support of the child is valuable. Nonoffending parents are in crisis too; they may not be making reasonable decisions or behaving responsibly; they need help in understanding what has happened and what options are available. Their feelings and confusion are as important as the victim's and must be addressed. A mother may think about separation or divorce, feeling that she cannot live with a person who would abuse her children. There are religious considerations for most women who are contemplating divorce. She may choose to prosecute the offender in order to get him into treatment and then wait to decide about divorce until after he completes treatment. She needs support so that she can support her child.[12]

ADULT SURVIVORS OF CHILD SEXUAL ABUSE

As the topic of incest becomes more openly discussed, more adults are beginning to acknowledge and discuss their experiences as child victims of sexual abuse in their families. These survivors may be realizing or acknowledging for the first time that they are not alone in their experiences and, by talking with others who were also victims, begin to resolve some of the feelings they have carried for years. A support group for adult women or men who were child victims of incest is an ideal place to deal with these experiences. Because a survivor may believe that she or he is the only person whose father (or other family member) was sexual with her or him, an adult survivor may have sustained isolation from other people for years. Believing that they carry a secret that no one else could comprehend, survivors may maintain a "safe" emotional distance from everyone. Depression and self-destructive behavior may be ongoing problems for adult survivors of childhood sexual abuse.

At some point, anger is a common feeling expressed by adult survivors. This anger, which may have lain under the surface for years, eventually comes out. The anger may be directed at themselves for not being able to stop the abuse or protect their younger siblings from abuse, at their mother for not protecting them, or at the offender. Survivors at this point should be encouraged to identify and express their anger, and direct it most appropriately toward the offender, the source of the abuse (see chapter 7, "The Healing Power of Justice").

Because for many survivors there was no intervention or assistance for them as children, as adults they have a strong sense of unfinished business. The survivor's anger, guilt, and confusion are unresolved. The adult survivor may choose to act on her or his own behalf at this point by confronting the offender. This can be done in person or by letter. Letters written expressing the victim's pain and anger may never be mailed and yet still be effective. If the offender is dead, the opportunity for confrontation is not there, but writing such a letter can be a valuable step for the survivor anyway. It is important to remember that a survivor's desire to confront the offender always carries with it the expectation that the offender will acknowledge his offense and ask for forgiveness, preparing the way for some form of reconciliation. In fact, the offender may well continue to deny that the abuse ever took place and may be unwilling to discuss the matter at all. A survivor should be prepared for this disappointment. Nonetheless, the survivor has done what needed to be done in confronting the childhood abuse.

Some victims of incest experience sexual difficulties as adults. They feel fearful of sexual contact with a partner or simply separate their emotions from sexual activity (as they did when they were children). Sexual dysfunction may also be a problem. Adult survivors may avoid sexual relationships altogether or may engage in frequent and indiscriminate sexual activity. Most sexual problems that face adult survivors are related to fear of intimacy (emotional, sexual, etc.), which comes from their childhood experience of betrayal in an intimate family relationship. Intimacy requires risk and vulnerability, both of which may be very difficult for adult survivors.

Having been sexually exploited in one's family, it is not easy to trust anyone again enough to be truly intimate with them. Adult survivors who have taken the opportunity to discuss their experiences and feelings with other survivors or with a trained counselor have found this a helpful means of breaking out of their isolation and beginning the healing process. Sexual abuse experienced as a child need not diminish one's relationships with others in adult life.[13]

THE GOSPEL CONTEXT FOR MINISTRY

Jesus lifts up children as blessed recipients of the kingdom of God. In this he is pointing out the vulnerability of children who, by definition having fewer resources than adults, deserve protection. He is also clear that someone who takes advantage of a child will suffer serious consequences.

In the early twenty-first century, as the disclosures of sexual abuse by priests in the Roman Catholic Church multiplied, hundreds of adult survivors of molestation by priests came forward. What became apparent was not only the individual acts of abuse of children by priests but also the ineptitude and cover-up that occurred in many dioceses. Long-standing patterns of abuse and movement of pedophiles from diocese to diocese were revealed. The abuse of children by the very persons entrusted with their care is a travesty. The damage to individuals, families, and the church will not be healed quickly.

They have treated the wound of my people carelessly, saying, "Peace, peace," when there is no peace.

They acted shamefully, they committed abomination; yet they were not at all ashamed, they did not know how to blush....

When I wanted to gather them, says the Lord, there are no grapes on the vine, nor figs on the fig tree; even the leaves are withered, and what I gave them has passed away from them. (Jeremiah 8:11–13 NRSV)

The potential for sexual abuse or exploitation of children and youth presents a huge challenge to children's and youth ministries in the church. For too long these problems have been ignored or overlooked by religious educators and youth ministers. Yet because we know that a significant number of our children and youth are abused, some on an ongoing basis in their families or dating relationships, it is critical that training and resources for children and youth ministries address these experiences and that adult leaders be sufficiently trained to respond to disclosures appropriately (see the discussion of mandatory reporting in chapter 10).

Wounded Healers and Bystanders

The Roles of the Pastor

In 1972, Henri Nouwen wrote an amazing book called *The Wounded Healer.* This was the year I entered seminary, and Henri was one of my teachers. Henri was congruent in his life in ways that few of us ever are. He taught that we must identify the suffering in our own hearts as a starting point for ministry. As ordained pastors, we are not set apart from the wounds and suffering of others. We carry many of the same wounds in us. It is foolish to pretend otherwise. Henri believed that recognizing our own woundedness would make us better pastors.

Nouwen's insights and courage in his teaching were important breakthroughs in theological education in the 1970s. He was certainly right about the importance of our recognition of our own wounds as we entered into ministry. But in his emphasis on this recognition at that point he overlooked the important corollary: we need to be about our own healing of those wounds if we are to be effective pastors. In other words, woundedness doth not a healer make. We need wounded healers who are committed to their own healing in order to be good pastors.

HEALING HEALERS

This notion of being a healing wounded healer is particularly significant in light of the painful phenomenon of sexual abuse by clergy. We are seeing the results of wounded clergy bringing their woundedness forward into the lives of those they serve by victimizing them, both children and adults. This is the best evidence we have that having been wounded does not make us a healthy and effective helper for others. And yet we also find that those who have recognized their past wounds and worked on their healing with the help of others may in fact bring exceptional gifts to ministry. Their capacity for empathy and sense of good boundaries in pastoral relationships are particular strengths in doing ministry especially with other survivors.

The caution here is that the purpose of going into ministry is not to be healed. In other words, ministry is not about us and our healing. The fact that we experience healing along the way is a bonus. Our healing is a process that is ours that we then bring to ministry, scars and all, to empower and encourage us to be of help to others. But we must be able to separate our needs and agenda from those of the people we serve. Otherwise we may end up using them for our purposes and inadvertently, perhaps, doing them harm.

BYSTANDERS

The other role that we need to be clear about in ministry is that of the bystander. In her now-classic work, *Trauma and Recovery,* Judith Herman asserts that there are three groups of people involved in any situation of abuse: victim/survivors, perpetrators, and bystanders. In other words, we all fall into one of these three categories. Over time we may fit into more than one category.

The role of bystander is ambiguous and complex. The bystander is present to a particular situation, whether she or he knows it or not. For example, there are victim/survivors and perpetrators in every congregation, whether the pastor is aware or not. But if we are aware, we then have two choices: we can pass by on the other side and deny our awareness or we can become involved as a Samaritan. The temptation to pass by is very strong, particularly when we do not feel prepared or competent to engage the situation. The key to effective pastoral ministry with abuse situations is to remember that we are never alone in our helping role. There are always others around us who can be part of the team to respond to specific situations.

The other temptation may be to become a super Samaritan. We may attempt to rescue a victim/survivor or convince ourselves that only we can "save" them. This may be particularly tempting for an adult survivor in ministry who is still early in her or his own healing. With the zeal of a convert, that person may want to be the hero who saves a congregant from the pain of abuse that the pastor knows too well. Needless to say, we do not need super Samaritans.

We need bystanders with good boundaries who are willing and able to be witnesses and advocates, who can walk with a victim/survivor or perpetrator as they confront their own particular experiences and choices. This is the fundamental role of ministry in response to sexual violence and abuse.

THE PRACTICE OF MINISTRY

So within the larger context of cautions about wounded healers and bystanders, what are the practical implications for ministry? Why would someone who has been raped or someone who has sexually abused another go to a pastor for help? For some people, the church is a primary reference point in their lives. When faced with a personal crisis they turn first to their pastor. For them, the pastor can be a trusted and known resource; they may assume that the pastor will know what to do in this situation. For others, the pastor may be the only resource. In a small town or rural area that does not have specialized community services (for example, a Rape Crisis Line), the pastor may be seen as the only "helper" available. Still others may seek out a pastor because this crisis of sexual victimization is also a crisis of faith; the experience may have raised basic spiritual questions for which the victim or offender needs counsel.

Yet just as often individuals or families coping with the trauma of sexual violence avoid pastors. Many clergy still say that they have never had someone involved in rape or sexual abuse come to them for assistance. Unfortunately, based on this experience, they conclude that there is no one in their congregation who is a victim, survivor, or offender. Given the large numbers of persons who have experienced sexual violence and abuse, this assumption is most likely erroneous. The more logical conclusion is that many people hesitate to go to their pastor when faced with such an experience.

There are several reasons for this hesitation. Generally, any experience of sexual abuse or violence is stigmatizing for the victim. Although society's attitudes are slowly changing, many victims are still afraid to tell anyone about their abuse, because they fear disbelief, judgment, ostracism, and lack of support. Unfortunately, the church has long adopted an attitude, not unlike society's, which says that experiences of sexual abuse or violence are unmentionable and unacceptable in the church and, because of confusion, the church tends toward blaming the victim. When the pastor and congregation do not initiate discussion of sexual violence, the silence reinforces the stigmatization. The message is clear that the church really doesn't want to know about this particular form of suffering. Thus, for many the church and the pastor (as representative of the church) are not viewed as potential resources in this situation.

Another reason for hesitation on the part of the victim/survivor or offender may be a perception that the pastor lacks knowledge, sensitivity, and/or experience in dealing with sexual assault. A level of trust between pastor and parishioner that is adequate to other situations may not be adequate to this one. The victim/survivor or offender fears that the pastor will not understand or know what to do, or perhaps the pastor will be so surprised and shocked that the person seeking help ends up having to help the pastor deal with his or her reaction.

Finally, male and female victim/survivors are sometimes hesitant to go to their pastor if their pastor is male (and if they were abused by a male). Having a male pastor may heighten the victim's fear that he would not understand or respond sensitively. A clergywoman is often preferred because the victim/survivor feels that her or his chances of being understood are better. By the same token, an adult male survivor of childhood sexual abuse by a woman may be more comfortable going to a male pastor. Pastors should be sensitive to this concern and have colleagues to whom they can refer a victim/survivor if gender is an issue.

The concerns that victim/survivors or offenders express about a pastor's possible insensitivity are real and reasonable. When one is facing a personal crisis of this magnitude, it is not a good time to risk rejection or lack of understanding from one's pastor. So for many people the silence continues. They do not seek help at all. A pastor can open the door and let it be known that he or she is available to help with the problem of sexual violence by giving permission for the subject to be discussed in church and by being prepared to help.

GIVING PERMISSION

At the end of a four-week seminar on sexual and domestic violence, a Lutheran pastor of a small congregation reported with some distress that in the past several weeks he had had a rape and two incest cases in his congregation. He could not understand why this "sudden outbreak" of sexual abuse in his congregation had occurred. The seminar coordinator explored this further with the group and discovered that the pastor, on the first Sunday after the first seminar session, had announced from the pulpit that he was taking a seminar on sexual abuse and domestic violence, which he was finding very helpful. In the weeks following that announcement, parishioners came forward for the first time with their concerns about sexual assault. Rather than "a sudden outbreak," each shared a past or chronic unresolved problem.

By making this announcement from the pulpit, the pastor in effect hung up a sign saying, "I am learning about these problems, I know that some of you are facing them, and I am available to help." It should come as no surprise that people then sought his assistance.

Giving permission to victim/survivors or offenders to seek help regarding sexual violence happens when the pastor communicates that talking about sexual violence in church is acceptable and that he or she has the knowledge and expertise to help. This can be accomplished through a sermon, educational presentation directed to different age groups, fliers posted in the narthex advertising local resources like a Rape Crisis Line, use of denominational curricula dealing with the topic, etc.

BEING PREPARED TO HELP

It is unlikely that any pastor is adequately prepared to respond to a victim/survivor or offender of sexual violence unless he or she has had some means to increase knowledge and counseling skills in this area (special training, experience, or materials, for example). The topic remains rarely addressed in most seminaries or ministry training programs. While most seminaries and training programs offer education in counseling and crisis intervention, this preparation is not sufficient to respond to sexual violence. Although sexual assault and abuse have some similarities with other life crises, they are, in many ways, unlike any other experience that a person faces. Some degree of specialized knowledge is necessary in order to respond effectively.

A pastor must be familiar and comfortable with the issue of sexual violence in order to help the victim/survivor or offender. Talking with a victim/survivor or offender is often a very disquieting experience. The pastor may be reminded of her or his own experience of violence or abuse as a victim or an offender. The important thing is that the pastor be aware of those feelings and of their source in his or her own experience. For example, a pastor who has been a victim of sexual assault or abuse, *may* be better prepared to empathize with a victim/survivor. But if the personal pain of the experience is still acute, it may have the opposite effect and block the pastor's response. In this case, the pastor should refer the victim/survivor to another pastor who is more able to respond.

The pastor may be confronted with things that he or she does not want to hear, particularly experiences that are horrendous and disturbing. The temptation is to minimize or not believe what is being said so as to soften its impact on one's psyche. Some of the stories may seem "unbelievable," things we would like to believe are not happening to people, but in fact are. For example, the daughter of the Sunday school superintendent who ran away from home finally returns only to reveal to the pastor that she ran away because her father was sexually abusing her. Such a situation has numerous ramifications and no simple solutions. While the gut reaction might be disbelief, horror, and minimization, none of these is helpful to a victim/survivor.

Developing a level of comfort can be accomplished by exploring one's experiences with, feelings about, and attitudes concerning sexual violence. Pastors (and other helpers) need to reflect on several questions:

- To what extent does the pastor identify with the victim/survivor or with the offender?

- What personal experiences of the pastor relate in some way, for example, when the pastor has felt powerless, frightened, or alone?

- What beliefs about sexual violence does the pastor have that are not based on fact, for example, the belief that some women ask to be raped or rapists are just sexually overactive?

A pastor can respond calmly and yet not minimize the situation by being knowledgeable about the subject of sexual violence, knowing what to do next, and not allowing feelings of anger, disgust, disbelief, or discomfort to dominate the response.

REASSURANCE AND SUPPORT

Following a sexual assault, victims need to hear that they are acceptable and worthy persons, that they are not to blame for their assault, and that they will not be abandoned in this crisis. The pastor's efforts to reassure and support a victim/survivor in these ways are much more meaningful if the congregation is also able to be supportive. Then the pastor can communicate that the church as a whole is prepared to be with the victim through this experience. Of course the victim/survivor needs to decide if and how much information (if any) is shared with the congregation.

Research suggests a commonsense outcome that positive responses are helpful and negative responses are harmful to victim/survivors. But negative responses appear to have a great impact on the healing process. The two most key positive responses are believing the victim/survivor and providing her or him with someone with whom to talk. Unconditional acceptance is an important early step in reducing psychological distress and moving toward healing.[1]

One frequent question is whether a male pastor can be of assistance to a female victim/survivor of sexual violence. The concern raised by this question is whether or not the maleness of the pastor may be too great an obstacle to the victim/survivor's feeling comfortable and trusting with him. Following the assault, some victims find it very difficult to feel safe talking with any male helper, be it police, medical personnel, or clergy. In such instances, the sensitive male pastor can refer the victim/survivor to a qualified female pastor or laywoman. For other victims, talking with a male they trust can be reassuring. In these cases, the pastor needs to avoid reacting in a patronizing or overly protective manner. A victim/survivor needs someone who can listen and be supportive rather than someone who wants to rescue her from the experience. When giving support, the male pastor should avoid any action that might be perceived by the victim/survivor as physically or sexually threatening; thus, touching should be kept to a minimum.

A male clergy colleague told of his initial meeting with a twenty-three-year-old woman rape victim. As they talked in his office, he got up from his chair, walked around behind her, and put his hands on her shoulders to reassure her and offer her physical support. She froze and stopped talking with him. His action was frightening and threatening to her. The man who had raped her had approached her from behind.

His action toward her, although well-intended, was entirely inappropriate and counterproductive. Reassurance and support may best be communicated in nontouching ways.

INITIAL ASSESSMENT

During the initial meeting with a victim or offender, the pastor needs to assess several areas in order to determine his or her appropriate role in the particular situation. If the assault occurred within the past forty-eight hours and if no other resources (rape crisis agency, police, medical personnel) have been contacted, then the pastor should assume a *crisis intervention role.* The way that the pastor carries out this role depends on what community resources are available for referral and on whether the person is a victim or offender. For a victim, the initial assessment should focus on safety and health. Is she or he now safe? Does the victim need medical attention? Does she or he want to report to the police (the sooner, the better, in order to preserve evidence for prosecution)? For an offender who is confessing a crime, in the context of confession (see discussion below), the pastor's role is to help the offender consider self-reporting to the police. If other crisis resources have been contacted and are being used, then the pastor's attention needs to be directed toward areas not covered by those resources, particularly spiritual or religious concerns.

If the assault or abuse is chronic (incestuous abuse) or has occurred earlier in the person's life, then the pastor's response should be less crisis-oriented and more focused on assessing the current needs of the person seeking help and the impact of the sexual violence on that person's life. In either case, the pastor's role in assessing the situation is a critical one, especially if the pastor is the only person outside of those crisis responders like police and medical personnel who has been told about the assault or abuse.

WORKING WITH OTHER COMMUNITY RESOURCES: COLLABORATION

Most urban and suburban communities and some rural communities in the United States now have sexual assault services available, either through a crisis line, a community mental health center, or a specialized service such as a rape crisis center. Services for sex offenders are not as common, but are sometimes available regionally. Persons providing these services are trained to respond to sexual violence whether it is a crisis or chronic problem. They are available as resources to pastors and congregations.

Unfortunately, some pastors hesitate to use secular resources in response to a problem like sexual assault. A gulf has developed over the years between mental health/social services and religious professionals, resulting from long-standing mistrust and skepticism. Social workers and counselors do not trust pastors to know what to do when faced with sexual assault or abuse, and pastors do not trust social workers and counselors to be sensitive to the spiritual needs of their parishioners. This attitude of mutual mistrust comes from experiences of poor communication, insensitivity, and inappropriate treatment or counsel on both sides. The resulting lack of cooperation means that persons who need help are often placed in a position of choosing either secular support or pastoral support. In some communities, little effort has been made in the interests of the victim by either side to overcome this gulf and to begin to relate to each other as professional peers who have special training and skills much needed by the people they serve.

In other communities, religious and secular resources have both sought to bridge the gap, and there has been remarkable success in sharing resources and developing a network of services. They work cooperatively in response to victims and offenders. For example, in one particular community, a group of pastors was trained by the rape crisis center to deal with sexual assault. In turn the rape crisis center staff and volunteers were trained by the pastors to respond sensitively to the religious concerns expressed by victims. Here, a mutual referral agreement exists where pastors refer victims for crisis counseling to the rape crisis center and the rape crisis center refers victims with religious questions to the pastors. In addition, pastors help with fundraising and community education and encourage lay participation in the center as volunteers. Such a collaborative relationship benefits victim/survivors most of all.

Seldom does a pastor have the training, time, and energy to adequately provide all of the immediate and long-term counseling that a victim/survivor or offender may need. A network develops when religious and secular professionals reach out to each other as peers, sharing information, providing training for each other, serving on boards of agencies, and offering to provide services when referred to by the other. Such working together to meet the needs of victim/survivors and offenders begins to build the mutual trust that is needed for effective work and provides adequate breadth of services and resources.

KNOW YOUR RESOURCES

Early research conducted in 1977 in a large urban area indicated that 76 percent of parish pastors in that area did not know of a single resource (general or specialized) that they could call upon to assist victim/survivors or offenders of sexual violence. At that time, this city had the highest concentration of sexual assault services of any area in the region. Yet parish pastors were not utilizing these services because they did not even know what was available.[2] Certainly awareness of available resources has increased, which hopefully has translated into increased referrals to these resources. The pastor's responsibility is to find out what services are available in his or her community. A pastor should contact any agency that sounds like it addresses sexual assault and request copies of brochures to keep on hand. Look in the community services section of the local phone book under "abuse," "rape crisis," or "sexual assault." If possible, go and talk to an agency staff person in order to clarify what they do offer and begin to build a relationship with the advocates. Attend any training events that the agency offers. Know and use the resources in the community. Responding to victim/survivors and offenders is not something we are adequately prepared to handle on our own.

MAKING REFERRALS

When resources are available, it is preferable to refer a victim/survivor or offender to a specialized agency prepared to deal with sexual assault. The staff and volunteers of these agencies have the knowledge and experience to provide the needed counseling and advocacy. They know the medical and legal systems and can minimize the difficulties that a victim may face dealing with them. For example, advocates at a rape crisis counseling center can accompany the victim/survivor in reporting to the police, dealing with prosecution, or getting a medical exam at the emergency room.

In making a referral to an agency, preferably refer to a specific person whom the pastor knows and trusts. This is another reason to get to know an agency's staff and volunteers either through self-introduction or through participation in a conference or training workshop. Giving a victim/survivor or offender a name of someone at the agency reassures them that they will connect with an individual who can help. A pastor's wise use of referrals comes from an awareness of his or her limitations and from a clear understanding of what one's role should be. Particularly from a parish pastor's point of view, limited expertise, time, and energy necessitate drawing on all available resources.

PASTORAL ROLE

The pastor, in a pastoral role, can offer a victim/survivor or offender a unique resource. Expertise in pastoral care, theology, and ethics can be invaluable to a religiously affiliated person facing the aftermath of a sexual assault. The pastor is the primary resource when a victim/survivor or offender faces questions such as: Why did God let this happen to me? Does God still love me? Can God forgive me for this?

Through prayer, spiritual counsel and reflection, and scripture study, the pastor can assist a person with primary issues in her or his life (see chapter 7, "The Healing Power of Justice," particularly for specific scripture passages that are helpful to victim/survivors).

When a pastor makes a referral to a secular agency, this does not mean that the pastor's responsibility ends. The pastoral and supportive role is often still needed by the person seeking help. A pastor who tries to pass total responsibility on to another helper is said to be "dumping the client." Even if the religious concerns seem to be initially resolved, it is important to check in with a victim/survivor for the next six months to a year, reminding that person of the continuing care and support of the church. Anniversaries of an assault are especially significant for many survivors, so checking in with a survivor around the anniversary can be very supportive. For an offender, weekly contact may be necessary to ensure that he or she remains in treatment and to assure that offender of the support of the church as he or she goes through that rehabilitation process.

CONFIDENTIALITY AND MANDATORY REPORTING

While all helping professionals have a responsibility to maintain confidentiality regarding interaction between them and their clients, clergy have an additional responsibility within the context of a pastoral and confessional role. A number of states recognize the special nature of the clergy-penitent relationship and provide the legal privilege for clergy not to be forced to divulge information learned within a pastoral relationship.[3] In sexual assault situations this can sometimes create a bind for the pastor. On the one hand, the pastor has a commitment not to repeat information shared in a counseling or confessional setting. On the other hand, when information comes from an offender or relates to the sexual abuse of a child, the pastor has an ethical responsibility to do whatever is necessary to prevent any further assault or abuse from occurring. This may involve reporting information to a law enforcement agency.

In some states, clergy are required by law (along with teachers, social workers, doctors, counselors, etc.) to report any suspicion of child abuse (including child sexual abuse) to a law enforcement or child protection agency.[4] In other states, clergy are exempt from this reporting requirement. Suspicion or confirmation that sexual abuse has occurred, coupled with the knowledge that unless the offender is stopped, he or she will offend again, may press a pastor to choose between conflicting ethical principles. Shall the pastor break confidentiality in order to protect a child, or shall he or she safeguard confidentiality and place the child at further risk? In this case, concern for the welfare of potential, or actual victims takes precedent, particularly for child victims who are at high risk and often powerless to stop the abuse.[5] Regardless of the state law requiring mandatory reporting, it is our pastoral responsibility to report child sexual abuse to law enforcement and work with these agencies to protect the child from further harm.

Acting on this concern may then mean reporting an offender to the authorities. This action is also a function of concern for the welfare of the offender. His confession or disclosure to a pastor that he is sexually offending may be a call for help. This help is only possible if he is held accountable for his acts and provided with appropriate treatment. For his sake as well as the sake of the victim, the pastor's responsibility is to intervene to stop the offender's abusive behavior. Allowing the offender to continue to offend with our knowledge is unfair to him or her and only multiplies the legal difficulties that person will face. It also makes us complicit in the abuse of a child — or children.

The church has addressed the question of confidentiality in a variety of ways. Within the Anglican Communion, for example, the "Seal of Confession" is defined as follows:

> The absolute obligation not to reveal anything said by a penitent using the Sacrament of Penance.... The obligation arises from a tacit contract between penitent and confessor, from its necessity for maintenance of the use of the sacrament by the faithful, and

from canon law. The obligation covers direct and indirect revelation, e.g., unguarded statements from which matters heard in confession could be deduced or recognized, and admits of no exception, no matter what urgent reasons of life or death, Church or state, may be advanced.[6]

The Roman Catholic provision is equally stringent. The United Methodist Book of Discipline is more straightforward but also strict: "All clergy of The United Methodist Church are charged to maintain all confidences inviolate, including confessional confidences."[7] Some denominations have addressed the issue with limited conditions, for example, the Evangelical Lutheran Church in America:

> In keeping with the historic discipline and practice of the Lutheran church and to be true to a sacred trust inherent in the nature of the pastoral office, no ordained minister of this church shall divulge any confidential disclosure received in the course of the care of souls or otherwise in a professional capacity, nor testify concerning conduct observed by the ordained minister while working in a pastoral capacity, except with the express permission of the person who has given confidential information to the ordained minister or who was observed by the ordained minister, or *if the person intends great harm to self or others.* [emphasis added][8]

This provision is very important in questioning the absolute nature of pastor-penitent privilege when communication is exchanged which indicates that there will be further sexual assault or abuse. It is important for the church to face the conflict in ethical values that results from an awareness of sexual assault or abuse committed by a counselee or penitent.

Yet the above rules for particular denominations leave many pastors in a quandary: despite the rules, how can they ignore the pressing needs of victims and perpetrators and remain true to their calling? When a pastor feels such an ethical mandate to report knowledge of sexual abuse or assault, I suggest that it need not be done secretively or in such a way as to deceive the offender. Rather, the pastor should inform the person at the time the information is shared that it needs to be reported to the appropriate authorities. The pastor can then ask the person's permission to notify police or a child protection service, or the pastor can suggest to the person that it is in their own best interest to report it himself or herself (in the presence of the pastor). These approaches hold the greatest potential for maintaining some level of trust between pastor and offender. In this way an ongoing relationship between pastor and offender may be maintained, and effective intervention can be carried out to stop the abuse. If the offender refuses to self-report, then the pastor is faced with the decision of whether to report the offender in order to protect others from harm or to maintain confidentiality even at the price of possible harm to others.

WORKING WITH OFFENDERS

Pastors or counselors may find themselves in a situation requiring early intervention with a sex offender, either because of specific information shared by the offender himself, such as in a confessional context; because the offender has been arrested; or because someone else in the family, such as an incest victim, has sought help. In any of these cases, the pastor or counselor needs to be aware of several factors in responding to the offender.

- Sex offenders seldom tell the truth about their behavior. They will minimize, deny, and lie about what happened. This is especially true for child molesters: "Nothing really happened...," "I was just giving him a bath...," "Don't believe that kid; she lies all the time...," "I was drunk; I don't remember a thing...."

- Sex offenders seldom express remorse or any sense that what they did was wrong.

- Sex offenders are most concerned with the consequences facing them once they are caught. In this regard, they can be very manipulative of those around them and may well try to mobilize a pastor's support as a character witness in their behalf.

- Sex offenders are repeat offenders who continue to assault and abuse others until they are stopped. Experience indicates that the legal system often provides the leverage needed to get an offender into a treatment program and keep him or her there as long as necessary. If treatment is not advised, then incarceration at least protects the community from the offender.

The pastor's or counselor's role at this point is a significant one; he or she can be an important link in the confrontation of the offender's assault. In conjunction with family members and legal and medical authorities, the pastor or counselor can provide the offender with the consistent message that what he or she has done is wrong and must stop *and* that help is available.

> *A man came into his pastor's office looking for help. He told his pastor that he had been "messing around" with his nine-year-old daughter. In response to the pastor's questions, the man admitted that he had finally decided that this was wrong and he wanted to know if God and the pastor could forgive him. The pastor replied, "John, you know that God forgives those who are truly sorry for their sins, and I can certainly forgive you. But first we are going to pray about this right now together and ask for God's presence and, as soon as we finish, we are going to call Child Protective Services and get you into treatment." This was not quite the response that the incest offender was looking for. He was mostly interested in some quick forgiveness and reassurance that everything would be all right. He had not bargained for a pastor who knew that, in addition to spiritual counsel, he needed treatment to make sure that he did not molest his daughter again. John did go into treatment and the pastor arranged to meet with him once a week for prayer and Bible study. In this way, the pastor was able to monitor John's involvement in treatment and to offer the encouragement and support that he*

needed for the long process of rehabilitation. Dealing with the issues of forgiveness came later. (See chapter 8)

The pastor or counselor needs to be able to confront the offender and *not* become a partner in minimizing what the offender is doing. In addition, the pastor should offer support throughout the treatment process. The pastor or counselor should not expect to be a primary therapist for a sex offender who needs a specially designed treatment program.

Offenders with a religious background may suddenly "get religion" in the midst of confrontation or prosecution for sexual abuse or assault.[9] The pastor must not be taken in by yet another effort by the offender to avoid the consequences of his or her behavior. Whether the "conversion" is fake or real, the pastor needs to address these conversion experiences always with a priority for protection of the vulnerable victims, which obviously requires some discernment and judgment by the pastor. We have two options:

1. *"Now, Jason, this is the fourth time in the past year that you have 'found Jesus.' And this time you are facing prosecution for sexual assault. I'm not buying it. God is merciful and compassionate, but God is not stupid. And God knows your heart and holds you accountable for the harm that you did to Susan. I will walk with you as you face the consequences, but I won't be a part of your attempt to avoid them."*

2. *"I am very thankful that you have opened your heart to God in the midst of this crisis. Jesus will be an enormous support to you as you face the consequences of your behavior. This means that when the court decides what to do, you will have God in your heart, and me and the congregation by your side as you face either incarceration or treatment."*

Successful treatment of sex offenders is extremely difficult because options are limited. Treatment of rapists focuses on the offender's violence and aggression, low self-image, covert fantasizing, and possibly unresolved childhood victimization. Working with child molesters is even more difficult in some ways because in contrast with most rapists, the offender does derive significant sexual gratification from his offense, which reinforces the behavior. It is clear with these offenders that insight, confession, and remorse are not sufficient to change their behavior. Long-term, behavior-oriented treatment is required. There is no cure: the optimal outcome is management of the offending behavior and protection of the community, which means that even a child molester who has completed treatment can never be trusted alone with children. So if this person is a member of our congregation, then we must provide structure for that person's participation in church activities. They must always be supervised by a responsible adult to support them in their effort to repent and not reoffend.

A number of treatment programs for sex offenders are now available in the United States. Contact your local rape crisis program or state sexual assault coalition for referrals. Programs for rapists are usually connected to a prison or inpatient mental health facility. Child molesters are most often treated in outpatient community-based programs or by private therapists. Treatment philosophies and approaches differ from program to program and have varying degrees of success. The first goal of any program should be the safety of the community (particularly the safety of the child in an incestuous abuse situation), and second, the effective treatment of the offender so that the offender does not repeat the assaultive behavior. For the incest offender, this may well mean being separated from the family during treatment, which is the only way to ensure the protection of the child victim from further abuse.

Some people advocate imprisonment for all sex offenders; others support capital punishment as the solution. They argue that treatment somehow excuses offenders and may allow them to repeat the offense. In fact, imprisonment of rapists, while it may be necessary at some point for the protection of society, does not rehabilitate them. For those who are treatable, effective treatment programs are a must. For those who are not treatable, imprisonment, with all its limitations and imperfections, remains the only option. Both represent a stopgap means of dealing with the symptom — the rapist's violent behavior — of a deeply rooted social problem.

WORKING WITH VICTIMS

To fulfill the pastoral role with rape victims, one must understand fully the nature of rape, its impact on the victim, and the healing process. The nature of the rape situation itself is significant in shaping a helpful counseling response. Rape experiences generally fall into two broad categories: blitz rape and confidence rape.[10] *Blitz rape* is the sudden, surprise attack by a stranger or strangers. Totally unexpected, the rape shatters the victim's sense of trust in her or his environment. The victim may feel that she or he was in the wrong place at the wrong time and is unable to make sense out of what has happened. Blitz rape may occur outside (park, alley, etc.) or inside (home, school, church, office, etc.). In either case, the victim is taken by surprise. The world is no longer safe and hospitable. Counseling issues should focus on grieving the loss of safety and security, accepting of the reality of a hostile environment without being unnecessarily limited by it, and learning to take risks again.

The much more common *confidence rape* or acquaintance rape[11] involves a rapist and victim who have had some degree of contact prior to the assault. The degree of previous contact varies.

- New acquaintance: A rapist may approach a victim in a seemingly safe situation, begin a conversation to develop trust on the part of the victim, and then betray that trust by taking advantage of the victim. For example, a new acquaintance rapist might be someone seeking information from a person waiting for a bus, a delivery or repair person, or a friend of a friend who just moved to town.

- Friend or family member: This rapist may be a neighbor, date, friend, classmate, coworker, family member, or partner. The rapist has some kind of prior relationship with the victim, which he or she uses as a way of establishing trust and then betrays. The rapist does not respect the bounds of the relationship or the wishes of the victim. The victim of this rapist in particular may be hesitant to seek assistance or report the assault because she or he feels that no one will believe it was rape because of the prior relationship with the person.

- Authority figure: In this case the rapist is a person who has authority over the victim and abuses that authority by sexually assaulting the victim, sometimes referred to as "getting sexual favors." This rapist could be an employer, doctor, pastor, counselor, or teacher.

In addition to the blitz and confidence rape situations described above, in which it is assumed that the victim was capable of expressing an unwillingness to have sexual contact, some rapes occur when a victim is unable to express lack of consent to sexual contact. This could occur in a blitz or confidence situation. Sexual contact without expressed unwillingness often involves children who, because of their lack of maturity and awareness, are unable to freely choose or resist sexual contact — for example, a four-year-old girl who simply does not know enough to comprehend what a sixteen-year-old babysitter is doing to her, much less express lack of consent, or a ten-year-old boy whose father not only demands sexual contact with him but threatens to beat him if he does not comply. Likewise, adults may be unable to express lack of consent, or to effectively resist unwanted sexual contact if they are developmentally disabled, intoxicated, or drugged — for example, a woman confined to a wheelchair by cerebral palsy, or a man who passes out drunk at a party. In all of these situations, a rapist can easily take advantage of a person who is in a vulnerable position. The counseling response for victims who were unable to express lack of consent should focus on clarification that what occurred was an assault, and that the victim was not to blame for it, but rather was taken advantage of while in a vulnerable state.

FROM VICTIM TO SURVIVOR

Although rape that culminates in the death of the victim is relatively rare, the life-threatening dimension of the experience of rape is very real and quite common. Fear, both during and following the assault, is the most widely reported reaction. In addition, the victim's entire world is turned upside down. She or he has experienced something that "only happens to other people," something that contradicts the ordinary "rules" of one's environment. The world is no longer a hospitable place: a rape victim's life is never the same again.[12]

In discussing the impact of rape, it is difficult to accurately convey the magnitude of the experience without falling prey to perpetuating the stereotype of the female victim whose life has been destroyed or who has been driven to the edge of insanity by the rape. Permanent, crippling damage to the victim is rare. Rape is not the worst thing that can happen to a person. However, rape is horrendous and destructive for any victim. Like other crimes of violence, rape may leave the victim with that sense that "I could have been killed." The physical, emotional, and spiritual violation is overwhelming. But whether or not that damage becomes permanent depends largely on the response of those around the victim and the process of recovery that she or he experiences.

The process of recovery from the rape begins immediately. Most important in shaping that recovery is the response that a rape victim receives from family, friends, the church, and the community. If the victim feels comfortable in sharing what happened with those around her or him and finds a sensitive and caring response, then the recovery process proceeds. If, for any reason, the victim cannot share the experience and seek support from such resources, then the recovery may be long and painful; the negative impact of the rape is maximized by the victim's isolation.

Support and understanding from family, friends, or helpers enables a rape victim to utilize his or her own strengths to move through recovery and to discover new strengths and learnings that result in growth and change. There are many examples of this growth and change. One victim discovered that with the support of an advocate, she could deal with the legal system, which had always intimidated her before. Another victim found that his family was able to support him in a way he had never expected and, consequently, a new level of family relationships resulted. One woman discovered that her anger was a positive, energizing emotion that she need not fear any longer. A victim who managed to fight off her assailant realized that she could effectively protect herself. Another victim decided that she need not tolerate an abusive relationship with her boyfriend. Through such recovery processes, victims become survivors, no longer victimized by the rape experience. Without supportive responses from family, friends, church, and community, all too often victims remain victims.

Victims may have unrealistic expectations of the people around them. They may want a rape crisis worker to take care of everything (police interview, medical appointments, etc.), or a clergyperson to make it all better, or a friend to "solve" all their problems by rescuing them. These expectations are understandable but are not in the best interest of the victim. Those who are trying to help need to be realistic about what they can provide: time to listen, genuine caring, information, advocacy, and support. They also need to be careful not to be pulled into rescuing the victim. Rescuing perpetuates the victimization by treating the victim as helpless and ignoring the person's inner strengths. The goal is not to rescue but to assist the victim in moving through the crisis to become a survivor.

Whether a clergyperson or lay counselor is working in conjunction with rape crisis services or is the only available resource to the victim, he or she needs to understand the impact of the rape as a particular form of crisis or trauma experience. A crisis is defined as an externally imposed event that creates a situation beyond a person's normal coping threshold which requires problem-solving abilities beyond that person's capacity at that particular time. It presents a person with a situation in which the person may feel powerless, overwhelmed, and out-of-control of one's life. When faced with a crisis like divorce, terminal illness, or natural disaster, most people first seek help from familiar resources like friends or family (primary resources). Next, they may go to individuals or agencies that are seen as trustworthy but not particularly familiar to the person in crisis, like clergy or police (secondary resources). As a last resort, they may call upon groups that are anonymous and unfamiliar like the Red Cross, food banks, Crisis Line (tertiary resources).

Unlike victims of other crises, many rape victims hesitate to approach primary resources for help for fear of being rejected or not believed or being blamed for the attack. Thus, they are more likely to use secondary or tertiary helpers first. Regardless of whom they approach — clergy, police, medical personnel, family, or friends — it is strongly recommended that that person encourage the victim to contact a local rape crisis service to assist with the initial crisis intervention. The specialized counseling and advocacy services available through such agencies are invaluable for the victim. There she or he will find trained advocates who can accompany the victim in seeking medical care and in reporting to the police and dealing with the criminal justice system. The advocate also provides a support presence as needed, and the organization may also offer a support group. The primary function of the advocate is to offer information and to advocate for victims in whatever system they may encounter.

RAPE TRAUMA SYNDROME

Ann Burgess and Lynda Holmstrom in 1973 provided the first comprehensive theoretical model through which to understand the experience of rape from the perspective of the victim. They interviewed rape victims who sought assistance from Boston City Hospital during this period and, based on their analysis of this data, developed the concept of the rape trauma syndrome.[13] This paradigm suggests a linear model to understand the impact of rape on a victim. Understanding what a "typical" victim's reaction to rape is enables a more realistic response on the part of helpers, family, and friends. It provides helpers with a way of anticipating some of the needs of a victim as she or he moves through the recovery process.

Rape trauma syndrome occurs in two phases. The acute phase is the initial period in which there is much disruption in the victim's life, during which fear remains the primary emotion. The reorganization phase begins two to three weeks after the rape, during which the victim begins the recovery process of reorganizing one's life.

A victim may experience a wide variety of reactions during the acute phase. Listen carefully to the victim's feelings and thoughts, acknowledge them as legitimate, and reassure the victim that her or his reactions are normal, that is, common for someone who has experienced rape. The pastor or counselor can provide this important educational function. A victim may be anxious that she "is going crazy" because she has never experienced such a range of emotions before. Reassure her and explain that in her situation, her feelings and thoughts make sense *and* that she will move into the next phase of recovery, the reorganization phase.

The limitation of rape trauma syndrome is important to keep in mind. RTS is a stage theory that assumes linear progress forward in healing and thus can move from being descriptive to prescriptive.[14] This approach can lead a helper to encourage movement forward prematurely or to not recognize that the healing process may move forward and backward or be cyclical.

POST-TRAUMATIC STRESS DISORDER AND MORE

Post-Traumatic Stress Disorder was first named in the DSM-III (*Diagnostic and Statistical Manual of Mental Disorders*) in 1980. This framework places rape alongside other traumas (for example, natural disaster, accident, combat, etc.) as a normal emotional response to an abnormal or unexpected situation.[15] Judith Herman was concerned that too often the sexual abuse of women and children is not "abnormal" or "unexpected" but rather common and becomes expected over time. So in her book *Trauma and Recovery*[16] she developed the concept of "complex post-traumatic stress disorder" to describe the syndrome that follows prolonged, repeated trauma, which is frequently the experience of child sexual abuse, marital rape/battering, or sexual harassment. As Leslie points out, one of the limitations of PTSD to describe the aftermath of sexual abuse or assault is its cultural limitations.[17] An individual's culture shapes one's response to abuse or assault. Unless there is a social context that recognizes sexual violence, a woman may not identify PTSD symptoms as a priority.[18]

COUNSELING IMPLICATIONS FOR THE STAGES OF CRISIS

Any counseling response to a victim needs to take account of the stages through which the crisis reaction progresses. The initial reaction of a rape victim is *shock and disbelief.* Victims seldom believe that such a thing can happen to them. Then, as the reality sets in, they begin to face the *awareness* of what has happened. Their reactions include fear, anger, crying, and withdrawal. Next comes some degree of *acceptance* of the fact that they live in a dangerous society. This may involve letting go of a somewhat naive view that regarded society as basically safe as long as one was careful. Then there is the stage of *restitution and resolution.* It is hoped that the victim will seek some form of restitution, perhaps through the legal system, and finally comes to some sense of resolution, which enables the victim to live with the reality of the experience, learn from it, and be willing to continue to take risks in order to live a meaningful life (see chapter 7, "The Healing Power of Justice").

For victims who were functioning adequately prior to the rape, this experience is best dealt with as a crisis reaction, and basic crisis intervention strategies are the best response. The counseling is issue-oriented, short-term, and educational. Long-term psychotherapy usually is not needed. For victims who have a history of physical or psychological problems (depression, psychosis, drug or alcohol abuse, battering, or sexual abuse), their response to the assault may be a *compound reaction.* Once these multiple problems are identified, multiple resources should be used, and long-term therapy with a psychotherapist may be necessary.

Pastors or counselors should be alert to what is called the *silent rape reaction.* The majority of victims never report rape, so it is not surprising that people who seek counseling or assistance for other problems may also be rape or abuse victims who have never told anyone and who have been carrying the psychological burden of the experience for months or years. This may also be true for persons who have just been raped and are seeking help, but who were also raped or sexually abused earlier in their lives. Indications of previous sexual assault may be evident in an interview — for example, long silences, blocking, distress, reports of phobic reactions, fear of relationships with men (for women), loss of self-confidence and self-esteem, feelings of self-blame, nightmares, or sexual dysfunction. If there is a suspicion of previous sexual abuse, ask the victim if she or he has ever had forced sexual contact or ever been assaulted. This will give the victim permission to share that information if she or he so chooses. The counselor can then evaluate what additional assistance may be needed from other sources.

PARTICULAR ISSUES FOR MALE VICTIMS

In general, male victims of rape experience all of the same reactions as female victims, though there are a few additional reactions and problems that are specific to the males who are sexually assaulted.[19] Because most men have been socialized to see themselves as invulnerable to sexual attack, they have rarely thought of themselves as potential victims of sexual violence, as powerless, or at the mercy of someone else. Rape, in the traditional male understanding, is something that happens to females. Yet men are raped by other men in institutions (mental hospitals, prisons, etc.) and in the general social setting.

When faced with someone bigger and stronger, when threatened with a weapon, or when confronted by a gang, a man may find that he is unable to effectively defend himself against sexual assault. A rape experience threatens a man's self-image and his view of his place in the world, both of which are traditionally defined by his masculinity.

This challenge to one's self-image is particularly apparent in the concerns that male victims, unlike female victims, express about sexual orientation. Many heterosexual male rape victims have high levels of anxiety about their own sexual orientation following the rape. The anxiety is expressed as a fear that somehow the rape will "turn them into a homosexual" or that they must actually be or appear to be homosexual to have elicited the attacker's attention. This anxiety stems not only from the confusion of sexuality with sexual violence, but is further complicated by the deep fear and misunderstanding of homosexuality that exists in our culture. These particular concerns of male rape victims result primarily from their ignorance about the crime of sexual assault and can be addressed most effectively through education of the victim. Male rape victims, regardless of their predominant sexual preference, need assistance in understanding that the motivation for rape is violence and has little to do with their individual sexual identity.

The confused sense of sexuality and identity that male rape victims often experience is compounded by the fact that, during rapes, ejaculation and erection may occur in the victim:

> People mistakenly think that if a man is in a state of fear or anxiety, he cannot achieve erection or ejaculation. Further, in misidentifying ejaculation with orgasm, the victim himself may not understand his psychological response and may come to doubt his own sexuality....A male also tends to equate manhood with independence and control, and when such control is lost, as it is in rape, and when another male gains sexual access to him, there may be a feeling of loss of manhood in the victim. He feels less of a man....Whereas a female victim may develop an aversion to sexual relations following an assault, a male victim may show increased need for sexual activity with a woman to reestablish and reaffirm his manhood. Because of existing social values, sexual contact with another male, even though coerced, may be stigmatizing for the victim, since now his manhood has been tampered with, and he himself may fear labeling or even actual conversion, especially if he is not secure in regard to his sexual identity.[20]

In addition, the male rape victim needs to understand that a sexual assault does not "change" a person's sexual orientation. If he has ongoing confusion or ambivalence about his sexual orientation, the assault may heighten that ambivalence. Such ambivalence about sexual orientation should be dealt with as a concern apart from the assault. This would assist the person in identifying and accepting his own sexual feelings, whether they be homosexual, bisexual, or heterosexual. For the victim who was comfortable with his sexual orientation prior to the rape, the anxiety about the impact of the assault on his sexual orientation will be minimal, and he will be better able to focus on his reorganization process.

In the face of confusion on the part of the victim about his sexual identity, it is important for a counselor or helper to assist the victim in understanding that his manhood, or more accurately his personhood, is not based solely on his ability to resist sexual attack. His feelings may be coming more from the socialization he has received about what it means "to be a man" than from what are the real bases of his personhood. He can then focus on the aspects of the rape experience that affect men and women similarly.

The victim who is gay may experience self-blame, anger, and guilt in addition to the trauma of the assault. He may be less likely to seek medical care or to report to the police for fear of the response. He will need support and advocacy in order to receive the services he requires. In addition, a gay male victim will be faced with the reality that he is more vulnerable than other men in the community to attack by heterosexual males (now viewed as "hate crimes") and that he has less recourse to prevent such attacks. This awareness may present difficulties as he attempts to reorganize his life following the assault. Especially for the closeted gay man, the circumstances of an assault are very difficult. He may face the dual questions of disclosing the assault and/or coming out in the midst of crisis.

In addition to all the concerns discussed above, men who are raped in the correctional or institutional setting also have to face the fact that they remain at high risk for further assault. The rapist has regular access to them, and victims have few effective means of protection from the assailant. In this setting, rape takes on the larger function of establishing a pattern of social power and hierarchy among males in a closed system. Thus the physical and psychological trauma to the victim may be more severe and long term than for men raped in the community.

Finally, because of homophobia and because the social definition of masculinity remains so rigid, the stigmatization of male rape victims is even greater than for females. When confronted with the reality of male victimization, the public response is usually one of incredulity, skepticism, and derision. The consequence of this is that very few male victims talk about their experiences or seek assistance from friends or community resources. They end up trying to cope with the victimization in complete isolation, with no support and little information that could help them clarify the experience and begin the process of recovery. The more openly that male sexual victimization is discussed, the more likely it is that men will come forward to seek assistance.

FAMILY REACTIONS

Family reactions to a rape are often very strong and have a significant impact on the victim's recovery. Anyone with whom the victim has a significant family relationship (partner, parent, sibling, etc.) and with whom the victim has shared some information about the rape experiences some degree of reaction to the news. Sometimes physical and emotional reactions mimic those of the victims, for example, sleeplessness, headaches, loss of appetite, and excessive fears. While these reactions are very real and legitimate, it is important to remind the family member who the victim is. For example, the mother of a fourteen-year-old rape victim said to the pastor, "I can't believe this happened to me." The pastor replied, "It didn't happen to you. It happened to your daughter, and she needs you to support her now." This is not to deny the impact on the family members, but the crisis belongs to the victim. When other family members take on the crisis as their own, then too often the victim feels a responsibility to stop and take care of them. Thus the recovery process is interrupted. A pastor can be very helpful at this point in dealing with the feelings of family members apart from the victim so that the family members have someone to talk to in order to provide effective support for the victim.

Family reactions may pose additional problems for the victim in several ways. Parents' need to explain the rape may take the form of blaming the victim: "I told you not to go to that party. If you hadn't disobeyed me, this would never have happened." Thus a teenage victim ends up feeling alienated from and punished by her parents at a time when she needs support and understanding. Male family members in particular will often express their anger at what has happened with bravado and talk of revenge. Consider, for example, the husband of a forty-seven-year-old rape victim who says, "I'm gonna find that son-of-a-bitch, and when I do I'm gonna fix him so he won't rape again." This reaction on the part of a family member is the most upsetting to a rape victim and presents an additional crisis with which she must cope. She realizes that the angry family member may do something irrational or violent. Such acts would have the potential to create additional problems for her and the family, so her attention is turned to the family member and away from her own needs. An angry, vengeful response by a family member who is unwilling to stop and consider the consequences of his actions is never helpful in resolving the situation or in speeding the recovery of the victim.

The desire for revenge on the part of male family members often arises from a sense on their part that *they* have been violated: "How could that guy do this to me?" They perceive themselves as the victim rather than their wife or child. Obviously, such a response is not helpful to the victim. This attitude on the part of the family member should be challenged. He should be reminded that he is not the victim, but that his wife or child is the victim and needs his support. His concern should be for the victim's feelings and how he can be supportive to her. Again, a pastor is in a good position to work with the male family member while he expresses and clarifies his feelings and decides what to do about them.

Part of the reorganization process for victims involves the reestablishment of relationships with sexual partners.[21] This can be difficult and stressful emotionally and sexually for both persons. The victim may be emotionally distant; sexual interaction often ceases for a period of time. It takes time for a victim to renew intimacy and trust, to be able to open up emotionally and to be vulnerable with a partner again. Sometimes partners hurry to reestablish the sexual relationship in order to prove to themselves that "everything is alright," that "the rape hasn't changed anything." This is often not the best course. If the sexual encounter is disappointing, both people may have increased anxiety about their relationship. Sometimes male partners of victims experience impotence and discover that they are ambivalent about reestablishing their sexual relationship. In all these circumstances, partners are most successful when they proceed slowly and avoid pushing a false sense of renewed intimacy. It is more productive to focus on the little things that are important to the relationship: for example, a special place that means a lot to both, a special meal to prepare for each other, etc. Physical affection without sexual expectations can be very reassuring to both partners; it can renew intimacy and prepare both for reestablishing sexual activity. It is especially helpful to discuss feelings and not assume what the other may be thinking or feeling.

Family members may find themselves in a quandary, wanting to help but not knowing how. Guidance from a rape crisis agency or pastor can assist them. They may feel anxious because they do not know what to say or how to act: Should they talk about the rape or not mention it? Should they reach out physically to the victim or carefully avoid touching? The victim should choose what she or he needs most from the family. Some victims need to talk about the rape a lot; some need to tell the story only once. Some may not want to mention it ever again. The victim/survivor should decide.

Family members can offer to listen whenever the victim wants to talk. Because the victim is in the process of becoming a survivor, she or he may not want a well-meaning family member to remind him or her every day of the victimization. However, family denial is also not helpful. Sometimes a family makes an unspoken agreement not to mention the rape so as not to upset the victim. In this case, the victim feels isolated and shut out, unable to share her or his thoughts and feelings when they do arise. Flexibility is the best guide. The family should try to adapt to the changing needs of the victim, encouraging her or him to set the limits for family discussion. Families can be an invaluable resource to a victim of rape if they are able and willing to listen and respond supportively, taking their lead from the survivor.

WORKING ALONE: A RURAL OR SMALL-TOWN SETTING

Pastors serving in a rural area or small town may find that they are _the_ primary resource for victim/survivors or offenders. In this case, they may be called upon to provide crisis counseling and support as well as advocacy with medical and legal systems. This role can be very demanding. The pastor needs to keep in mind his or her time and energy limitations and develop additional support resources within the congregation. Ideally, members of the congregation can assist, for example, by accompanying a victim to a medical appointment or prosecutor interview if the victim is comfortable with disclosure to individual members of the church. The pastoral role of providing spiritual guidance and counsel is basically the same as for the urban or suburban pastor. For the rural pastor, this role may be more integrated into the overall assistance provided for the victim, offender, and their families.

Often confidentiality arises as an additional complication in a rural or small-town setting. Where everyone knows everyone else and news travels fast through informal networks of communication, keeping anything confidential is difficult. Fears about having their experience become public knowledge may prevent victim/survivors from seeking help from clergy, police, or doctors in their own community. Pastors especially need to be sensitive to this fear so that a victim can be assured that confidences will be respected. A pastor should specifically mention awareness of the need for extra care in safeguarding privacy and assure the victim that he/she will not share any information about the victim's situation without permission. The pastor should be careful not to share *any aspect* of a story that might identify the victim.

An additional responsibility that may arise for the rural pastor in response to an incident of sexual violence is the need to pastor to the community as a whole (if news of the incident becomes public). The community may react with some of the same characteristics as the victim: fear, panic, anger, grief, etc. The local pastor(s) can provide factual information about sexual violence, help direct the community's anger in appropriate channels to minimize tendencies toward revenge, and generally assist the community in working through its feelings.

Regardless of the setting of ministry, be it parish, hospital, jail, or university, a pastor will encounter both victim/survivors and offenders. Regardless of the geography or demographics of the community, sexual violence is a fact of life. This is a challenge to and opportunity for ministry for a pastor. Awareness, self-awareness, and courage makes it possible for a pastor to be a healing presence in church and community.

Chapter 11 ——————————————————————

Asking the Church to Be the Church

The community of faith as we experience it in the Christian tradition is made up of believers, those who confess faith in God, who follow Jesus, and who seek to live their lives accordingly based on the Gospels. It is no surprise that the community of faith is a diverse grouping ranging from those with fundamentalist theologies to those with liberation theologies. The community of faith gathers in a structured format (congregation or parish) or a nonstructured one (house church, community based ministry, etc.). Wherever and however the community of faith gathers, it claims to be a part of the body of Christ and, through it, we are called to ministry. One aspect of this ministry is a pastoral responsibility to victims and offenders of sexual violence.

But the other reality is that congregations are made up of victim/survivors, offenders, and bystanders, which always complicates the situation where someone has assaulted or abused another person. Given the large numbers of persons who are directly affected by sexual assault and abuse, we can safely assume that in virtually every church gathering, from Sunday worship to the occasional potluck, we are all in the room — victim/survivors, offenders, and bystanders. So our consideration of effective ministry has to take account of this reality.

CONGREGATIONAL RESPONSES

In the context of sexual violence, how can a congregation individually and collectively respond to victims of sexual violence or offenders and their families? It is important to recognize that congregations (and individuals) react to the suffering of sexual assault with deep ambivalence. Congregations seem to respond to people's pain based on an unspoken standard of differential suffering. If a member shares with the pastor and congregation the news that her father died yesterday, the congregation would respond with cards, prayers, flowers, visits, assistance with the funeral, family meals, and hosting out-of-town guests. If that same member shares that she was raped yesterday by her employer, the congregation would most likely not know what to do and might well do nothing.

In some situations of pain, pastors and congregations are comfortable in the Good Samaritan role. In other situations such as sexual assault, they will be tempted to play the Priest and the Levite and pass by on the other side. So it is no surprise that victims may hesitate to seek the support of their congregations, anticipating the ambivalence and discomfort they may well likely encounter. Congregational ambivalence is but a reflection of our own individual ambivalence. Most people, even those who are more aware, have a lingering question as to whether a rape victim is not somehow responsible for the assault. Like Job's comforters, we may try to be helpful, but we may also be trying to discern what the victim must have done to deserve this suffering (see chapter 7, "The Healing Power of Justice").

Part of our motivation for focusing on how the victim may have deserved this suffering is to reassure ourselves that it will not happen to us. We simply will never let ourselves be in a position to "deserve" this suffering. In addition, we have a need to dissociate ourselves from a victim, particularly a victim who is similar to us (in age, race, class, lifestyle, etc.). If we allow ourselves to acknowledge that this victim is very much like us and that she or he was assaulted, then we have to face the reality that we may also become a victim. To keep this realization at a distance, we keep the victim at a distance. Being with the victim is a too-painful reminder of our own vulnerability. So the person who was victimized is isolated and denied the support of the community of faith.

An alternative congregational response to a victim of sexual violence would focus on presence. Rather than shying away from the victim and from the crime, we can be present, available, and willing to listen. Some victims prefer to tell their story to others; other victims prefer not to repeat it. In either case, we should not avoid the issue by talking about the weather; the pretense of normality leads victims to believe we do not want to talk about the assault at all. We can reassure the victim that we still care about her or him. We should be honest about our feelings by being willing to say that what has happened makes us uncomfortable or frightened. Our pretense to be unaffected by the experience sets us apart from the victim. We can also be present by offering to help, for example, by taking a woman's children on a day's outing or preparing dinner for her family one evening. In these ways, the members of the victim's community of faith can be present, supportive, and caring, and thereby help the victim to avoid feeling isolated from a potentially significant source of support.

How a congregation responds to a sex offender is equally ambivalent and difficult. Often a congregation mistakenly assumes there to be only three choices: support an offender's denial that he is responsible for the offense; believing his guilt, ostracize him completely from the congregation; or ignore the whole issue altogether. But all that these responses communicate is that we as a congregation cannot deal with someone among us who is a sex offender. So we deny the evidence that he or she is an offender ("How could he be? He teaches Sunday school and sings in the choir."), and support the denial even to the point of providing character witnesses at the trial. If we accept the evidence, we make it clear that the offender is unwelcome in the community of faith, or we pretend to be unaware of the situation entirely. None of these responses is helpful to the offender nor to any efforts to make justice possible.

The community of faith, particularly in the form of the congregation, seems to find it virtually impossible to confront a sex offender by indicating unequivocally that his or her behavior is harmful to others and is wrong and must stop, and refuse to excuse, explain away, or minimize what the person has done. Simultaneously, we seem unable to be supportive and affirming of the offender's efforts to change, to make restitution, and to seek reconciliation. In short, we have difficulty speaking the truth in love and holding each other accountable for something as serious as sexual violence.

A person who rapes or sexually abuses others is not aided by our denial of the evidence of this fact, just as an alcoholic is not helped when we overlook his or her periodic intoxication. Likewise, our minimization of the offense serves no useful purpose. Comments like "these things just happen sometimes," or "it could have happened to anybody," or "boys will be boys," give the offender the impression that what happened was not really serious, and hence the offender feels no motivation to change. Instead, we must be willing to communicate clearly and directly our disapproval of the offending behavior; we must be willing to speak the truth.

A sex offender who is confronted with the offense by the victim, the legal system, his or her congregation, friends, or family is not helped by being ostracized. This only furthers isolation and hostility, which makes it difficult for the offender to try to change. He or she is not helped by being the focus of vengeful attacks, verbal or physical. A group of people who are willing to be supportive, to strengthen the offender's resolve to stay in a treatment program, to be present with that person through the process of change is what is needed most. Ostracism is punishment that does not bring change. To be present in love to the offender is to bring a supportive and firm hand to bear in order to enable his repentance.

Preaching

Preaching about a subject like sexual abuse and violence is always a challenge. Yet to not preach about it only sustains the church's silence and leaves victim/survivors and offenders in isolation. If there has been a public report of an incident in the community, particularly if it involves someone known to church members, the pastor absolutely should address the situation in a sermon. People need education and reassurance. The sermon can provide a basic framework of information about sexual violence and abuse as well as the assurance that the pastor and the church are prepared to be supportive. It can also lay out an ethical framework for understanding the nature of the sin of sexual violence and the possibilities for justice making.[1]

Liturgical Supports

One of the unique aspects of the community of faith as it seeks to respond to victims of sexual violence is its potential for supporting a victim's recovery through a liturgical form. Just as we give form to other significant experiences through baptism, weddings, and funerals, it is also appropriate that we seek liturgical ways to bring healing and resolution to victims. Most of the liturgical activities that have arisen in response to victims have taken place informally, outside of a congregational setting. The following three examples illustrate the ways liturgy has been used to further a victim's healing process.

> *A woman who had been raped realized that she felt somehow stained by the assault. It was not that she felt dirty or stigmatized by the sexual contact per se. Rather, in the violation of her person, she felt that something had been put on her that she could not cast off. So she decided that she wanted to experience some form of ritual cleansing in order to be cleansed of the violation. She sought the help of a woman pastor friend who suggested that she gather her close friends and then use water to wash away the stain of violation.*

With her friends present, her community of faith affirmed her worth as a person and provided a reminder that she was not alone in her experience. The ritual restored her sense of wholeness and well-being physically, emotionally, and spiritually. She felt renewed and no longer defined by the rape experience.

> *A woman was raped in her own apartment. As the first anniversary of her rape approached, she began to feel anxious. She was fearful of making it through the night which would be one year since her rape. Because she is Roman Catholic, she decided to*

use a traditional liturgical form to assist her. She arranged to hold a vigil throughout the night of this anniversary. She held vigil alone in her apartment. She knew that her friends were also awake in their homes praying with her through the night. The next morning she and her friends gathered with a priest to celebrate mass.

This vigil experience enabled her to redeem that date, to regain control over the night that a year ago had been so devastating to her. By staying awake and sharing prayer with her community of faith, she knew that the night itself would no longer hold power over her.

A seminary intern was raped by a stranger early one afternoon as she was working alone in the church where she was employed for the summer. A man cornered her in the church office and sexually assaulted her. The safety that she had felt in this quiet suburban congregation was shattered by the attack. Like any other rape victim, she began the long and painful process of recovery, which was made all the more difficult by her having to go to work each day at the church where her assault took place. At the end of the summer, the woman left the community to return to seminary, unsure about the future of her vocation as a woman in ministry. In some ways, the rape had become a symbol of her relationship with the church — a relationship that was painful, angering, sobering, and yet which still held potential for new life.

The next year of seminary and a lot of counsel and support from friends and colleagues brought clarity to her vocational commitment, and she responded to a call to the ordained ministry. She chose to be ordained in the church where she was raped. She chose to return to that place where not only had she known the ultimate vulnerability, but also the joy of fellowship and the promise of celebration. She chose to lay claim to that place which had claimed her several years before.

Her ordination became a significant moment of transition for her. She moved from being a victim to being a survivor, from _being a victim to being a pastor. In that event, she was made new and the place was made new. Her ordination redeemed that physical space for her. It once again became a place of joy and celebration, a source of new life which empowered her rather than rendering her powerless._

This woman could very easily not have returned to seminary to complete her training and enter the ministry. She could have quietly withdrawn and privately nursed her wound. But because of her courage and her willingness to receive the support of her community of faith, she remained open to her call. She refused to allow a rapist to hold her back from the ministry she knew she must do. Because of her experience as a victim, her response to victims of all kinds has special integrity; her compassion for their suffering and her anger at the sources of their suffering carry her forward uniquely prepared to minister with the people.

The community of faith can be a valuable resource to victims and offenders if its members are able and willing to open their eyes to the reality of sexual violence. A congregation's fear and discomfort can be reduced as information is presented and discussed. By being more informed, a community of faith can become prepared to respond to the pain of a member dealing with sexual violence. An individual's community of faith can provide the pastoral and liturgical support she or he needs and be the key to justice making.

Where Do We Want to Go?

Responding to sexual violence is like responding to the problem of cancer. Effective strategies are implemented in multiple ways: there are after-the-fact and before-the-fact strategies, individual and collective actions. Millions of dollars are spent each year to find a "cure" for cancer. This is basically an after-the-fact approach. The dollars are used to answer the question of how to cure a cancer that has already taken hold in the body. Responses to this problem are certainly necessary, but they are only Band-Aids; they are necessary but insufficient to eliminate cancer. Before-the-fact strategies include health precautions: avoiding too much sun, not smoking, etc. These precautions are helpful but are limited to those things over which we as individuals have control. The larger sources of cancer must also be addressed — for example, workers must be protected from occupational hazards like asbestos poisoning; poisonous emissions must be controlled more stringently throughout the world. Finally the sources of carcinogens must be eliminated, such as the water supply contaminated by chemical dumping, pesticides, and leaks from nuclear reactors. Our efforts in response to sexual violence are similar.

Pastoral responses to victims and offenders, rape crisis services, and other forms of care are after-the-fact responses. While vital for the well-being of victim/survivors, they do very little to prevent sexual violence. Our efforts to respond to sexual violence must also be preventative, before-the-fact. When people begin to ask what can be done before-the-fact about sexual violence, their questions are usually very personalized and individual. For example, "How can I keep from being raped? How can I protect my children from a child molester?"

Their proposed solutions are equally individualized: "I never go out after dark anymore. I do not allow my children to walk to school anymore." The problem with most people's strategies in response to sexual violence is that they focus on avoiding personal attack, are often based on misinformation about sexual assault, and do not use collective resources for action. In addition, these individualized efforts to avoid attack often result in limiting people's activities. Such limitations serve in turn to increase people's passivity and fear. For example, the churchwoman who no longer goes to evening meetings because she is afraid to go out at night may avoid an attack but she becomes more isolated and passive. This is a high price to pay for a sense of safety. Furthermore, this woman is still at risk even though she stays home. She is as likely to be attacked in her own home as she is on the street, and so in fact her sense of safety is somewhat illusory. An individual's limitations on her or his activities may protect that person from a sexual assault, but these actions do very little to prevent sexual assault in general from occurring.

An effective before-the-fact strategy to end sexual violence must include activity in three areas: precautions, protection, and prevention. Precautions are steps taken to minimize or avoid potential dangers; protection includes steps taken when someone is faced with immediate danger; and prevention describes activity to address the danger at its roots and to eliminate it. Precautions, protection, and prevention are strategies that are implemented by persons working both individually and collectively.

Precautions are steps taken by individuals or groups to minimize potential dangers. These include measures such as keeping doors locked, avoiding hitchhiking, maintaining adequate street lighting, and organizing a block watch. Precautions are intended to help a person avoid contact with a potential attacker. It is critical that precautions be based on accurate information about sexual assault. For example, people who decide that they will never open their door to a stranger are only addressing 40 percent of the dangerous situations: 60 percent of rapists are known to their victims — friends, acquaintances, family members, coworkers. Another example is that people who resolve never to go out of their home alone in order to avoid rapists are only safe half the time: 50 percent of all rapes occur in one's own home. Or the child who is taught to stay away from strangers or not to take rides from strangers is only prepared for 15 percent of assaultive situations: 85 percent of all sexual abuse against children is inflicted by someone known to them and usually someone well-known. Precautions are helpful only if they are based on the reality of sexual abuse situations. Thus we need to teach our children and teens about sexual abuse to prepare them for the possibility that an adult or older teen might approach them sexually. It is far more frightening for someone to be faced with sexual assault or abuse with no information than it is to be prepared with the facts and what to do if it happens.

Protection refers to the steps a person takes when confronted by an attacker. Protecting oneself means defending oneself physically or verbally. In order to be effective, self-defense also has to be based on an accurate understanding of sexual assault. For example, if a person is approached at a bus stop by a suspicious-looking person who attempts to begin a conversation, ignoring that person may not be as effective as assertively and verbally turning down such conversation. Being able to defend oneself adequately requires training and practice. For example, persons who carry guns or mace cans without having specific training may increase their danger. The weapons of unprepared victims are often used against them. Self-defense programs are a means of protection. Through specialized programs, children, teenagers, and adults can learn physical and verbal skills, gain self-confidence, and overcome fears about being able to defend themselves.

For some Christian women, the whole idea of preparing to protect oneself from the violence of sexual assault is difficult to consider. Our religious training may make it hard for us to consider seriously the possibility that we too may be victims; even if we do accept that possibility, our religious training may prevent us from adequately preparing to protect ourselves. Several aspects of religious teaching (primarily directed at girls and women) get in the way of consideration of our own self-protection.

- *A belief that "good" women do not get raped; only "bad" women get raped.* Proper, virtuous behavior or religious piety does not guarantee one's safety. God does not "protect" the righteous and allow the unrighteous to be harmed. Rape is not something that girls and women bring on by the way they dress or behave or by where they go. Every female in our society is at risk for some form of sexual attack. Being a "good, Christian woman" does not lessen vulnerability.

- *A confusion between propriety and appropriateness.* As women we have been taught to be kind and polite to others; as Christians, we have been taught kindness and concern, not to speak harshly to others, etc. Under ordinary circumstances, these are reasonable and admirable ways to interact with someone else. But when we are confronted by a rapist, gentle, kind words are seldom effective; this response will be seen as passive and weak, rendering the potential victim more vulnerable in the face of her attacker. A definitive verbal and/or physical response that might otherwise be interpreted by someone as being rude is most appropriate. It is better to be rude than raped.

- *A desire to be helpful, compassionate, involved.* A common ploy that rapists use to test a potential victim is to ask for assistance: "May I use your phone? Could you show me how to get to Oak Street? Could you tell me what time it is?" Because of our religious teaching emphasizing helping those in need and loving our neighbor, many of us want to respond to a request for help. However, in a rape-prone society, to respond to a request from a strange male may set us up for rape. If we are alone (at home or on the street) and a man asks for help, it may be more appropriate not to respond. This choice not to respond is the price we all pay for the prevalence of rape in our society.

- *A desire not to be "self-centered."* A concern for others but not for ourselves is a dominant theme in Christian teaching. The suggestion to respond assertively and firmly when confronted by a potential rapist may be interpreted as selfish and self-centered. Yet the commandment to "love one another *as you love yourself*" provides a model of equal concern for both oneself and the other person. Anyone who attempts to do violence to us does not deserve our compliance. Fulfilling the love commandment begins by loving oneself enough to stand up for oneself and refusing to be someone's doormat.

- *A belief that physical force is never an acceptable response to any situation.* For many Christian women, nonviolence is a primary value. They regard Jesus's teaching to love your enemies and turn the other cheek as mandates for a nonviolent response to assault. When threatened with rape, we all face the question: "Is there a situation in which an aggressive, physical response may be necessary and appropriate to protect myself? If so, am I prepared to make such a response?" This is a question that each person, finally, must answer. Jesus's teaching was not intended to encourage us to allow ourselves to be victimized and abused. Yet the question of what specific response we are willing to make to physical attack is one that requires our prayerful consideration.

- *A desire to protect our virginity.* Contrary to Roman Catholic doctrine, St. Maria Goretti is not a role model for young women faced with a violent assailant. If an assailant has a weapon, the wisest response may be not to physically struggle because we could be seriously injured or killed. Life is more important than virginity.

- *A willingness to tolerate abuse in a marriage or parent-child relationship.* A misinterpretation of scripture (for example, Ephesians 5:21f and 6:1–4) can present a roadblock to a victim of abuse in the family. Neither the teaching to "be subject to one another" in marriage nor to "honor your father and mother" as a child or teen mean that a person should accept abuse in those settings.

To the extent that Christian teaching prevents women from even considering self-protection seriously, it does us a disservice. We must recognize that we are vulnerable to sexual attack or abuse, which is contrary to God's will for our lives. As persons created in God's own image, we are worthy of protecting ourselves from injury and abuse, which contradict God's image within us.

Children in particular need to be taught how to protect themselves from a child molester. Too often children are not given the information and skills necessary to protect themselves. Furthermore, they are often taught to obey their elders without question. Children need to be taught what sexual abuse is; they should be given permission to refuse to obey an adult who intends to sexually exploit them. They should know that there are adults who they can trust to help them when confronted by a child molester. We spend time and energy teaching children what to do if a fire breaks out in their home or school; each year schools provide Fire Prevention Week to call attention to this problem. We must teach children what to do if an adult approaches them sexually, because the chances that a child will be sexually molested are far greater than the chances that a child will be caught in a fire. In addition to Fire Prevention Week, we need Abuse Prevention Week in schools and churches.

Prevention of sexual violence requires addressing the root causes of the problem. Sexual violence is not an occasional, isolated incident experienced by individuals in an extraordinary situation. Sexual violence is a widespread problem taking place in a broad social context that allows and even encourages it to occur. Rape and child sexual abuse are life threatening by-products of a violent, sexist, and racist society. Our society accepts sexual violence as tolerable and inevitable. We encourage sex role differences that accentuate masculine aggression and feminine passivity. We confuse sexual activity with sexual violence to the extent of often equating the two. We tend to blame the victim or blame God instead of holding the offender responsible for his or her acts. Until we begin to address these attitudes and practices in our society, we will not see a significant decrease in the incidence of sexual violence, for they create a climate of tolerance of sexual violence in our society.

The media contributes greatly to this climate of tolerance and must be examined and considered as a root source of the problem of sexual violence. As a major source of socialization and learning for most people, the media is a powerful means of conveying attitudes about women, men, sexuality, and violence. Unfortunately, it plays a significant role in perpetuating sexual violence. Advertising and entertainment media (including television, films, radio, print, and music) provide images of women and men and how they relate to each other. Such images significantly affect our self-perceptions and behaviors.

Discussion about sexual violence and the media inevitably leads to questions about the impact of pornography. What is the connection between pornography and sexual abuse and violence? To address this issue is to step into a morass of controversy that raises questions about the meaning of sexuality and the nature of pornography, its effects on human behavior, and the question of censorship.

In the past, research and discussion about pornography have arisen from two different perspectives.[1] In one, there is the assumption that sex is bad, that pornography equals sex, and therefore pornography is bad. Those who use this logic often also oppose sexuality education materials and see control of all sexually explicit materials through censorship as advisable. The opposing view assumes that sex is good, that pornography equals sex, and thus pornography is good. These people are in favor of pornography and at the same time support sexuality education and defend First Amendment rights against censorship. We find Christians in both camps.

Both groups equate pornography with sex. Only in the late twentieth century with the feminist critique of pornography (led by Andrea Dworkin, Susan Griffin, Catharine MacKinnon, and others) has the notion that pornography is merely sexually explicit material been called into question. (Of course, some other feminists defend pornography as harmless or beneficial.) Pornography is not just the portrayal of explicit sex; it is the portrayal of explicit violence or abuse in a sexual setting. It objectifies women and men. If children are involved, it is in and of itself child sexual abuse. It creates a fantasy world portraying unreal people and promotes the false belief that women enjoy being objectified and brutalized in a sexual setting. The pairing of sex and violence in pornography promotes the equation of sexual activity with sexual violence and abuse.

T. Walter Herbert in his book *Sexual Violence and American Manhood* quotes a pornographer who explains that the appeal of pornography is its solitary release: "You grab a video, run home, slam it into your machine, never have to have any contact with anybody else in the world."[2] The X-rated film director goes on to say that he wants to bring more violence into his films: "I'd like to really show what I believe the men want to see: violence against women."[3] Herbert places the fact of pornography within an economic context:

> The porn industry has continued to proliferate [since 1993], largely through a greatly enlarged market that embraces the Internet, videocassettes, and X-rated films for rent on hotel movie channels.... The business totals annually between $10 billion and $14 billion in the United States, [which is] a bigger business than professional football, basketball, and baseball put together.[4]

The easy accessibility of both child pornography and other X-rated pornography on the Internet has significantly contributed to its proliferation. Privacy makes perusal possible. Violence and exploitation are eroticized in a solitary setting devoid of social norms or values.

In understanding pornography, we need to distinguish it from other forms of sexually explicit materials such as erotica, sexuality education materials, and documentary or moral realism.

- *Pornography* is sexually explicit material that portrays abuse, violence, and degradation for the purpose of arousal and entertainment.

- *Erotica* describes sexual materials that may or may not be sexually explicit and which are used for the purpose of arousal and entertainment. Erotica does not include any violence, abuse, or degradation of a person.

- *Sexuality education materials* are sexually explicit materials used for the purpose of education or therapy, and which do not include violence, abuse, or degradation.

- *Documentary* or portrayals of *moral realism* are sexually explicit and/or violent and abusive materials that depict acts of sexual abuse or violence for the purpose of documentation and critique. In these materials, the truth of the pain caused by sexual violence is accurately portrayed and the perspective taken is one of sympathy for the victims of sexual violence. The victim's humanity is always reaffirmed.

These distinctions are important if we are to understand the impact that pornography has on individuals and on society. Pornography, or explicitly violent sexual material, is common and readily available.

Recent research on pornography used a research design (based on social learning theory) which is similar to the one used to determine that violence on television resulted in aggressive behavior in viewers. The results from these studies on pornography were predictable. Edward Donnerstein concludes:

> ...films which depict violence against women, even without sexual content could act as a stimulus for aggressive acts towards women.... There is ample evidence that the observation of violent forms of media can facilitate aggressive responses, yet to assume that the depiction of sexual-aggression could not have a similar effect, particularly against females, would be misleading.[5]

A study conducted by Seymour Feshbach and Neal M. Malamuth provided disturbing evidence of the impact of pornography:

> College men who viewed pornography that fused sex and violence tended to be more sexually aroused by the idea of rape

and less sympathetic to victims than a control group.... In addition, both groups of men not only identified with the rapist, but 51 percent said that they might commit rape if they were assured they would not be caught.... "The juxtaposition of violence with sexual excitement and satisfaction provides an unusual opportunity for conditioning of violent responses to erotic stimuli."[6]

It certainly seems reasonable that exposure to images that portray rape and sexual abuse as positive and pleasurable experiences for the victims would eventually create an impression in the observer that the aggressive exploitation of persons is normative and acceptable. In addition, the portrayal of erotic, sexually explicit images together with violent images invariably leads to the eroticization of violence. When sexual violence becomes normative and violence becomes eroticized, sexual activity and sexual violence become thoroughly confused. The cultural context is set for the toleration of sexual assault and abuse. This is why we have to examine the historic and contemporary presence of violence in the social construction of sexuality and of gender (see chapter 2, "The Social Construction of Sexuality and Sexual Violence").

The complex and widespread social phenomenon of pornography does appear to be one factor related to acts of sexual violence. The question then is, what do we do about it? In formulating strategies for action that address this particular root cause of sexual violence, three things are needed.

- We need to agree that pornography does present a problem to our society and that it does have a negative impact on the lives of women, men, and children. Dismissing pornography as harmless and jumping to justify its existence by protecting pornographers' First Amendment rights ignores a serious social problem in our midst.

- We need an anti-pornography strategy that is not based on government censorship. Censorship is not an effective tool to deal with pornography. Like prohibition, censorship only drives the pornography industry underground. (The exception to this is child porn, which is illegal because the sexual contact with children that is often depicted in child porn is illegal.) Too often, censorship is used against materials other than pornography. Censorship has been used to limit erotica and sexuality education materials simply because they are sexually explicit. An anti-pornography strategy should be focused on economics. Pornography is a multimillion-dollar industry because of consumers. Discouraging consumers from buying pornography will begin to limit its profitability. Men talking to men about why they use pornography and how it affects their relationships is a beginning point. Zoning restrictions, advertising restrictions, pickets, and demonstrations have been successful in many communities in limiting the commercial viability of distribution of pornography. Taxation should be explored with revenues going to support services for victims.

- Most important, we need to develop a competing message. We need sexually explicit, factual materials that portray caring, affectionate, erotic, mutually consenting relationships between people. If the only sexually explicit materials available are violent and abusive, then people will learn from them that sexuality is degrading, exploitative, and nonconsensual. Erotica and sexuality education materials can provide a much-needed alternative to pornography.

Pornography is a disturbing fact of life in our society. Its presence says something very disquieting about sexuality as we know it. More and more people are becoming eroticized to violence and abuse; more and more acts of sexual violence are being committed against women, children, and men. We must face the connection that exists between these two realities. As we strategize, we must also be clear in our analysis of the problem and seek effective solutions. We must be clear that the problem with pornography is not that it is sexual but that it is violent. Concern comes not from a prudish, Victorian reaction to sexually explicit images but from a concern about the distortion of human sexuality that pornography represents and the damage that it does to our lives and relationships. Pornography is the propaganda of sexual violence.

Pornography is only one aspect of our society that helps to create a climate of tolerance of sexual violence, but it is a significant aspect because it is so common and widespread. Our task must be to create a climate of intolerance of sexual violence. To do this we must tell the truth, and education is one means to that end. We must tell the truth about the pain of victimization, about the responsibility that offenders carry for their actions, and about the message conveyed by pornography. Every strategy for action to bring about a climate of intolerance of sexual violence begins with education.

Herbert concludes his reflection:

> Not that violent pornography leads to rape in some lockstep causal sequence, but that both pornography and sexually abusive conduct arise from chronic dilemmas of male gendering. Stemming from a shared source, the interplay between pornography and sexual violence is complex and various....This argument explicitly refutes the claim that sexual violence is "natural," meaning that it is determined by genetically hard-wired biological imperatives. Dispelling the mythology of "natural" male violence, and demonstrating the historical conditions in which it acquired its present form, so I hope and believe, will enlarge the resources available to those who seek justice in the intimate relations of women and men.[7]

Men and women must be willing to face the truth about the sexual violence that pervades this society. Our survival depends on it. When we name the unmentionable sin, we deny its power over our lives. In naming it, we reclaim the truth which we know, that the way things are is not the way they have to be.

In Alice Walker's novel in which she confronts the practice of female genital mutilation, she concludes with the affirmation that "resistance is the secret of joy."[8] For those of us most vulnerable to sexual abuse and violence, resistance is our only option. It is how we survive every day in spite of being bombarded with images and experiences that contradict our very existence. Resistance for Christians arises from the conviction expressed by Paul in the letter to the Romans:

> No, in all these things we are more than conquerors through him who loved us. For I am convinced that neither death, nor life, nor angels, nor rulers, nor things present, nor things to come, nor powers, nor height, nor depth, nor anything else in all creation, will be able to separate us from the love of God in Christ Jesus our Lord. (Romans 8:37–39 NRSV)

With this assurance, we can and must address sexual violence as both a personal and social problem in our midst.

My colleague Judith Beals wrote an editorial for the *Boston Globe* in the aftermath of the early disclosure in 2000 of the extensive sexual abuse by priests and subsequent cover-ups in the Boston archdiocese. In it she observed:

> The turning point in every social justice movement occurs when the authentic leadership of survivors is met with the genuine commitments of our most powerful social institutions. The result, inevitably, is the strengthening of existing systems that work and the continual development of new innovations, protections, and partnerships that we have yet to even imagine. If there is any silver lining to the recent tragic events, it is the opportunity to channel public outrage into lasting structures and commitments that will rid society of sexual violence. If we fail to do this, the shame is ours.[9]

If the church can find its way to trust the leadership of survivors and to use its considerable resources (in collaboration with others) to challenge the acceptance of sexual violence and abuse as facts of life and to offer an alternative affirmation of healthy and just sexuality, we have the capacity to change the way things are into the way they can be.

Afterword

At the American Academy of Religion annual meeting in San Antonio, Texas, in late November 2004, my colleagues Carol Adams, Mary Hunt, Nantawan Lewis, and Traci West, and I discussed publicly this thoroughly revised book, *Sexual Violence: The Sin Revisited,* a discussion moderated by Andrea Smith. The conversation prompted by the book continues and I am deeply grateful for it.

It was perhaps ironic that this occasion followed the 2004 U.S. presidential election won by George W. Bush, an election that, according to much of the media, hinged on issues of "moral values" — political code for abortion and homosexuality. *Sexual Violence: The Sin Revisited* is of course about moral values, which in the sexual sphere must be grounded in an awareness of sexual violence. So perhaps the timing is fortuitous.

One of the goals I wanted to accomplish in this major revision of *Sexual Violence: The Unmentionable Sin,* was to think further about the moral wrong of rape. In all my work on this issue I am still amazed at the experiences — including rape — that many people accept as "just the way things are" and the unmitigated confusion that remains as to why sexual violence is wrong to begin with.

So in this revision I have explored the options both philosophical and theological: a property crime (against men), an assault, the absence of consent. But I have concluded that none of these is adequate. Instead I argue for the moral wrong of *harm.* I suggest it not as a subjective category per se but as a community norm that on occasion is also translated into law, e.g., statutory rape laws that seek to protect underage teens from exploitation by adults. Likewise this ethical framework must stand beside any discussion of sexual ethics. So any discussion of sodomy must focus on rape as a sexual sin rather than on the morality of anal intercourse between any two consenting adults. Ultimately this insight is what led to the U.S. Supreme Court ruling that eliminated state sodomy laws.

So my colleagues and I engaged in a further conversation as they responded to the new developments in my work as well as my insights from the first edition; and I responded to them. This is how we all bring our best to the table and through our shared insights perhaps advance the cause a few steps. Adams, Hunt, Lewis, and West are all scholar/activists both in and out of the academy. They bring a remarkable breadth of perspective to the discussion, a breadth that helps all of us engage more deeply with this book.

Traci West,[1] in her role as a seminary professor, found merit in the practical focus of addressing theological concerns for clergy such as sin, forgiveness, and adultery. In addressing these concerns my comments are both grounded in scripture and suggest bridges between secular feminist ideology and Christian theology.

West notes that this book addresses guidelines about behavior at a time when ideas about sexuality are remarkably fluid, and guidelines are susceptible to manipulation. This discussion of guidelines is inclusive, begins with women's experiences as the focus of gender analysis, and addresses the particular responsibilities of clergy in their own professional behavior. But she also points to the problem that guidelines in and of themselves suggest the false perception of universality. Any discussion of guidelines, ethics, theology, etc. is culturally bound. Our analysis is always partial.

In her book *Wounds of the Spirit* (1999), West critiqued the first edition of this book for the limits of my self-understanding about white victim-survivors and their communities. Subsequently she has graciously engaged in a deeper dialogue with me on these issues. She rightly points to the bind for white feminists who may write too much about "white" experience ending up being exclusive or who include discussions of the experiences of women of color ending up being appropriative. The third alternative is in ignorance to suggest a flawed analysis, which only spreads misconceptions that can certainly be damaging.

As a white feminist, I live with the bind that West describes and try not to be immobilized by it. We are responsible to speak the truth of our own particular experience and to lift up the experience of others within our limited understanding of it as we engage the points of intersection of the two. This is why dialogue is absolutely critical.

West also lifted up the dilemma for white liberals who hesitate to confront male offenders of color and are willing to sacrifice women victims of color in the process. She framed her remarks in a story of a woman of color who was raped by a man of color, and when she sought help from a rape crisis center, encountered white women who ultimately supported the man and denied the woman's experience. This story encapsulates the complex layers of race, gender, status, etc. that are always present in situations of sexual violence. West rightly urges engagement and not denial of these complexities if we are to comprehend and act on the demands of social justice.

Feminist author Carol Adams[2] readily asserted at the panel discussion that ethics, theology, and pastoral care together either are complicit in sexual violence or can be liberating. It is from this perspective that she is uneasy with Judith Herman's term "bystander," which she sees as passive by definition. She urges a different term to distinguish between passive and engaged pastoral presence. I resist this solution to limiting the understanding of "bystander," for I intend "bystander" to describe everyone who is neither victim nor perpetrator because I think that distinction is important. But then it is equally important, following Adams here, to make the distinction between the passive bystander and the engaged bystander. In Luke's parable (10:25–37), the priest, Levite, and Samaritan are all bystanders and they all have a moral choice to make. The priest and Levite choose to be passive and to pass by. The Samaritan chooses to stop and engage the suffering of the wounded man by the side of the road. This is the model I am advocating, and it requires first the recognition that one is a bystander and then the choice to pass by or to engage. This is the point of convergence for ethics, theology, and pastoral care.

Adams rightly identified my wrestling with Catharine Mac-Kinnon's analysis. I have come to appreciate MacKinnon's insight that lack of consent is an inadequate criterion for identifying sexual assault and that "as sexual inequality is gendered as man and woman, gender inequality is sexualized as dominance and subordination."[3] But Adams also rightly identifies my concern as theological. I am unwilling to concede that the fallen world, the way things are, is created by God or is immutable. Given that violence is context (Hunt), then to suggest an understanding of sexuality sans violence is a statement of faith as the writer of Hebrews suggests: "Now faith is the assurance of things hoped for, the conviction of things not seen" (11:1).

Catholic feminist theologian Mary Hunt[4] appreciated the importance of how we frame the issues: clearly naming the agency of the perpetrator of sexual violence rather than describing the passive experience of the victim and shifting the ethical focus away from "adultery" and on to "theft." In addition Hunt supports the reframing of the issue of forgiveness for both victim and perpetrator: forgiveness is a process made possible by experiences of justice and accountability.

Hunt pondered the limits of single-tradition (in this case the Christian) discussions of issues, given the pluralism of our society, and questions whether any tradition has within it adequate resources for self-critique. I see this as a both/and problem. There is need for both in-depth deconstruction/reconstruction within our own tradition and for dialogue among various traditions in order to learn from each other and bring an external critical eye to the discussion.

Likewise she raised the cultural limitations of the discussion of clergy ethics, which for me highlights the need for further conversation *within* each of our communities, whether racial/ethnic communities or the L/G/B/T community. We must take responsibility for guiding leaders to avoid taking advantage of community members even though our norms and expectations may differ.

Finally Hunt asserts: "I believe it is time to shift our default assumption from one that claims that violence is episodic and justice part of the social fabric to a more realistic one that assumes that violence is contextual and justice episodic." This important insight from Hunt is a reality check for all our work in addressing sexual violence. It also is to recognize that our goal is for a world in which violence is episodic and justice is context. We have a way to go yet.

Teacher and activist Nantawan Lewis[5] found traction in my placement of sexual violence in a socio-cultural context, naming it as "sin," challenging the enduring silence within the Christian tradition (especially with regard to sexual ethics and sexual violence), and paradoxically calling the church to be the church.

She wants the Epilogue to go further! Lewis wants the definition of sexual violence to include other challenges to women's health and safety, by adding reproductive rights, forced prostitution, female genital mutilation, etc. I resist this desire in spite of its merits. I have always felt strongly that if we are finally to discuss the unmentionable sins of sexual violence, we need to stay focused on this portion of sins against women. So a woman's right to live free from fear of sexual violence should not get lost in the temptation for it to remain unmentioned. However it is critical that work on *sexual* violence interface with the work on other harms done to women, because seldom are any of these experiences singular.

Lewis also wanted an even deeper discussion of sexual violence in the interconnections of various oppressions. I welcome this discussion and the dialogue necessary to comprehend the complexities of it. Finally, she invited the academy to pursue a further comparative and interreligious dialogue on sexual violence. Again my support is for the both/and approach. We need in-depth study of our own traditions *and* interaction between and among our traditions.

May the conversation continue.

Finally as I have reflected on David and Bathsheba further I offer my comments as a summary of *Sexual Violence: The Sin Revisited*. Recall the story. King David spots Bathsheba and wants to have sex with her. So he sends for her and impregnates her. We are not told how she felt about any of this, so consent is not altogether in the picture. But now that she is pregnant, David has to create a cover-up. So he sends for Bathsheba's soldier husband, who is away fighting the war. Uriah comes to David, who rewards him and tells him to go home and have sex with his wife. Uriah refuses because his comrades are still fighting, and he does not feel that he should take advantage of this special treatment. The next night David gets him drunk but still Uriah does not go to his wife. David's plan to get Uriah to have sex with his wife in order to appear to be responsible for her pregnancy fails.

So the next plan is to send Uriah back to the front with instructions to his commander that he be put in the front line where he will surely be killed. The report comes back that he was in fact killed in battle. Bathsheba mourns the loss of her husband. Then David sends for her and marries her so that the child she bears then is assumed to be his.

The ethical analysis of this situation follows in the text: God was not pleased with David and God sent Nathan to confront him. But see how Nathan frames the confrontation. *He does not talk about adultery or even about sex.* He talks about power.

He tells David a story: There was a rich man and a poor man. The rich man had many sheep. The poor man had one lamb which he had bought and raised in his family. She was "like a daughter to him," the text says. The rich man had a visitor and instead of taking one of his own sheep to provide for the visitor, he instead took the poor man's lamb to be the meal for his guest.

David responds with anger and condemns the rich man to death, adding that he should restore the poor man fourfold what he took from him. Nathan responds with those now classic words, "You are the man."

God's confrontation of David delivered through Nathan and the story of the rich and poor man are the heart of the ethical analysis here. David is called to account not for having sex per se but for misusing his power over and over to take things that were not his: Bathsheba herself and Uriah's life. His sin is theft, which was an option for him only because he was king. Few others could have accomplished these deeds with impunity.

Nathan is unrelenting in his call to accountability. And the consequences he pronounces are far reaching: "The sword shall never depart from your house." David finally comprehends and confesses his sin. Nathan tells him that he will not die because of God's mercy, but that his child will die, which he does right after being born. David is held accountable.

What does this have to do with sexual violence or even sexual ethics? Everything. A story like this taken from our religious tradition offers us remarkable insight into the profound ethical issues at stake when boundaries are crossed and power is misused. It also gives us a deeper understanding of the nature of sexual sin. If our society spent more time worrying about the misuse of power by powerful men (or women) rather than about deciding who can marry whom, we would all be better off. If we brought our moral values to bear on the real moral issues of our time, we might see the day when safety, healing, and justice are context and sexual violence is episodic. I believe this day will come if we persist in asserting that the way things are is not the way they have to be. This is my statement of faith.

Notes

Prologue: Unnatural Acts

1. *Seattle Times,* September 1, 1982.

2. Laura Lederer, ed., *Take Back the Night* (New York: William Morrow, 1980), 203.

3. Ibid.

4. As reported in Beryl Lieff Benderly, "Rape Free or Rape Prone," *Science* (October 1982): 40–43.

5. Ibid., 42.

6. See Randy Thornhill and Craig Palmer, *A Natural History of Rape* (Cambridge, Mass.: MIT Press, 2000), in which they argue that rape is biologically determined by the need for reproduction. Men are driven to copulate with women. If women resist, the act becomes rape.

7. Kathleen Barry, *Female Sexual Slavery* (Englewood Cliffs, N.J.: Prentice Hall, 1979), 174–214.

8. For example, Theodore Reik, *Psychology of Sex Relations* (New York: Rinehart, 1945), 9; and Havelock Ellis, "Analysis of Sexual Impulse," in *Studies in the Psychology of Sex,* I, part 2 (New York: Random House, 1942), 65, as quoted in Barry, *Female Sexual Slavery,* 217.

9. Marquis de Sade, from "La philosophie dans le boudoir," in *Marquis de Sade: Selections,* ed. Paul Dinnage, 132–33, as quoted in Barry, *Female Sexual Slavery,* 190.

10. Sigmund Freud, *Three Contributions to the Theory of Sex* (New York: E. P. Dutton, 1962), 22, as quoted in Barry, *Female Sexual Slavery,* 193.

11. Barry, *Female Sexual Slavery,* 193.

12. Kathleen Zuanich Young, "The Imperishable Virginity of Saint Maria Goretti," in *Violence against Women and Children: A Christian Theological Sourcebook,* ed. Carol J. Adams and Marie M. Fortune (New York: Continuum, 1995), 282.

13. Barry, *Female Sexual Slavery,* 218. Masters and Johnson's work is based on this thesis, as is Zilbergeld's sex therapy. Zilbergeld comments: "Human sexuality

is basically a learned phenomenon. Very little of our sexual behavior can properly be called instinctive." Bernie Zilbergeld, *Male Sexuality* (Boston: Little, Brown, 1978), 12.

14. Ibid., 218–19.

15. Ibid., 219.

16. But these myths are still held as truths by many. For example, a psychologist made the following statement in response to a discussion on sexual harassment in the workplace: "Every psychologist knows that biologically driven behavior [that is, sexual] will occur in spite of proscriptions and restrictions" (personal communication).

17. Barry, *Female Sexual Slavery,* 217. Once again the moral agency here belongs to the object (that is, woman or child) of a man's sexual interest.

18. Nicholas Groth with Jean Birnbaum, *Men Who Rape* (New York: Plenum Press, 1979), 2.

19. Quoted in ibid., 15.

20. Ibid., 27.

21. One finds the writing about sexuality and sexual violence in the late twentieth century beginning to provide valuable resources in understanding sexual violence and its relationship to sexuality. For example, Groth with Birnbaum, *Men Who Rape,* and Bernie Zilbergeld, *Male Sexuality,* 12–20.

Chapter 1: Introduction

1. *Webster's New Collegiate Dictionary* (Springfield, Mass.: G. & C. Merriam Co., 1961), 950.

2. Sandra Butler, *Conspiracy of Silence: the Trauma of Incest* (San Francisco: New Glide Publications, 1978), 49–50.

3. "After murder, rape is the most serious crime against the person, and it is among the most challenging to count." Mary P. Koss, "Detecting the Scope of Rape: a Review of Prevalence Research Methods," *Journal of Interpersonal Violence* 8, no. 2 (1993): 198–222.

4. Albert Bandura, *Aggression: A Social Learning Analysis* (Englewood Cliffs, N.J.: Prentice-Hall, 1973), 5.

5. "Justices, 6–3, Legalize Gay Sexual Conduct in Sweeping Reversal of Court's '86 Ruling," *New York Times,* June 27, 2003.

6. See Lori B. Girshick, *Woman-to-Woman Sexual Violence* (Boston: Northeastern University Press, 2002).

7. See Barrie Levy, ed., *Dating Violence: Young Women in Danger* (Seattle: Seal Press, 1998).

8. See also Ron Clark, "The Silence in Dinah's Cry: Narrative in Genesis 34 in a Context of Sexual Violence," *Journal of Religion and Abuse* 2, no. 4 (2001).

9. See Anita Diamant, *The Red Tent* (New York: Picador USA, 1997), for a very different interpretation of Dinah's experience and the aftermath.

10. We can assume that this matter would have been handled in later years according to the Deuteronomic laws rather than arbitrarily by the victim's brothers. The laws appear to have developed as a means of dealing with the violation of property which sexual assault of a woman represented. See chapter 4, "A New Sexual Ethic."

11. Susan Niditch, "Genesis," in _The Women's Bible Commentary_, ed. Carol A. Newsom and Sharon H. Ringe (Louisville: Westminster/John Knox Press, 1992), 23.

12. See Ron O'Grady, _The Hidden Shame of the Church: Sexual Abuse of Children and the Church_ (Geneva: World Council of Churches, 2001).

13. "Underage" refers to boys and girls under sixteen or eighteen years of age depending on state statutes. The more effective statutes indicate that underage persons are by definition unable to consent to sexual contact with an adult. See chapter 4, "A New Sexual Ethic."

14. U.S. Department of Health and Human Services, _Child Sexual Abuse: Incest, Assault, and Sexual Exploitation_ (Washington, D.C.: U.S. Department of Health and Human Services, 1981), 1.

15. David Finkelhor, "What's Wrong with Sex between Adults and Children? Ethics and the Problem of Sexual Abuse," _American Journal of Orthopsychiatry_ 49 (October 1979): 694–96.

16. U.S. Department of Health and Human Services, 1.

17. U.S. Federal Equal Employment Opportunity Commission.

18. Marie M. Fortune et al., _Clergy Misconduct: Sexual Abuse in the Ministerial Relationship_ (Seattle: FaithTrust Institute, 1992), 26.

19. The story of David and Bathsheba echoes the political crisis in the United States in 2000 created by President Bill Clinton's sexual liaison with a young White House intern. This led to his impeachment and subsequent acquittal but not before the political establishment was shaken to its core. We were left with many questions: Was Bill Clinton chastened and sobered? Did he comprehend what all of this is about? Did he have the character to really repent, that is, change, not only his assumptions of sexual access to women, but his sense of entitlement and use of power that comes to straight, white men who happen to also be president?

We don't have the right to expect our leaders to be saints. We do have the right to expect them to be aware of the importance of their role in public life and the sacrifices that go with it, to be able to acknowledge mistakes and take responsibility for them, to use some common sense, and to think first of the well-being of the people they serve. No one is required to take on the role of minister, judge, teacher, or president. A person seeks these roles and with them is given the public's trust. Once in such a position, a person is expected to exercise leadership with some degree of humility, self-discipline, and self-reflection.

The issues here are not about prudish finger-wagging at a bad boy caught with his pants down. The issues are far greater and their implications deeper than Bill

Clinton ever wanted to acknowledge. Bill Clinton wanted this scandal to be about sex. David wanted his taking of Bathsheba to be about sex. But neither was.

20. "Relationship" here is not limited to an intimate, primary relationship but refers to any interaction with another person. In relating to others, we know Immanuel, "God with us."

21. This theological insight is concretized in the concept of "covenant," used in scripture to describe the relationships among people and between people and God.

22. James B. Nelson, *Embodiment* (Minneapolis: Augsburg, 1978), 72: "A variety of polar concepts can thus be used, bearing common meanings with different shadings: sin and salvation, alienation and reconciliation, fragmentation and wholeness, death and life, law and gospel, death and resurrection."

23. Ibid.

Chapter 2: The Social Construction of Sexuality and Sexual Violence

1. Py Bateman, "The Context of Date Rape," in *Dating Violence: Young Women in Danger*, ed. Barrie Levy (Seattle: Seal Press, 1998), 95, discusses the research by Miller and Marshall (1987) finding that one in six women interviewed believed that when a man was sexually aroused, it was impossible for him to stop himself.

2. See Bernie Zilbergeld, "Learning about Sex," in Zilbergeld, *Male Sexuality* (Boston: Little, Brown, 1978), 12–20.

3. Florence Rush, *The Best Kept Secret: Sexual Abuse of Children* (Englewood Cliffs, N.J.: Prentice-Hall, 1980), 170.

4. In same-sex relationships the same romantic love prototype may function that requires artificial gender roles (butch-femme) to be imposed in order to create and sustain a subordinate-dominant relationship.

5. Susan Griffin, *Rape: The Power of Consciousness* (San Francisco: Harper & Row, 1979), 7.

6. Rush, *The Best Kept Secret*, 170.

7. James B. Nelson, *Embodiment* (Minneapolis: Augsburg, 1978), 46.

8. See Phyllis Tribble, *God and the Rhetoric of Sexuality* (Philadelphia: Fortress Press, 1978), 12–23, and Susan Niditch, "Genesis," *The Women's Bible Commentary*, ed. Carol A. Newsom and Sharon H. Ringe (Louisville: Westminster/John Knox Press, 1992), 10–25.

9. For extensive discussion of Western creation stories from scripture and their impact on church doctrine, see Elaine Pagels, *Adam, Eve, and the Serpent* (New York: Vintage Books, 1988).

10. Griffin, *Rape*, 7.

11. Ann Cahill, *Rethinking Rape* (Ithaca, N.Y.: Cornell University Press, 2001), 185.

12. Pamela Foa, "What's Wrong with Rape," in _Feminism and Philosophy,_ ed. Mary Vetterling-Braggin, Frederick A. Elliston, and Jane English (Totowa, N.J.: Littlefield, Adams, 1977), 356.

13. Sexuality education for girls in Catholic schools frequently focused on the lesson based on St. Maria Goretti, the young woman who was martyred as she resisted the attack of a rapist. See Kathleen Zuanich Young, "The Imperishable Virginity of Saint Maria Goretti," in _Violence against Women and Children: A Christian Theological Sourcebook,_ ed. Carol J. Adams and Marie M. Fortune (New York: Continuum, 1995), 279–86.

14. _Celebrating the Saints_ (New York: Pueblo Publishing Co., 1973), 171–73.

15. In the 1969 self-help book widely used in couples' counseling, _The Intimate Enemy — How to Fight Fair in Love and Marriage,_ Bach and Wyden prescribe the game to their readers: "And some women like to resist and protest too much. When they say 'no, not now,' they really mean 'yes if' (you really passionately want me). Then such a wife can give herself to the rapist [her husband] and say 'I'm overcome by you....'" Men should not simply assume that their partners don't at times feel like being raped; and that 'no' can mean 'yes' if the pursuit is persistent, skillful and genuinely passionate" (262). If women so often say "no" when they mean "yes," what do women say when they mean "no"? The authors then point out that: "Women, especially during the uncertainties of seduction and early courtship, will accommodate to the male level of aggression assigned to them. They usually keep secret their own desire for more or less tenderness" (261). The woman is expected to play the game and is blamed for it at the same time. Finally, the authors reassuringly conclude: "As partners learn how to fuse sex and aggression, their sex satisfaction gradually increases and their need to injure others verbally or physically decreases" (261). In no way is male sexual aggression questioned nor are men held accountable for their sexually aggressive activity. George R. Bach and Peter Wyden, _The Intimate Enemy_ (New York: William Morrow, 1969).

16. Dr. Anne Ganley, a therapist who worked with men who were violent towards their intimate partners from 1978 to 1998, comments: "Men define 'being in control' as having control over another person or a situation, not as self-control."

17. Otto A. Piper, _The Biblical View of Sex and Marriage_ (New York: Charles Scribner's Sons, 1960). This passage from Piper's _Biblical View of Sex and Marriage,_ published in 1960, is an extraordinary statement that reflects a cultural norm for male sexuality and discounts women's objections to this norm because women who object do not know their place: "The fact that erotic personal love and sexual desire are not necessarily connected causes some _modern_ [italics mine] women to look upon sexual intercourse as a degrading experience. They charge that in the sexual relationship they serve only as the means of satisfying a man's sexual appetite. However, this experience is not a universal one. There are women who find full contentment in the fact that they should be physically fit to satisfy a man's passion. On the other hand,

it is not accidental that in our days this feeling of degradation should be found especially among educated women with an articulate sense of personal value who engage in extramarital sexual relations" (62).

18. See John Stoltenberg, *The End of Manhood* (New York: Dutton/Penguin Books, 1993).

19. In the fall of 2003, preceding the 2004 U.S. presidential election, President George W. Bush cultivated a classic John Wayne image: "David Gutmann, a professor emeritus of psychology at Northwestern, notes that Mr. Bush 'bears important *masculine stigmata* (italics mine): he is a Texan, he is not afraid of war, and he sticks to his guns in the face of a worldwide storm of criticism.' " Maureen Dowd, "Gotta Lotta Stigmata," *New York Times,* August 24, 2003.

20. Nelson, *Embodiment,* 66–67.

21. Homophobia is the irrational fear of homosexual feelings in oneself; of lesbians, gay men, bisexuals and transgender people; and of homosexuality in general.

22. T. Walter Herbert, *Sexual Violence and American Manhood* (Cambridge, Mass.: Harvard University Press, 2002), 13–14.

23. *Webster's New World Dictionary of the American Language* (New York: The World Publishing Company, 1966), 1208.

24. *Spokane Daily Chronicle,* January 8, 1982. This captain, who was responsible for rape investigations, also wore a T-shirt with this comment printed on it. Community groups immediately requested his dismissal but were unsuccessful.

25. Similarly, hyperventilation is a physiological response in which one takes shallow, short breaths. It may result from either sexual excitement or fear.

26. Sandra Butler, *Conspiracy of Silence: The Trauma of Incest* (San Francisco: New Glide Publications, 1978), 49–51

27. Arlene Swidler, "It's No Sin to Be Raped," *U.S. Catholic* (February 1979): 12.

28. *San Francisco Chronicle,* May 27 and 28, 1977, as cited in Susan Griffin's *Rape,* 86. Following this incident, Judge Simonson was defeated in a recall election and no longer sits on the bench.

29. In fact it is seldom the case that women who are raped are engaged in "morally suspect" activity. For these victims, it is especially hard to "explain" the rape to others and to themselves.

30. Traci West, *Wounds of the Spirit* (New York: New York University Press, 1999), 96–97.

31. "Justices, 6–3, Legalize Gay Sexual Conduct in Sweeping Reversal of Court's '86 Ruling." *New York Times,* June 27, 2003.

32. See also Marie M. Fortune, *Love Does No Harm: Sexual Ethics for the Rest of Us* (New York: Continuum, 1995).

33. Ibid.

34. This cautionary tale of a woman crying "rape" falsely is reflected in the case of the Scottsboro Boys in the 1930s. Here two white women falsely accused a group of

black men of rape. The innocent men were convicted and all served prison sentences. These gender and racial dynamics were repeated throughout the South, often resulting in the lynching of black men by white mobs. These practices were challenged by anti-lynching campaigns led by Ida B. Wells-Barnett and others.

35. See also Niditch, "Genesis," 25.

36. See Rosemary Radford Ruether, ed., _Religion and Sexism_ (New York: Simon & Schuster, 1974).

37. Mary Pellauer, "Augustine on Rape," in _Violence against Women and Children: A Christian Theological Sourcebook,_ ed. Carol J. Adams and Marie M. Fortune (New York: Continuum, 1995), 207–41.

38. Ibid., 215–16.

39. Ibid., 218.

40. Ibid., 232.

41. Ibid., 235.

42. Rossell Hope Bobbins, "Malleus Maleficarum," _Encyclopedia of Witchcraft and Demonology_ (New York: Crown, 1959), 337–40.

43. _Malleus Maleficarum,_ quoted in Rosemary Radford Ruether, _New Woman–New Earth_ (New York: Seabury Press, 1978), 97–98.

44. Ibid., 102.

45. Florence Rush, _The Best Kept Secret: Sexual Abuse of Children_ (Englewood Cliffs, N.J.: Prentice-Hall, 1980), 39.

46. Anne Llewellyn Barstow, _Witchcraze_ (San Francisco: Pandora/HarperCollins, 1994), 12. For additional discussion of issues of colonization, see Nantawan Boonprasat Lewis and Marie M. Fortune, eds., _Remembering Conquest: Feminist/Womanist Perspectives on Religion, Colonization, and Sexual Violence_ (New York: Haworth Pastoral Press, 1999).

47. "Sex" is placed in quotation marks here so as to distinguish it from "sexual activity" as it is used in Continuum III.

48. "Proactive" refers to initiating behavior during sexual activity.

49. Lorenne M. G. Clark and Debra J. Lewis, _Rape: The Price of Coercive Sexuality_ (Toronto: Women's Press, 1977), 175.

Chapter 3: Sexual Violence

1. See Neil M. Malamuth, "Aggression against Women," in _Pornography and Sexual Aggression,_ ed. Neil M. Malamuth and Edward Donnerstein (Orlando: Academic Press, 1984), reporting that an average of 35 percent of men studied indicated a likelihood that they would rape if assured they would not be caught and punished.

2. See the work of Lois Livezy, Toinette Eugene, Traci West, Pamela Cooper-White, and others.

3. Anthony Kosnik et al., _Human Sexuality_ (New York: Paulist Press, 1977), 43–44.

4. Ibid., 43.

5. We even see this challenge in the reaction to extensive disclosures (early twenty-first century) of child sexual abuse by priests. The focus has been on the male victims of male priests and the ethical wrong has then focused on "homosexuality." Otherwise church and society have had difficulty coming up with the reasons it is wrong to be sexual with a child regardless of gender.

6. Carol Adams in her discussion of MacKinnon asserts: "But we have to shift our perspective to see that sexual victimization is to be expected, rather than that sexual victimization is the exception, not the rule. In this shift, we come to perceive not that men who commit sex crimes must be 'sick' but that this is exactly how male sexuality is constructed.... From this perspective, we can see that the very, very few men who are prosecuted for acts of sexual victimization may be the 'failures,' that is, those who get 'caught,' and therefore it is not accurate to build our understanding of sex crimes on this pool of individuals." Carol Adams, "Toward a Feminist Theology of Religion and the State," in *Violence against Women and Children: A Christian Theological Sourcebook,* ed. Carol J. Adams and Marie M. Fortune (New York: Continuum, 1995), 22.

7. "Rape is here understood as part of an interlocking set of practices, demands, and behaviors that serve to perpetuate the social and political domination of men over women. From this perspective, rape is constituted not as a horrific aberration from normal, healthy sexual encounters, but rather as a necessary element of a particular political structure. 'What is wrong with rape, then, is that it is really not wrong at all' (MacKinnon)." Ann Cahill, *Rethinking Rape* (Ithaca, N.Y.: Cornell University Press, 2001), 184.

8. Ibid., 167–68.

9. See also Tikva Frymer-Kensky, "Deuteronomy," *The Women's Bible Commentary,* ed. Carol A. Newsom and Sharon H. Ringe (Louisville: Westminster/John Knox Press, 1992), 56–59.

10. Raymond E. Brown, S.S., Joseph A. Fitzmyer, S.J., Roland E. Murphy, O.Carm., *The Jerome Biblical Commentary* (Englewood Cliffs, N.J.: Prentice-Hall, 1969), 79.

11. The only exception to this is the son-father prohibition, which is included because the father is obviously not the possession of the son.

12. In addition to the Levitical sources, Florence Rush suggests that there is evidence in the Talmudic writings of sexual license taken with young girls who were not close kin. "The Talmud held that a female child of 'three years and one day' could be betrothed by sexual intercourse with her father's permission. Intercourse with one younger was not a crime, but invalid. If a prospective groom would penetrate the child just once more after her third birthday, he could legitimately claim his promised bride." Florence Rush, *The Best Kept Secret: Sexual Abuse of Children* (Englewood Cliffs, N.J.: Prentice-Hall, 1980), 17. The practice of child rape in order to acquire a wife rests exclusively on the designation of female children as property who grow up to become wives. The property status never changes, only the owner.

The only control over this practice of child rape was exercised by the girl's father, who could withhold his permission for her to be raped. But he was unlikely to refuse an opportunity to have her designated to her husband at an early age.

13. "The laws focus mainly upon external threats to the man's authority, honor and property, though they may occasionally serve to define and protect his rights in relation to members of his own household." Phyllis Bird, "Image of Women in the Old Testament," in _Religion and Sexism,_ ed. Rosemary Radford Ruether (New York: Simon & Schuster, 1974), 51.

14. Cahill, _Rethinking Rape,_ 168: "The wrong committed here is not one of violence against the female victim, but of trespass on another man's property, which constitutes a threat to the rights, and therefore the political and social identity, of the owning male. This trespass (especially insofar as it represented a financial loss on the part of a father whose daughter was now damaged goods relative to the market of marriage) was perceived with social outrage and therefore punished severely. . . . In certain cases, most notably if the victim was a virgin, rape could be understood as a theft of an irreplaceable piece of property for which the real victim (usually the father in this case) deserved financial compensation."

15. See chapter 6, "Just Responses to the Sin of Sexual Violence," for a discussion of racism, slavery, lynching, and property rights.

16. Cahill, _Rethinking Rape,_ 169.

17. Ibid., 171. "Liberal theories of rape depend on a certain understanding of consent that demands that it be freely given. . . . Yet this conceptualization of consent, when taken against political and social structures that seriously limit women's agency and autonomy under many circumstances, proves problematic."

18. In the United States, women still do not have a guarantee of equal rights under the constitution in the absence of the Equal Rights Amendment. We are not yet even approaching economic parity between women and men.

19. Cahill, _Rethinking Rape,_ 173.

20. Ibid., 174–75: "Specifically with regard to rape, consent theory falters on locating the ethical wrong of rape in the absence of the victim's consent. To approach the wrong of rape as embedded in the nonconsensual nature of the act is inevitably to place the ethical burden on the victim. The ethical question that courts must pursue becomes whether the victim sufficiently communicated her nonconsent, or whether that nonconsent was likely given the history of the victim." In 2003, basketball star Kobe Bryant was charged with sexual assault of a nineteen-year-old woman employee who came to his hotel room. His defense was "consensual sex." He is African American; the alleged victim is Anglo. The courts were asked to address (1) what happened? and (2) was it wrong?

21. Robert Davis, "Condom-Rape Case Brings an Outcry," _USA Today,_ September 10, 1992.

22. Cahill, _Rethinking Rape,_ 179: Cahill cites Michael Davis's distinction as "simple rape as being 'compelled by brute force to have sexual intercourse (but be

otherwise unharmed),' whereas aggravated rape includes the explicit threat and/or imposition of further violence."

23. Ibid., 181.

24. John T. Noonan, "Genital Good," *Communio* 8 (Fall 1981): 200–201.

25. Karl Menninger, *Whatever Became of Sin?* (New York: Hawthorn Books, 1973), 140.

26. *Baker's Dictionary of Christian Ethics,* ed. Carl F. H. Henry (Grand Rapids: Baker Book House, 1973), 565.

27. Ibid.

28. *Dictionary of Moral Theology* (Westminster, Md.: Newman Press, 1962), 1017.

29. Ibid.

30. Ibid., 1017–18.

31. Ibid., 1018.

32. In this we see the reflection of Thomas Aquinas, who was most concerned about injury done to husband or father rather than to the rape victim herself. Oscar E. Feucht et al., *Sex and the Church* (St. Louis: Concordia Publishing House, 1961), 70.

33. *Dictionary of Moral Theology,* 1018.

34. This text is the only one cited here that addresses the question of what happens if a woman does conceive from rape: "It is a disputed question whether, immediately following intercourse, the woman may use positive means to prevent conception or must let nature take its course." Ibid., 1018. While moral theologians discuss the intricacies of this question, women are left to decide with little moral guidance or pastoral help from the church whether to abort a fetus that results from rape.

35. Otto A. Piper, *The Biblical View of Sex and Marriage* (New York: Charles Scribner's Sons, 1960), 62.

36. Ibid.

37. *Baker's Dictionary,* 319; *Dictionary of Moral Theology,* 614.

38. *Dictionary of Moral Theology,* 614.

39. Noonan, "Genital Good," 203.

40. Ibid., 205.

41. William Countryman, *Dirt, Greed, and Sex* (Philadelphia: Fortress Press, 1988), 248.

42. James B. Nelson, *Embodiment* (Minneapolis: Augsburg, 1978), 262.

43. James B. Nelson and Sandra Longfellow, eds., *Sexuality and the Sacred* (Louisville: Westminster John Knox Press, 1994).

44. Cahill, *Rethinking Rape,* 194–95.

45. Ibid., 192–93.

46. This idealistic notion assumes that the assailant's sociopathy or narcissism does not obliterate the potential for empathy.

47. The 2002 revisions to the U.S. Roman Catholic Bishops' Dallas Policy on the sexual abuse of children held some interesting revelations. The bishops directly tied the definition of sexual abuse to a moral standard based on the Sixth Commandment in Hebrew scripture: "You shall not commit adultery." If this is the basis of their ethical understanding of sexual abuse, then no wonder the perception persisted that the bishops simply didn't "get it." The average layperson would rightly ask, "I thought adultery was about adults having sex with someone they are not married to. What does sexual abuse of kids have to do with adultery?"

48. The exception is found among feminist biblical scholars and preachers, for example, Phyllis Trible in _Texts of Terror: Literary-Feminist Readings of Biblical Narratives_ (Minneapolis: Fortress Press, 2003).

49. Toinette Eugene, " 'Swing Low, Sweet Chariot!': A Womanist Ethical Response to Sexual Violence and Abuse," in _Violence against Women and Children: A Christian Theological Sourcebook,_ ed. Carol J. Adams and Marie M. Fortune (New York: Continuum, 1995), 186–87.

50. "Folly" defined as "wickedness or wantonness."

51. Adams, "Toward a Feminist Theology of Religion and the State," 26.

Chapter 4: A New Sexual Ethic

1. For a concise history of sexual ethics in Western culture, see Margaret Farley, "Sexual Ethics," in _Sexuality and the Sacred,_ ed. James B. Nelson and Sandra B. Longfellow (Louisville: Westminster John Knox Press, 1994), 54–67.

2. In this regard, Nelson's discussion of "Love and Sexual Ethics" is most helpful (_Embodiment_ [Minneapolis: Augsburg, 1978])..

3. See Adrienne Rich's discussion of trust in _Women and Honor: Some Notes on Lying_ (Pittsburgh: Motheroot Publications, 1977).

4. In some traditions past and present, an additional concern was the procreative potential of sexual activity, that is, sexual activity that could lead to conception within marriage was acceptable while nonprocreative sexual acts were wrong.

5. Margaret Farley, "Sexual Ethics," _Encyclopedia of Bioethics_ (New York: Free Press, 1978), 1578.

6. Ibid., 1582.

7. Accepting the option to say "yes" carries with it responsibilities, such as protecting oneself against disease and unwanted pregnancy.

8. See "Love — All That and More," video series produced by FaithTrust Institute, Seattle, 2001 (www.faithtrustinstitute.org).

9. Fifty-four percent of women victims were under eighteen years old at the time of the first rape, and 83 percent were under the age of twenty-five. Patricia Tjaden and Nancy Thoennes, "Prevalence, Incidence, and Consequences of Violence against Women: Finds from the National Violence against Women Survey Office of Justice Programs," U.S. Department of Justice, November 1998.

10. See "Love — All That and More" video series.

11. David Finkelhor's fine article provides an excellent argument for the consent standard to be applied to sexual contact, especially between adults and children. See "What's Wrong with Sex between Adults and Children? Ethics and the Problem of Sexual Abuse," *American Journal of Orthopsychiatry* 49 (October 1979): 692–97.

12. See "Working Together," the newsletter of the Center for the Prevention of Sexual and Domestic Violence, 2 (December 1981–January 1982).

13. It has long been assumed that humans share an incest taboo universally. In fact, the taboo itself has not limited the conduct of sexually abusing children. It has only limited the revelation and discussion of this social problem.

14. Diana Russell, *Rape in Marriage* (Bloomington: Indiana University Press, 1990).

15. Alan Abrahamson, "Defendant Says He Has Right to Sex with Wife," *Los Angeles Times,* January 29, 1996.

16. Marie Fortune, *Is Nothing Sacred? When Sex Invades the Ministerial Relationship* (San Francisco: HarperSanFrancisco, 1989; Cleveland: United Church Press, 1999).

17. See www.survivorsnetwork.org.

18. For further discussion of child sexual abuse in the Catholic Church, see Marie M. Fortune and Merle Longwood, eds., *Sexual Abuse in the Catholic Church: Trusting the Clergy?* (New York: Haworth Pastoral Press, 2003).

19. See American Academy of Pastoral Counselors at www.aapc.org.

20. "Bodily integrity" is a term used by social ethicist Beverly Wildung Harrison to describe the right (particularly for women) to control one's own body and to establish personal physical boundaries. "Theology of Pro-Choice: A Feminist Perspective," *The Witness* 64 (September 1981): 20.

21. See also Katherine Hancock Ragsdale, *Boundary Wars* (Cleveland: Pilgrim Press, 1996), for a further discussion of the complexities of boundary issues in helping relationships.

22. This section is a summary of my book *Love Does No Harm: Sexual Ethics for the Rest of Us* (New York: Continuum, 1995).

Chapter 5: Scripture Resources for Reframing Ethical Approaches to Sexual Violence

1. Margaret Farley, "Sexual Ethics," *Encyclopedia of Bioethics* (New York: Free Press, 1978), 1576.

2. "There are lusts of many kinds, but when the word is used simply without addition it would not occur to anyone that it mean anything but sexual emotion. This affects not only the whole body in an external sense, but also in an interior sense. It moves the whole man by a combined appetite of both body and mind. That is why it produces the greatest pleasure of which the body is capable, so that at the moment of consummation practically the whole watch and ward of reasoned thought is overwhelmed." Augustine, *City of God* (London: Oxford University Press, 1963),

235–36. Unfortunately, Augustine regards this expression as "the greatest pleasure of which the body is capable," implying that male sexuality is dependent on "violent sexual appetite."

3. James Nelson also makes this distinction in his interpretation of Matthew 5:28: "And if lust is untamed, inordinate sexual desire which is not only the passion for _possession_ of another but which also becomes, by its very centrality in the self, an expression of _idolatry,_ then we are dealing here with something different from the usual erotic awareness expressed in sexual fantasy." James B. Nelson, _Embodiment_ (Minneapolis: Augsburg, 1978), 162.

4. See also Exodus 22:21–22, where widows, orphans, and aliens or strangers are indicated.

5. "The laws focus mainly upon external threats to the man's authority, honor and property, though they may occasionally serve to define and protect his rights in relation to members of his own household." Phyllis Byrd, "Image of Women in the Old Testament," in _Religion and Sexism,_ ed. Rosemary Radford Ruether (New York: Simon & Schuster, 1974), 51.

6. This is the case for Protestant and Hebrew scriptures. Jerome's Latin translation includes three additional stories about Daniel translated into Latin from Greek, attributed to Theoditus. Raymond E. Brown, S.S., Joseph A. Fitzmyer, S.J., Roland E. Murphy, O.Carm., _The Jerome Biblical Commentary_ (Englewood Cliffs, N.J.: Prentice-Hall, 1969), 459. But the emphasis here is on the use of the passage to encourage chastity and discourage sexual activity. Although included, it misinterprets the events and results in an antisexual message more than an antiviolence one.

7. Ibid., 459.

8. E.g., this chapter does not appear in the Protestant canon but rather is placed in the Apocrypha. In the Roman Catholic Jerusalem Bible, it appears as the last chapter of Daniel.

9. Esther is remembered and celebrated by Jews during the holiday of Purim. Esther saved the Jews from extermination while in Persia.

10. See Phyllis Trible, _Texts of Terror: Literary-Feminist Readings of Biblical Narratives_ (Minneapolis: Fortress Press, 2003).

Chapter 6: Just Responses to the Sin of Sexual Violence

1. T. Walter Herbert, _Sexual Violence and American Manhood_ (Cambridge, Mass.: Harvard University Press, 2002), 14.

2. Judith Herman, _Trauma and Recovery_ (New York: Basic Books, 1992), 7–9.

3. This was the issue for a number of Republicans who led the impeachment process against President Clinton in 2000. Their own extramarital activities finally came to light, which pointed to their hypocrisy.

4. I have not attempted here to address the ways in which the legal system itself contributes to justice or injustice in resolving incidents of sexual violence. A guilty

plea or a conviction may be the first step toward acknowledging the wrong done, moving the offender to repentance, treatment, or incarceration.

5. Eighty percent to 90 percent of crimes against women are committed by someone of the same racial background as the victim (U.S. Department of Justice, 1994, Bureau of Justice Statistics). This figure appears to hold steady over time: "The ten years' experience of rape crisis centers have shown that the large majority, 90 percent, of the rapes committed are intraracial, confined within racial groupings, as opposed to the dominant myths that most rapes are inter-racial." Loretta J. Ross, "Rape and Third World Women," *Aegis* no. 35 (Summer 1982): 46.

6. Traci West, *Wounds of the Spirit* (New York: New York University Press, 1999), 14. Dr. West continues citing first-person narratives of slave women's experiences of sexual violence.

7. Wells estimated that more than ten thousand lynchings occurred in thirty years at the end of the nineteenth century. Lori Robinson, *I Will Survive: The African American Guide to Healing from Sexual Assault and Abuse* (New York: Seal Press, 2002), 225.

8. Research in the 1990s as to the rates of intimate violence by race were inconclusive. Patricia Mahoney, Linda M. Williams, Carolyn M. West, "Violence against Women by Intimate Relationship Partners," *Sourcebook on Violence against Women*, ed. Claire M. Renzetti, Jeffrey L. Edleson, and Raquel Kennedy Bergen (Thousand Oaks, Calif.: Sage Publications, 2001), 164–65.

9. Alice Walker, "Advancing Luna – and Ida B. Wells," *You Can't Keep a Good Woman Down* (New York: Harcourt Brace Jovanovich, 1982), 93.

10. Andrea Smith, "Sexual Violence and American Indian Genocide," in *Remembering Conquest: Feminist/Womanist Perspectives on Religion, Colonization, and Sexual Violence,* ed. Nantawan Boonprasat Lewis and Marie M. Fortune (New York: Haworth Pastoral Press, 1999), 31–52.

11. The National Violence against Women Survey in 1998 found that 17.7 percent of white women and 34.1 percent of American Indian/Alaska Native women reported rape victimization. Patricia Tjaden and Nancy Thoennes, "Prevalence, Incidence, and Consequences of Violence against Women: Findings from the National Violence against Women Survey," Washington, D.C.: National Institute of Justice, Office of Justice Programs, U.S. Department of Justice, 1998.

12. Rachel Bundang, "Scars ARE History: Colonialism, Written on the Body," in *Remembering Conquest: Feminist/Womanist Perspectives on Religion, Colonization, and Sexual Violence,* ed. Nantawan Boonprasat Lewis and Marie M. Fortune (New York: Haworth Pastoral Press, 1999), 64.

13. Daryl L. Jones, June 11, 1999: www.directionaction.com/roserep.htm.

14. Toinette Eugene, "Swing Lo, Sweet Chariot!" in *Violence against Women and Children: A Christian Theological Sourcebook,* ed. Carol J. Adams and Marie M. Fortune (New York: Continuum, 1995), 187.

15. This double bind exists in any minority community, for example, the lesbian/gay/bisexual/transgender community or the Jewish community.

16. For additional discussion of sexual violence and African American women in the 1970s and 1980s, see Angela Davis, "The Dialectics of Rape," _Ms. Magazine_ (June 1975), 74ff.; Gerta Lerner, ed., "The Rape of Black Women as a Weapon of Terror," _Black Women in White America: A Documentary History_ (New York: Vintage Books, 1972); Beverly Smith, "Black Women's Health: Notes for a Course," _But Some of Us Are Brave_ (Old Westbury, N.Y.: Feminist Press, 1982), 112–13. See also West, _Wounds of the Spirit_.

17. Traci West, "Spirit-Colonizing Violations: Racism, Sexual Violence and Black American Women," in _Remembering Conquest: Feminist/Womanist Perspectives on Religion, Colonization, and Sexual Violence,_ ed. Nantawan Boonprasat Lewis and Marie M. Fortune (New York: Haworth Pastoral Press, 1999), 29.

Chapter 7: The Healing Power of Justice

1. Harold Kushner, _When Bad Things Happen to Good People_ (New York: Schocken Books, 1981), 88.

2. Judith Herman, _Trauma and Recovery_ (New York: Basic Books, 1992), 7–8.

3. Ibid.

4. "The legal system is designed to protect men from the superior power of the state but not to protect women or children from the superior power of men." Ibid., 72.

5. Ibid., 177.

6. Traci West, _Wounds of the Spirit_ (New York: New York University Press, 1999), 178.

7. Herman, _Trauma and Recovery,_ 181.

8. Christie Cozad Neuger, _Counseling Women_ (Minneapolis: Augsburg Fortress, 2001), discusses narrative counseling theory as a framework for work with survivors: "We make meaning and live our lives through the stories that we have created to give our lives coherence" (86).

9. Toinette Eugene, "Swing Low, Sweet Chariot!": A Womanist Response to Sexual Violence and Abuse," in _Violence against Women and Children,_ ed. Carol J. Adams and Marie M. Fortune (New York: Continuum, 1995), 188.

10. Augustine asserted "original sin," Eve's eating the apple in the Garden as the source of human suffering. The creation stories in Hebrew scripture are an attempt to explain suffering theologically.

11. But the explanation does not adequately explain the cause of suffering unrelated to human activity, for example, earthquake, volcano, or hurricane. Kushner's book entitled _When Bad Things Happen to Good People_ grapples with understanding our experiences of suffering.

12. This question reflected a common belief in Hebrew theology at that time. Raymond E. Brown, S.S., Joseph A. Fitzmyer, S.J., Roland E. Murphy, O.Carm., _The_

Jerome Biblical Commentary (Englewood Cliffs, N.J.: Prentice-Hall, 1969), 443, and C. K. Barrett, *Gospel According to St. John* (London: SPCK, 1955), 294.

13. Rita Nakashima Brock and Rebecca Parker, *Proverbs of Ashes* (Boston: Beacon Press, 2001), 30.

14. Ibid., 249–50.

15. Ibid., 250.

16. West, *Wounds of the Spirit,* 153.

17. Ibid.

18. Herman, *Trauma and Recovery,* 181.

19. The desire to conceal sexual assault is particularly strong among teenagers, who may fear the reaction of their peers and risk ostracization from the group. Also in the case of date rape, the assailant is likely to be one of their peers, which only further complicates their reactions.

20. "The 'goodness' of women was defined in terms of their desirability as objects of an exclusive sexual relationship; a 'good' woman, therefore, was a woman who resisted all temptation to squander her limited resources and who fought to preserve her assets for the man who could rightfully lay claim to them.... Since women's sexual and reproductive capacities were the qualities which men bargained and paid for, female sexuality became a commodity, and like any other commodity it had various price tags. It was thus inevitable that valuable female sexual property would on occasion be stolen." Lorenne M. G. Clark and Debra J. Lewis, *Rape: The Price of Coercive Sexuality* (Toronto: Women's Press, 1977), 172–73.

21. This specific concern about loss of virginity may be a priority for particular ethnic or religious groups, for example, Latina or Muslim women, and should be dealt with sensitively, respecting the individual's religious and cultural heritage. Other groups may not emphasize a woman's virginal status.

22. A cautionary note: as helpers, we cannot carry every burden that someone brings our way. Sustained by prayer and self-care, it is important to set some limits on what we can do. We can only do what we can do and then rely on others and the Holy Spirit to share the burden as well.

23. West, *Wounds of the Spirit,* 60.

24. See also Psalm 55:

> Give ear to my prayer, O God;
>   do not hide yourself from my supplication.
> Attend to me, and answer me;
>   I am troubled in my complaint.
> I am distraught by the noise of the enemy,
>   because of the clamor of the wicked.
> For they bring trouble upon me,
>   and in anger they cherish enmity against me.
>
> My heart is in anguish within me,
>   the terrors of death have fallen upon me.

Fear and trembling come upon me,
    and horror overwhelms me.
And I say, "O that I had wings like a dove!
    I would fly away and be at rest;
truly, I would flee far away;
    I would lodge in the wilderness;   _Selah_
I would hurry to find a shelter for myself
    from the raging wind and tempest."

Confuse, O Lord, confound their speech;
    for I see violence and strife in the city.
Day and night they go around it
    on its walls,
and iniquity and trouble are within it;
    ruin is in its midst;
oppression and fraud
    do not depart from its market place.

It is not enemies who taunt me —
    I could bear that;
it is not adversaries who deal insolently with me —
    I could hide from them.
But it is you, my equal,
    my companion, my familiar friend,
with whom I kept pleasant company;
    we walked in the house of God with the throng.
Let death come upon them;
    let them go down alive to Sheol;
    for evil is in their homes and in their hearts.

But I call upon God,
    and the LORD will save me.
Evening and morning and at noon
    I utter my complaint and moan,
    and he will hear my voice.
He will redeem me unharmed
    from the battle that I wage,
    for many are arrayed against me.
God, who is enthroned from of old,   _Selah_
    will hear, and will humble them —
because they do not change,
    and do not fear God.

My companion laid hands on a friend
    and violated a covenant with me
with speech smoother than butter,
    but with a heart set on war;

> with words that were softer than oil,
> but in fact were drawn swords.
>
> Cast your burden on the LORD,
> and he will sustain you;
> he will never permit
> the righteous to be moved.
>
> But you, O God, will cast them down
> into the lowest pit;
> the bloodthirsty and treacherous
> shall not live out half their days.
> But I will trust in you.

25. Willard Gaylin, *The Killing of Bonnie Garland* (New York: Simon and Schuster, 1982), 341.

26. Ibid., 336.

27. Dietrich Bonhoeffer, *Life Together,* trans. John W. Doberstein (New York: Harper & Row, 1954), 116.

28. "For the Jew the Hebrew term *teshuvah* is the word for repentance. *Teshuvah* literally means 'return,' clearly denoting a return to God after sin. In Judaism there is a distinction between sins against God and sins against people. For the former only regret or confession is necessary. For sins against people, *teshuvah* requires three steps: first, admission of wrongdoing; second, asking for forgiveness of the person wronged (here abused); third, reconciliation which can be accomplished only by a change in behavior." Marie M. Fortune and Judith Hertz, *Family Violence: A Workshop Manual for Clergy and Other Service Providers* (Seattle: Center for the Prevention of Sexual and Domestic Violence, 1980), 78.

29. This notion is not intended to open a debate between justification by faith versus justification by works. It is rather to suggest that repentance is not only in word but in deed as well.

30. Accountability through incarceration following conviction on criminal charges is one way to deny an offender access to vulnerable potential victims. However, it also raises fundamental issues about criminal justice reform in the United States and is not a satisfactory answer to long-term social problems like sexual violence and abuse.

31. Herman, *Trauma and Recovery,* 235–36.

Chapter 8: What about Forgiveness?

1. Linda Hollies as quoted in Lori Robinson, *I Will Survive: the African American Guide to Healing from Sexual Assault and Abuse* (New York: Seal Press, 2002), 131–32.

2. Fred Keene, "Structures of Forgiveness in the New Testament," in *Violence against Women: A Christian Theological Sourcebook,* ed. Carol Adams and Marie M. Fortune (New York: Continuum, 1995), 128.

3. See also Laura Davis, *I Thought We'd Never Speak Again* (New York: HarperCollins, 2002).

Chapter 9: Children and Youth

1. Barbara Myers, "Developmental Disruptions of Victims of Incest and Childhood Abuse," unpublished paper (1978).

2. Florence Rush has provided a valuable discussion of the "Freudian Coverup" in *The Best Kept Secret: Sexual Abuse of Children* (Englewood Cliffs, N.J.: Prentice-Hall, 1980), 80. In this chapter, she quotes Freud's conclusions: "Almost all of my women patients told me that they had been seduced by their fathers. I was driven to recognize in the end that these reports were untrue and so came to understand that the hysterical symptoms are derived from phantasies and not real occurrences."

3. David Finkelhor et al., "Sexual Abuse in a National Survey of Adult Men and Women: Prevalence, Characteristics, and Risk Factors," *Child Abuse and Neglect* 14 (1990): 19–28.

4. Lawrence A. Greenfield, "Sex Offenses and Sex Offenders: An Analysis of Data on Rape and Sexual Assault," Washington, D.C.: Bureau of Justice Statistics, Office of Justice Programs, U.S. Department of Justice, 1997.

5. American Association of University Women, "Hostile Hallways: The AAUW Survey on Sexual Harassment in America's Schools" (Washington, D.C.: AAUW Educational Foundation, 1993).

6. Barrie Levy, ed., *Dating Violence: Young Women in Danger* (Seattle: Seal Press, 1998), 9.

7. See Levy for further discussion and suggestions for intervention and prevention.

8. Myers, "Developmental Disruptions of Victims of Incest and Childhood Abuse."

9. For religious education curricula and videos, see www.faithtrustinstitute.org. Kathy Reid's curricula for children and the video series *Love — All That and More* for teens and young adults are valuable tools for work with children and youth in a religious setting.

10. Suzanne M. Sgroi, *Sexual Abuse of Children* (Seattle: Harborview Sexual Assault Center, 1977).

11. See also Carolyn Byerly, *The Mother's Book: How to Survive the Molestation of Your Child,* 3rd ed. (Dubuque: Iowa: Kendall-Hunt, 1997).

12. Groups for mothers of incest victims are an excellent means of helping them rally resources and benefit from support from others in the same situation. These groups are offered by some rape crisis or sexual assault agencies in local communities.

13. See also Ellen Bass and Laura Davis, *The Courage to Heal: A Guide for Women Survivors of Child Sexual Abuse* (New York: HarperPerennial, 1994), and Judith Herman, *Trauma and Recovery* (New York: Basic Books, 1992).

Chapter 10: Wounded Healers and Bystanders

1. Rebecca Campbell, Courtney E. Ahrens, Tracey Self, Sharon M. Wasco, Holly E. Barnes, "Social Reactions to Rape Victims: Healing and Hurtful Effects of Psychological and Physical Health Outcomes," *Violence and Victims* 16, no. 3 (2001): 287–302.

2. This research was conducted by Shannah Hormann in Seattle, Washington, for the then Center for the Prevention of Sexual and Domestic Violence (now FaithTrust Institute). Partial results were published in *JSAC Grapevine* 11, no. 3 (September 1979): 1–2.

3. A great deal of controversy surrounds this provision, including the question of who is a clergyperson, what about clergy in churches that do not have a doctrine of sacramental confession, what about nonsacramental confidential communications, etc. For additional discussion of the legal issues involved, see Seward Reese, "Confidential Communications to the Clergy," *Ohio State Law Journal* 24 (1963): 55–88.

4. It is not the pastor's role to investigate or question the child in detail. We do not have the expertise to do this. We can make a good faith report of *the suspicion* that a child is being harmed or may be at risk and not be liable for making a false report. The trained investigator then gathers the information and determines what is best for the child.

5. See Marie M. Fortune, "Reporting Child Abuse: An Ethical Mandate for Ministry," in *Abuse and Religion*, ed. Anne Horton (Lexington, Mass.: D. C. Heath, 1988).

6. *The Oxford Dictionary of the Christian Church* (London: Oxford University Press, 1957), 1234, as cited in Seward Reese, "Confidential Communications to Clergy," *Ohio State Law Journal* 24 (1963): 68.

7. *The Book of Discipline of the United Methodist Church* (Nashville: United Methodist Publishing House, 2000), par. 332.5.

8. Evangelical Lutheran Church in America, Constitutions, Bylaws, and Continuing Resolutions (November 2003), sec. 7.45.

9. See discussion of forgiveness in chapter 8, "What about Forgiveness?"

10. Ann Wolbert Burgess and Lynda Lytle Holmstrom, *Rape: Victims of Crisis* (Bowie, Md.: Robert J. Brady, 1974), 4, 6.

11. See Kristin Leslie, *When Violence Is No Stranger* (Minneapolis: Fortress Press, 2003), for a very helpful discussion of the pastoral counseling issues for survivors of acquaintance rape.

12. See Lori S. Robinson, *I Will Survive* (New York: Seal Press, 2002), for an in-depth discussion of survivor issues for African American women. Also Susan J. Brison, *Aftermath* (Princeton, N.J.: Princeton University Press, 2002), for a powerful discussion of healing from a brutal stranger rape, and Migael Scherer, *Still Loved by the Sun* (New York: Simon & Schuster, 1992).

13. "Rape trauma syndrome is the acute phase and long-term reorganization process that occurs as a result of a forcible rape or attempted forcible rape. This syndrome of behavioral, somatic, and psychological reactions is an acute stress reaction to a life-threatening situation." Ann Wolbert Burgess and Lynda Lytle Holmstrom, "Rape Trauma Syndrome," *American Journal of Psychiatry* 131, no. 9 (September 1974): 982. The discussion of rape trauma syndrome reflects primarily the experience of women victims. The general issues are similar for both female and male victims. Additional information follows discussing the particular needs of male victims. See also Burgess and Holmstrom, *Rape.*

14. Leslie, *When Violence Is No Stranger,* 38.

15. Ibid., 42.

16. Judith Herman, *Trauma and Recovery* (New York: Basic Books, 1992).

17. Leslie, *When Violence Is No Stranger,* 53.

18. Ibid. Leslie cites Myung-Sook Lee's work with Korean women survivors in this regard.

19. See Michael Scarce, *Male on Male Rape: The Hidden Toll of Stigma and Shame* (New York: Insight Books, 1997).

20. A. Nicholas Groth with H. Jean Birnbaum, *Men Who Rape* (New York: Plenum Press, 1979), 139.

21. See, for example, Robinson, *I Will Survive,* chapter 5 "Sexual Healing."

Chapter 11: Asking the Church to Be the Church

1. See also John McClure and Nancy Ramsay, eds., *Telling the Truth: Preaching about Sexual and Domestic Violence* (Cleveland: United Church of Christ Press, 1998).

Epilogue: Where Do We Want to Go?

1. See Irene Diamond's article, "Pornography and Repression: A Reconsideration of 'Who' and 'What,' " prepared for delivery at the Annual Meeting of the Western Social Science Association, Denver, Colorado, April 1978.

2. T. Walter Herbert, *Sexual Violence and American Manhood* (Cambridge, Mass.: Harvard University Press, 2002), 82–83, quoting an article by Robert Stoller and I. S. Levine.

3. Ibid.

4. Ibid., 212, referencing an article by Frank Rich, "Naked Capitalists," *New York Times Magazine,* May 20, 2001.

5. Edward Donnerstein as quoted in Laura Lederer, *Take Back the Night* (New York: William Morrow, 1980), 230.

6. Seymour Feshbach and Neal M. Malamuth as reported in Lederer, *Take Back the Night,* 215–16.

7. Herbert, *Sexual Violence and American Manhood,* 10–11.

8. Alice Walker, *Possessing the Secret of Joy* (New York: Pocket Star Books, 1992), 281.

9. Judith Beals, "Action on Sexual Violence," *Boston Globe,* April 1, 2002.

Afterword

1. Traci C. West is an Associate Professor of Ethics and African American Studies at Drew University Theological School. She is the author of *Wounds of the Spirit: Black Women, Violence, and Resistance Ethics* as well as several articles on issues of justice in church and society. She is also an ordained United Methodist minister and conducts workshops on antiracism and violence against women in church and community settings.

2. Carol Adams is the author of the groundbreaking *Sexual Politics of Meat: A Feminist-Vegetarian Critical Theory,* of the pastoral care guide *Woman-Battering,* and co-editor of *Violence against Women and Children: A Christian Theological Sourcebook,* among many others. She is an activist, yoga practitioner, and popular college speaker.]

3. Catharine MacKinnon, *Toward a Feminist Theory of State* (Cambridge, Mass.: Harvard University Press, 1989), 241.

4. Mary Hunt is a Catholic feminist theologian who specializes in theo-ethical issues. She is the co-director of WATER, the Women's Alliance for Theology, Ethics and Ritual in Silver Spring, Maryland. For 1999–2000 she was a Research Fellow at Harvard University in the Center for the Study of Values in Public Life. She is the co-editor (with Patricia Beattie Jung and Radhika Balakrishnan) of *Good Sex: Feminist Reflections from the World's Religions.*

5. Nantawan Boonprasat Lewis is Professor of Religious Studies and Ethnic Studies at Metropolitan State University, St. Paul/Minneapolis, Minnesota. She is co-editor of *Sisters Struggling in the Spirit: A Women of Color Theological Anthology* and *Remembering Conquest: Feminist/Womanist Perspectives on Religion, Colonization, and Sexual Violence.* Dr. Lewis is a member of the editorial board of the *Journal of Religion and Abuse* and the board of directors of FaithTrust Institute.

Selected Bibliography

Adams, Carol J., and Marie M. Fortune, eds. *Violence against Women and Children: A Christian Theological Sourcebook*. New York: Continuum, 1995.

Brock, Rita Nakashima, and Rebecca Ann Parker. *Proverbs of Ashes: Violence, Redemptive Suffering, and the Search for What Saves Us*. Boston: Beacon Press, 2001.

Butler, Sandra. *Conspiracy of Silence: The Trauma of Incest*. San Francisco: New Glide Publications, 1978.

Byerly, Carolyn. *The Mother's Book: How to Survive the Molestation of Your Child*. Dubuque, Iowa: Kendall/Hunt Publishing, 1997. Originally published 1985. See www.faithtrustinstitute.org.

Cooper-White, Pamela. *The Cry of Tamar: Violence against Women and the Church's Response*. Minneapolis: Fortress Press, 1995.

Fortune, Marie M. *Is Nothing Sacred?: When Sex Invades the Pastoral Relationship*. San Francisco: HarperSanFrancisco, 1989; Cleveland: United Church Press, 1999.

——— . *Love Does No Harm: Sexual Ethics for the Rest of Us*. New York: Continuum, 1995.

——— . *Sexual Violence: The Unmentionable Sin*. Cleveland: Pilgrim Press, 1983.

Heggen, Carolyn, H. *Sexual Abuse in Christian Homes and Churches*. Scottdale, Pa.: Herald Press, 1993.

Herman, Judith. *Trauma and Recovery*. New York: Basic Books, 1992.

Levy, Barry, ed. *Dating Violence: Young Women in Danger*. Seattle: Seal Press, 1998.

Lew, Mike. *Victims No Longer*. New York: Harper & Row, 1988.

Lewis, Nantawan Boonprasat, and Marie M. Fortune, eds. *Remembering Conquest: Feminist/Womanist Perspectives on Religion, Colonization, and Sexual Violence*. New York: Haworth Pastoral Press, 1999.

McClure, John, and Nancy Ramsay, eds. *Telling the Truth: Preaching about Sexual and Domestic Violence*. Cleveland: United Church Press, 1998.

Poling, James N. *The Abuse of Power: A Theological Problem*. Nashville: Abingdon Press, 1991.

Poling, Nancy Werking, ed. *Victim to Survivor: Women Recovering from Clergy Sexual Abuse*. Cleveland: United Church Press, 1999.

Reid, Kathy Goering. *Preventing Child Sexual Abuses, Ages 5–8*. Cleveland: United Church Press, 1994.

Reid, Kathy Goering, with Marie M. Fortune. *Preventing Child Sexual Abuse, Ages 9–12*. New York: United Church Press. 1989.

Trible, Phyllis. *Texts of Terror: Literary-Feminist Readings of Biblical Narratives*. Philadelphia: Fortress Press, 1984.

West, Traci C. *Wounds of the Spirit: Black Women, Violence, and Resistance Ethics*. New York: New York University Press, 1999.

Scripture Index

271

General Index

abandonment, 148–51

abuse victim/survivors, scriptural foundation for formulating response to, 124–27

accountability, 156, 158
  avoidance of, 111–13
  church's role in assuring, 127
  judgment for actions, 113–15

acknowledgment, 144–45

acquaintance rape, 5–6, 204–5

Adams, Carol, 72–73, 239, 240, 241–42, 254 n. 6, 268 n. 2

adultery, in Christian scripture, 101–2

advertising, sex and violence in, 32

agape, 93

aggravated rape, 256 n.

anger, 151–57

Anglican Communion, "Seal of Confession," 198–99

anti-pornography strategy, 235–36

anti-rape movement, 15–16, 50–51, 122

Aquinas, Thomas, 256 n. 32

Ashanti society, xv

atonement, 140–45

Augustine, 258–59 n. 2
  on lust, 102
  on rape, 35–36

avoidance, 112–13

awareness, 219

Bach, George R., 251 n. 15

Baker's Dictionary of Christian Ethics,
  defining rape, 60

Ballou, Hosea, 141

Barry, Kathleen, xvi, xvii–xviii

Barstow, Anne Llewellyn, 37

Beals, Judith, 238

behavioral guidelines, 240

Belliotti, Raymond, 59

Biblical View of Sex and Marriage
  (Piper), 61, 251–52 n. 17

blitz rape, 204

bodily integrity, 258 n. 20

Bonhoeffer, Dietrich, 157

Brock, Rita Nakashima, 141, 142

Brownmiller, Susan, 50, 51

Burgess, Ann Wolbert, 65, 208

Bush, George W., 252 n. 19

bystander, 241

Cahill, Ann, 22, 52, 55, 56, 58–59, 65

censorship, 236

child rape, as predecessor to marriage, 254–55 n. 12

children, teaching about sexual abuse, 231

child sexual abuse, 7–9, 83–84, 171–84
  adult survivors of, 181–83
  behavioral signals of, 178–79
  confusion of victims, 29
  coping mechanisms for incest victims, 174–76
  disclosure of, 178–80
  by person known to victim, 173–74

Christian ethics
  overemphasis on form of sexual activity, 33
  silence on sexual violence, 47–48

Christians, responses to anger, 152

273